T.H.A.N.K. Y.O.U.

THOMAS MAVITY

PAGE PUBLISHING, INC.
New York, NY

First originally published by Page Publishing, Inc. 2018

ISBN 978-1-64138-397-4 (Paperback)
ISBN 978-1-64138-396-7 (Digital)

Printed in the United States of America

CONTENTS

FOREWORD

I grew up in Northwest Indiana, The Region, Illiana, Blue Collar Row, The Rust Belt or whatever rough and tumble name the speaker calls this strong, diverse and ethnic area. People were proud of their families and traditions. The competitive environment in academics, athletics, business, politics, and religion was instilled into generations of families and communities. Strength in all these areas was the focus and key to growing up.

Mental, physical and psychological toughness was what each man, woman, and child needed to succeed in this geographical region. The cohesiveness of neighborhoods, celebrating local heroes, and a sense of loyalty to friends was the norm. Many races, cultures and creeds created diverse backgrounds and perceived differences. Everyday life was filled with anecdotes which required thick skin.

This great melting pot taught the author to have a vigor for life. In those days, steel was king, as the blast furnaces blared twenty-four hours a day, seven days a week. Friday nights in the fall meant high school football. It was not uncommon for ten thousand fans to pack a stadium. Many times, extra bleachers were flown in by helicopter the day before the big game. The Chicago media traveled to the location broadcasting the event live. Obviously, no added pressure was put on these teenage boys to perform. Emotions, feelings and pent-up aggressions were unleashed as the local gladiators fought for the pride of their schools. These memories are what molded me into the man I am.

If you are not from this area, others mistake your passion and aggressive nature as arrogance, conceit or haughty. I am so thankful for my remembrance of what was bestowed from such a diverse and impregnable space. This mental and physical toughness gave me desire and determination to succeed. I learned not to let anyone or anything stand in the way of my dream.

The steel mills withered away, social norms changed to a political correctness, and we grew into a litigious society. People became afraid to speak their minds and make everyday decisions. People were worried what others might think. People lost confidence and emotions of fear, anger, mistrust, and uneasiness became predominant. Negativity when augmented with feelings and emotions of everyday life equals an equation for failure. All the strong traditions learned became overshadowed by today's challenges.

I have been blessed with a family I love with all my heart, a solid education from Wabash College, and a dream career. I've grown from a boy to a man. I have worked tirelessly to achieve my goals and help others. I know God loves me and surrounds me daily. I am fortunate to have all I have acquired. I am cognizant of those who may not have had the same opportunities. I feel compassion for those in need, but question why people cannot achieve success. Life sometimes is not fair, but what I learned early in athletics was to have a fire burn inside your gut. When running wind sprints and gasping for air at football practice, a football coach screamed, "You gotta have want to!" and "Pain is the purifier!" These vivid memories taught magical life lessons that built character and perseverance.

I have proudly spent nearly twenty-five years in law enforcement monitoring and changing behavior. I have been in many households dealing with family, social, and criminal issues. I constantly read spiritual, leadership and self-help books to keep a positive mental attitude and enrich my life while I assist in dealing with much negativity in this world.

Everyone needs a plan of action or positive influence moving forward in life. Even though I am truly blessed and I am confident who I am, I have always felt there was more for me to accomplish. I told my father this thought, and one day, I finally figured it out. I wanted and needed to provide a positive method for people to feel good about themselves and strip away the negative layers holding them back.

I have studied the law of attraction learning the value of positive focus. These important building blocks led me to a simple answer: Demand from yourself and others a thankful attitude each and every day. Say thank you until it hurts. Thank-you is not only good manners but shows an attitude of gratitude. Your positive ideas, thoughts, and goals will multiply while the negative ones will disappear. In this book, the simple term *T.H.A.N.K. Y.O.U.* will have many words inside to help you achieve and succeed in life. You have many choices in life. Choose to say thank you and act grateful. I hope and pray this book opens your eyes and heart to a loving and abundant life.

T.H.A.N.K. Y.O.U.,

Thomas P. Mavity

ACKNOWLEDGMENT

I would like to thank the following pillars who strengthened my life, shared their life's experiences, and helped me develop into the man I have become one day at a time.

GOD - You brought me into your world and surrounded me with light. You covered me with love and a passionate heart. You protected me too many times to recall with your power. You always walked with me through every hill and valley. Thank you, GOD, for all these gifts you bestow on me.

TERRY (Father) - You demanded a strong work ethic, and you told me this effort would always receive the benefit of the doubt. You told me to be honest in my endeavors. You always made time to play catch and supported me at all of my extracurricular events. You taught me to have a healthy suspicion of people and their motives. You instilled in me commonsense thinking. You showed me the value of a dollar. You forgave me for breaking a window. You always loved me and were not afraid to tell me. You made sure I was educated. Thank you for all the gifts you gave me to succeed.

MARY (Mother) - You brought me into this world. You took naps with me when I was little. You taught me honesty and integrity. You always told me "good, better, best." You loved me like a rock. You gave me praise and discipline when I needed it. You listened when I hurt. You sacrificed to make sure I was educated. You introduced me to spirituality and explained the consistency needed. You gave me the abilities and resources to make sound decisions. You always told me I was special. You forgave me in our disagreements. Thank you for all the gifts you gave me to succeed.

TERYL (Sister) - You cared for me when I was young. You were interested in and supported me at my school activities. You always strove for excellence in your personal and life's endeavors. You set a positive example and listened to any problems I incurred. You put up with a little brother who was a terror. "What was the score!?" You are a great wife, mother, sister, friend, and teacher. You care for the collective world. You are like a good book; we can pick up our conversation without missing a beat. You are my hero. You always told me you loved me. Thank you for being the best sister in the world.

TED (Brother) - You always included me and took me with you even though I was four years younger. You were a role model with unimpeachable integrity. You made me want to follow you as an athlete, police officer and human being. You listened to me during hard times and were not judgmental. You made Guido hats fashionable! You showed me an ink pen appears to have one hundred gallons of ink! You are the toughest person I know. You always told me, "Tom, you are my brother, and I love you." You are my hero. Thank you for being the best brother in the world.

MICHELLE (Wife) - You are a well-rounded person who served in the United States Air Force for thirteen years. You are a strong and independent woman who does not need me. (I am glad you do though.) I am glad you chose me and asked God to bring us together. You have the patience of a saint and trust me implicitly. You love me wholeheartedly. You never complain about anything. You talk through our problems even when you are unhappy with me in the moment. You are a spiritual warrior and my best friend. You laugh and play jokes on me and for me. You treat me like a KING. You made me a precious gift, a "jar of light," to help me get through tough days at work. You gave me an awesome daughter in Emily. You proved to me visiting a place *is* better than photographs. Thank you for your exceptional culinary skills and making healthier choices for us. You allowed me to realize my dream and buy our retirement home early. You accepted Jacob and Caitlin as your own with love. You work on our vision board, and we see the benefits of thinking positively. Thank you for being the incredible woman you are and the best wife in the world.

JACOB (Son) - Thank you for the yellow beetle bug on the interstate with your mother's name on the license plate to let me know you arrived in the world. Your laugh when I tickled you as a baby was priceless. You proudly wore your custom-made police uniform daily. You told your kindergarten teacher "the only person who tells anyone what to do is my daddy, and he is an Illinois State trooper." (Such Loyalty.) How could I possibly me mad? You were brave every day I was gone. (I am sorry.) You loved me no matter what. You made drawings of a doughnut shop every time I came to see you. Thank you for the time we do spend together. You have the keen ability to look to the future. You are my son, and I am proud of you. You have learned integrity and leadership through Boy Scouts and achieved Eagle Scout. You are a true man who is not swayed by peer pressure. You have love for God. You accepted Michelle and Emily into our lives. You always tell me you love me. Thank you for being the best son in the world. I love you, buddy!

CAITLIN (Daughter) - Thank you for being my daughter and a gift from God! You had an infectious laugh as a little girl. "Caitlin, did you eat the candy bar?" "No, Daddy." "Please go look in the mirror." "HEEEEEEEEEE!" You are beautiful inside and out. You have an incredible personality and can adapt to any situation. You created the comic strip *Dirty Rat*. You have a love of song and dance. You have a voice of an angel. You played the role of Memaw awesomely. You took a club and smacked me in the back when I told you to; unfortunately, I was joking. You always put a smile on my face. You stand up for yourself and others. You are incredibly kind and compassionate. You love me no matter what. You were strong every day I was gone. (I am sorry.) You are incredibly smart and articulate. You have an incredible love for God. You accepted Michelle and Emily into our lives. You wear your heart on your sleeve. You are my daughter, and I am proud of you. Your feelings are important to me. Thank you for being the best daughter in the world. I love you with all my heart!

EMILY (Daughter) - Thank you for showing me the wonder of and the fun of make believe and fairy tales and tickling me with your wonder and innocence. You accepted me into your world. You showed me insight from a child's perspective and point of view. You believe the world is fair, and the world is good. You called me Dad. You have an incredible love of dance, piano, hunting, family, and friends. You have become more thick-skinned. You can now argue until the cows come home. (You're welcome.) Your love of God is evident. You are loving and caring to the nth degree. You create jokes to play on me. You LOVE the Chicago Cubs! Hah! (You caught a ball from Mr. Strode showing you can catch more than a cold!) You collect nutcracker figurines. You care about family and friends. Thank you for being such a great daughter. I love you without a doubt!

TONY CANDIANO - You and I, since we were children, have an unconditional friendship. We still call each other daily and communicate about the inequities of society. You make me laugh until I cry. You have been a sounding board for nearly forty years. You are the hardest working person I know and truly walk the walk. You keep me in check and tell me when I am wrong. You are my pea in a pod. You have made it on your own and continue to strive for perfection in your personal and private life. You are a competitive warrior and a role model to your family and all the kids you coached. You have created an awesome family, and their future is incredibly bright. You allowed ridiculous behavior by "Uncle Tommy" so the beat can go on. Thank you for being the best friend in the world and always making me a priority. I love you with all my heart.

JOE MAGINOT (Deceased) - You were my family's home delivery milkman. You shared your love of the Chicago Cubs and baseball. You gave me my first job on the farm as a milkman. You laughed until you cried watching me fall on the ice breaking a gallon of milk.

You never cut off families with children when they could not pay their bills. You were a role model at church as a steward. You were a pillar in the Tri-Town community. You taught me about business and working with people. You were my friend. Thank you, Joe, for all you did for my family and me.

WILLIAM "BILL" RICKS (Deceased) - Thank you for being the most well-rounded person I ever met. You served your country during World War II in the Pentagon in Washington D.C. You were the grandfather I never had. You loved me like your grandson and treated me with love and respect. You always told me "everything will be alright." You taught me how to work with wood. You told me it was okay for a man to cry. You loved animals and hunting. You talked to me for hours and laughed at the same jokes. You were loyal to me and loved me with all your heart. Thank you for letting me know when Rachel met you in heaven. I miss you, and I will cherish your friendship forever.

JEFF KEILMAN (Retired Police Officer) - You are a true friend and took me under your wing. You showed me how politics rear their ugly head. You showed me it was okay to not go with the flow. Your unique perspective telling me, "What are they going to do to you, make you work midnights?" You helped my family move to Illinois. Thank you for being my friend and making me laugh about trivial things.

KEN AND SHERRY SCHUTTE - Thank you for your friendship and neighborly advice. Ken, sure enjoyed watching football with you in your easy chair, sharing your popcorn and your perspective on women. (LOL!) You are the better fisherman. Sherry, you shared your strong spirituality and guidance when I needed it the most. You both shared with me the love of your family and your grandchildren, and we've created many fond memories. I'll always be grateful for all the cookouts and blamed for you having to "choke down the shoe leather." You came to my wedding and accepted my new family.

Thank you for all your love, kindness, and generosity throughout the years.

LELAND BURNETT - Thank you for answering your telephone on New Year's Eve 2007 and being at the right place at the right time. You and I were meant to be friends. You are the most genuine person and have the most integrity of anyone I know. You gave me much perspective as a retired trooper. You invited me into your home and showed me there were still great people in the world. You have a unique sense of humor. You gave me perspective on a career after law enforcement. Thank you for being a true friend.

STEVEN SNOW (Retired ISP Senior Master Trooper) - You came into my life when I truly needed a lifelong friend. You have an open-eyed perspective on life. You showed me everything in life is negotiable. You brought me down to the SNOW FAMILY FARM and shared your loving family with me. You showed me how to fish better. You allowed me to pick your brain for hours on end. You showed me how to dream big and listen to your inner self. You shared your love of real estate. We laughed at all the inequities of society. You learned Super Bowl Sunday was a football game. Thank you, Steven, for all you have done for me. Too bad your better half is a Chicago Bears fan! (Just kidding, Julie, only Packers for you.)

MIKE PIGG (Retired ISP Sergeant) - Thank you for being a true-blue friend with incredible insight. Thank you for your entrepreneurial spirit and ability to look outside the box to solve problems. Thank you for all the workouts playing basketball and racquetball. Thank you for showing me humility and humbleness when things did not go our way. Thank you for sharing your incredible family with me and the honor of seeing your children grow to adulthood. Thank you for always putting your family first. Thank you for your compassion with people as you understood their dilemmas.

TROY RUPERT (ISP Sergeant) - You are a role model. You believe in God, provide for your family, and protect society. You were my true friend throughout the years. Thank you for listening to my problems about work and home. You told me the truth even though it broke my heart. You helped us get through tough situations on the night shift and made work a breeze because I could always count on you. You always had my back. Thank you for trusting your own abilities and never giving up. You always have a positive attitude. You have the patience of a saint. Thank you for sharing your family and their accomplishments. Thank you for knowing when to ask, "Where you staying?" So you were not "bamboozled." We had fun!

MARKE BOBBITT (Retired ISP M/Sgt.) - You allowed cops to do their jobs and stood up for what was right. Your leadership taught me how to lead today. Thank you for many talks pointing me in the right direction. You are a genuine human being. I miss you. Thelma and Louise did not out run us!

PAT STAPLES (Retired ISP Captain) - You recognized me for two promotions because of my integrity, service, and pride. You had incredible leadership skills and charisma, always knowing what to say at the right time. You demonstrated care and compassion for the citizens of Illinois. You are a class act! Thank you.

MARJORIE PHILLIPS (Kindergarten and First Grade Teacher) - You showed love to all of your children and made them feel special. You baked a birthday cake for every child and had a toy treasure chest each could pick out a present. You made a special day for each student whose birthday fell in the summer. You are a role model for all teachers to follow. Thank you! You touched my life.

CINDY BALLOU (High School Spanish Teacher) - You wrote a thank-you note to my parents as I was the third Mavity to come through your classroom. You explained it was an honor to teach the Mavity children. You found ice for my injured pitching arm when I strained my elbow during a game. Thank you for your kindness. Thank you also for not holding a mistake I made against me. You taught me a valuable lesson.

SANDY WRIGHT (High School Guidance Counselor) - You recognized me as the most well-rounded student in my senior class presenting me with the Ralston-Purina Danforth Award at senior night. You wrote an outstanding acceptance letter for me to get into Wabash College. Thank you for caring about your students. You made a difference for me. Thank you.

AL PILARCIK (Deceased / Former Major League Outfielder and High School Baseball Coach) - You started me as a freshman on the varsity, which made many upperclassmen angry. You gave me channels to develop my baseball skills. Thank you.

TERRY TILLETT (High School Baseball Coach) - You helped me reach and realize my abilities in baseball and life. You always explained things constructively and in a positive manner, helping me grow as a man. Thank you for exemplifying the true meaning of teacher. We are similar as we wear our hearts on our sleeve. I now know what a "honacher" is!

ELMER BRITTON (Indiana High School Hall of Fame Football Coach) - You believed in and utilized an undersized player. You told me "pound for pound" I was "the toughest kid" you "ever coached." You showed me "the eye in the sky never lies," "a sixteen-pound canary was fat," and "the pope was Catholic." Thank you for all the valuable life lessons. Your stories live on as vividly as if it were yesterday.

SCOTT ZAJAC - You are a lifelong friend, former neighbor and the little brother I never had. Thank you for all the shenanigans we laugh about through the years: catching punts in the front yard (DRILLED!), remembering Three Stooges lines in sequence, having someone to verify the chaos on Springhill Drive, The Siren, and laughing until our stomachs cramped. We have deep discussions about God, family, life, and knowing and figuring out what makes us tick. You are the godfather for my son. You are a gift from God who makes the world a better place. I am proud of you.

INTRODUCTION

Each person is shaped by their attitudes, morals, upbringing and values. Their life's experiences are based on positive and negative thoughts and actions. These learned traits and behaviors build how we handle situations and grow. Choose to succeed. Sometimes, life's conditions make the playing field unequal. No matter what we have learned, by whatever means, we all remember powerful words that were spoken to us.

Words are the most powerful influences that affect our emotions. One positive or negative word can change the meaning of a sentence. One word can brighten a day or cause a misunderstanding. The purposeful choice of how and when to use our thoughts and words can change the outlook of the world.

We must train our mind with positive words, which will create the emotions of joy, happiness, love and a grateful attitude. Well-thought, positive words and actions create pride in ourselves, build a selfless work ethic, and a burning motivation to achieve greatness. Believe as more positive words flow, self-perceived barriers will crumble. This in turn will release many gifts to the universe. Imagine words inspiring us, so nothing can stop our will to succeed.

Every day, we must generate and duplicate with our positive thoughts and actions a grateful and winning spirit. Mentally, physically, emotionally and spiritually, our actions and words must lead the way to our goals we want to achieve. In this book, I have chosen words that burn an indelible image of gratitude. Once we make these positive words a consistent part of our day, thoughts, events and success will fall into place with ease and grace. Say yes to a new positive mind-set where we can accomplish all our goals and have a passion for life. Thank you! Now begin our voyage to a phenomenal, positive life filled with gratitude. Take the torch and visualize the changes we will generate for generations to come.

Proverbs 23:7 says, "As a man thinks in his heart, so is he."

TRUST

Trust is one of the most important words a person incorporates into their daily life. The moment we become a gift from God until we enter the kingdom of heaven, trust enters every aspect of our inner and outer experiences. Our first experience of trust as a newborn is knowing we are nurtured and loved by our parents. Trust enters every decision, thought, emotion and feeling. Trust is a loving, healthy, positive value that affects the whole world.

Trust is finishing a deal with a handshake. Trust is knowing someone is making a good decision for the best interest of all mankind. Trust is never defaming the proud heritage of the name our parents gave us. Trust is earned, granted, and allows freedom.

When we live by the Golden Rule, honestly working with and for people in all life's endeavors and knowing they are too, a happy, confident feeling occurs. This is trust. We have to trust consistently and pray that community and world leaders make strong collective decisions. Trust is paramount, and without it, negative vibes and emotions arise. We cannot ask someone, "Can I trust you a little or a lot?" Trust must be implicit. Trust must be unwavering as taking an oath from God. Visualize trust at work each and every day.

When there is no trust, negativity befalls all that is good. Doubt rises about people, their abilities, decisions and surrounding issues. This leads to a bombardment of negative energy that kindles manufactured stress. Always channel your thinking positively and get rid of all the unhealthy feelings.

Trust God first and believe we can achieve anything. Then trust our inclinations about people and surround ourselves with only trustworthy ones. Instill a can do, grateful attitude; and if our name is mentioned others will say, we can trust him or her with anything. Knowing we are trusted makes us the mortar that holds the bricks in place. Strive to be the most trusted person anyone knows.

Psalms 20:7 says, "Some trust in chariots and some in horses, but we trust in the name of the Lord our God."

TRANQUILITY

We toss and turn. Our mind will not shut down from the daily grind. The thoughts of bills, family strife, and stressors at work pull at our emotions and feelings. All we want to do is fall asleep and feel at peace. We have all encountered this at some point in our lives, and we are hoping for calmer waters ahead. How can we start feeling balanced again? Norman Vincent Peale explained, "Tranquility is one of the most beautiful and melodic of all English words, and the saying of it tends to induce a tranquil state."

Repeat tranquility over many times a day and see what it does. A friend of mine used to tell me when he traveled four hours home from the daily work week, "I can feel my blood pressure drop when I get about halfway there." I used to think he was a bit full of it until I bought my retirement home three hours from where I work. I now know the feeling he spoke about. The feeling we get is like a pressure gauge releasing steam. A tranquil feeling that makes my whole body go ahhhh!

Achieving a tranquil state daily with all life's factors takes consistent practice. Any book we read or anyone we have spoken to about this topic all agree on three things. Alone time with God, daily meditation, and a grateful heart are the keys. An extra five minutes upon awakening gets us in focus so our thoughts do not spiral out of control. The proper frequency stops negativity and can even change how the rest of our day unfolds. When the seas get rough, trust in him, and the waters will calm. Matthew 8:23–26 illustrates this point. "He got into a boat, and his disciples followed him. Suddenly, a violent storm came up on the sea, so that the boat was being swamped by the waves; but he was asleep. They came and woke him, saying, "Lord, save us! We are perishing!" He said to them, "Why are you terrified, O you of little faith?" Then he got up, rebuked the winds and the sea, and there was great calm.

When living in a consistent tranquil state, situations are manageable instead of stormy problems jolting our emotions. Our thoughts are positive, and reflection occurs. Our conversations are loving and kind resulting in answers instead of disagreements. We feel happier inside and can pay it forward to others. It is a daily decision to be free from agitation. Tranquility aligns our heart, mind, and body to be the best we can be. Say *tranquility* three times and see if a smile appears on our face. We caught you smiling.

TARGET

In life, we can target our goals and reach for the sky or have a target on our back and ask, "Why do all these negative circumstances keep happening?" Have a healthy respect for ourselves, decide to have a positive mental attitude, and be grateful for what we already have, even if we believe we do not have a lot. There is always someone out there who does not have what we do. Decide we deserve good things and believe it will occur. We must get inspired thought, which will lead to action. Say it over and over again. Do whatever it takes to attract all the good we want to accomplish. Make it happen by visualizing our targets. Henry Ford said, "Whether you think you can or can't, either way you are right."

Proverbs 4:25–27 says, "Let your eyes look straight ahead and your glance be directly forward. Survey the path for your feet, and let all your ways be sure. Turn neither to your right nor your left, keep your feet far from evil."

Our targets should be intended for good, enriching ourselves and those around us. An archer practices to hit the bull's-eye on a target, and without significant work cannot reach the goal. It is okay to fall short of our target, but like many world inventors who failed multiple times, they keep pushing forward diligently until their target is struck. We can learn much from failure as it nurtures growth. Many times, as we fall short of our target, we learn many lessons that we otherwise would not have known how to accomplish.

Sometimes, targets are moving, so we adapt and persevere as we go along. Think of all the soldiers in the great wars on the battlefields. They had to be mentally, physically, emotionally, and spiritually strong to survive. Their mental preparedness, ingenuity, and esprit de corps were paramount for survival. Think of munitions coming from all directions, terrain changing by the hour, nightfall, and being an active participant with the terror surrounding them. Their focus on the mission's target first and their target to stay alive were the norm. The rules of our game can change throughout our process. Focus to stay on target and listen inside what our body is telling us. Do not worry what others think. As long as we are working toward a healthy, meaningful target, the how's will come, and we will succeed. Remember, we can do anything we put our mind to; and with a positive mental attitude and grateful heart, we are on target!

TEACH

Teaching is one of the most powerful sources that influences and shapes a person's life. Everyone remembers and has been around good and bad examples of teaching. When we were in school, either in the classroom or participating in extracurricular activities, we remember mentors and those methods they taught to empower us. We also recall those who were non-inspirational and were only putting in their time.

These creative, inspirational and powerful leaders made the fire burn inside us to achieve success. Their examples, stories, and words are as vivid today as when we were young. As an adult, the life lessons learned as a child empower us tenfold. As we lead in the workplace, we take a little from many to shape our skill set and manifest what works versus what does not. Their teaching turns us into a better boss, communicator, leader, mentor, and parent for those looking up to us. When we realize all we have learned from our teachers, mentors, and coaches, it all comes to fruition. We know the value a good teacher has instilled.

Proverbs 15:1–4 says, "A mild answer calms wrath, but a harsh word stirs the anger. The tongue of the wise pours out knowledge, but the mouth of fools spurts forth folly. The eyes of the Lord are in every place, keeping watch on evil and the good. A soothing tongue is a tree of life, but a perverse one crushes spirit."

I remember as a teenage boy a classmate of mine was taking flying lessons. I thought this feat was remarkable. I communicated this fact to my father, and I said it would be great to do. My father's response was, "You couldn't afford the gas." This was an inspirational teaching moment missed. I always remembered those words, and it taught me a powerful life lesson. We must not step on other's joy. A great teacher never criticizes negatively but turns a negative into a positive thereby motivating. Teach from our heart good, life lessons, speak positive words and work with others to help visualize their dreams. Our teaching will inspire and be remembered by the words and actions we choose.

If we never taught, coached, mentored or parented a young person, challenge ourselves to get out of our comfort level and volunteer. We will gain more insight to life skills that will enrich our teaching abilities. Teaching will also give us a happy heart when we see a person learn a skill because of our efforts. So get out there and teach!

TRADITION

Everyone has traditions that they learned and followed. Whether they are cultural, social, family, religious, business, athletic, or whatever activities they participated, what was important was they were positive and inspired with God. 1 Peter 1:13 states, "Therefore gird up your loins of your mind, live soberly, and set your hopes completely on the grace to be brought to you at the revelation of Jesus Christ." We strive to duplicate what works well and follow those who inspire us.

What happens when traditions and norms we have been accustomed to have been damaging and hurtful? What will we do about it? We must break these cycles for ourselves and future generations. As an adult, it is our duty not to pass down unhealthy traditions. We must stop this tumultuous and problematic behavior. Our desire for traditional changes must manifest, and it all starts with us. The law of attraction talks about we attract what we think about. An example would be a family with an alcohol problem. This family probably for generations has coincided their social occasions and life around alcoholic beverages. They look at it as just a way of life and do not think of some of the damaging affects it had on themselves, others, and the next generations. When a family member had some inspired thoughts and looked at the consequences, they made a valid choice to change this tradition. As a law enforcement officer for nearly twenty-five years, this is one tradition I have dealt with on an almost daily basis. I arrested nearly one thousand DUIs in my career, and hopefully, I am able to help people change their behavior from drinking and driving. Ultimately, it was up to them to change their ways. Also, know we have the God-given abilities to change negative traditions that cause pain and hurt. Ask for help from above to change the behavior. Lou Holtz says in his book, *Winning Every Day,* "Tackle adversity. You are going to be knocked down. I have been on top and been at the bottom. To achieve success, you are going to have to solve problems."

Act grateful for the opportunity to accept traditions that are loving and healthy working in our life. These memories will be cherished and passed on with gratitude because of the outstanding joyful and happy feelings generated. A winning tradition of a sports team brings positive self-esteem to the players and coaches, a glowing sense of pride for the community, and long-lasting memories passed down from generations to come. Reflecting back, we can remember everything about a positive tradition on a winning sports team. It vividly affected our cognitive abilities, emotions, and senses. Recalling a great tradition, we can remember people, the weather on that day, the smell of air and a life lesson learned. The strong positive tradition outweighs any negative situation encountered. Create excellent traditions in our life that will last a lifetime. Remember, anyone can be average. We are in charge of our life, so shoot for the stars.

TOUGH

The word tough is a very positive and endearing characteristic to bestow on someone. This label brings all mental and physical aspects to the table, shaping the sculpture of a warrior; body, mind, and soul. We must be grateful for people who naturally have these qualities to lead. This is something that can be developed and learned through life's experiences and with the help of God.

Mentally tough means when situations become difficult, our negative emotions do not get in the way to complete a daunting task. An example would be a firefighter running into a burning building to save lives when others are running out. Mentally tough people do the right thing even when the decision is unpopular or an ethical dilemma. A police officer arrests their best friend or another police officer for driving under the influence. Galatians 6:9 states, "And let us not lose heart and grow weary and faint in acting nobly and doing right, for in due time and at the appointed season we shall reap, if we do not loosen and relax our courage and faint." This means do not become weak-minded. Even when these people are attacked for doing what was right, they are thick-skinned enough to carry on. These tough people use their mental abilities, so they are counted on to always get the job done.

Physically tough people will not be outworked. They labor longer and harder asking for more. They have a higher pain threshold and know the difference between an ouch and a hurt. They outlast others in endurance and have a warriorlike quality they will not be beat. They stand up for those who cannot stand up for themselves. The ultimate compliment for a mentally and physically tough person would be someone saying they would go to war with them. John Quincy Adams stated, "Courage and perseverance have a magical talisman, before which difficulties disappear and obstacles vanish into thin air." Physically tough people can make difficult situations go away as they stand their ground and hold the line.

It is important to know how to use our toughness while leading in life or mentoring. This is called tough love, which allows the mentored to make mistakes that will provide a learning experience for growth. The law of attraction helps this process by learning what we want on the inside and being strong enough to not let outside influences steer us off course. Anyone can do and be anything they want in life if they decide they are going to do it. We must be tough mentally and physically, act grateful for all we are and have, and give all our heart to the world in a loving and generous way. This is the definition of tough we have grown to understand.

TACTFUL

Words flow from us to speak our minds to others about everyday topics in the world. How we choose to respond is a choice that we must monitor. Today's technology has created instant gratification or embarrassment when in either written or verbal conversation, the world sees or hears what comes from our tongue and heart. Knowing what to say, how to say it, and the timing is tact. We can learn what to say in certain circumstances by life's examples. We know when to congratulate someone, offer thanks or extend our condolences. These are easy. What about everyday situations? We attract what we are thinking about, so if our thinking is not tactful, we may say words or phrases that are inappropriate for the time, topic, or audience. If our thinking is negative, it affects our emotions, so garbage in equals garbage out! This lack of tact causes uneasiness resulting in embarrassment of us or others. If we think we should not say something, then don't. Choose to control our emotions that will control our tongue. Colossians 4:6 says, "Let our speech always be gracious, seasoned with salt, so that you know how you should respond to each one."

Learn to have a time delay before responding to a question, accusation, or discussion. This will communicate a well-thought response with tact. Engage our brain with positive dialogue, which are successful, and educate ourselves how and when to use them. A good dictionary or thesaurus is a great place to learn about words and their proper meanings. This is another fantastic way to learn the tactful art of appropriate speaking with an audience. Learn other social codes and norms of the audience we are addressing. This shows a knowledge of their background and generates appreciation. One word may be used or understood in a different light depending on age, gender, or language a person speaks. Know your audience! This tactful process will show we care how we use our words, so if a mistake is made, our audience will be more forgiving.

In two and a half decades of law enforcement, I learned the tactful art of negotiation. This served me well resolving disputes and making each party believe they won the battle. The good cop/bad cop scenario we have all heard about really works. Tact is the key because even if you disagree with the situation, words can still show respect. Words are powerful and everlasting. Are you using tact with love and kindness or spewing vile with negative consequences? As said from the beginning, how we choose to respond is a choice. Develop into a role model with our tongue and learn to only say things with gratitude and tact. When this behavior is consistent, we will feel confident and calm when we tactfully speak.

TABOO

Everyone has verbally or acted on something they were less than proud of in their lives. Telling a small white lie or committing a moral sin, which is taboo, has a negative impact; and the damages are devastating. Using obscene words toward the Lord, others, or about situations comes from the heart, which has been affected by negative emotions. We need to stop the turmoil, eradicate taboo behavior, and be grateful for all our gifts.

What happens when taboo behavior goes against social norms but is being practiced anyway? This is defiant behavior, and when someone reaches this point, they have reached rock bottom. All their mental, emotional, physical and spiritual decisions are no longer sensible. They turn to alcohol, drugs, sex, gambling, and other taboo behaviors justifying their bad decisions and killing their inner pain. They know their actions are wrong, but continue down the path of destruction. They see no recourse for their actions. When these taboo sins and laws are broken, a price has to be paid. Bad behavior leads to bad consequences is how the law of attraction will work. These taboo actions will lead to serious injuries and possibly death. Numbers 15:30–31 states, "But anyone who sins defiantly, whether he be a native or an alien, insults the Lord, and shall be cut off from among his people. Since he has despised the word of the Lord and has broken his commandment, he must be cut off. He has only himself to blame." Remember, these people who seem to have nine lives in the physical world on Judgment Day will pay the price.

How do we avoid taboo words and behaviors while standing up for what is right? We build a strong relationship with GOD and visualize good behaviors and goals. Say, we are going to do our best every day. Refuse to hurt anyone with taboo language or actions. Have a grateful and loving heart. When this happens, we will not be tempted by taboo actions and words. Leaders care about people and also listen what others think about them. Someone who practices taboo behaviors does not care about others. Powerful positive words and actions along with a grateful spirit builds character. Someone who has great character will not fall into taboo habits because of the strong mental, physical, and emotional toughness built over years of work. God is always testing us with different temptations that go all the way back to Adam and Eve. Be the role model who everyone else says, what do they do that makes them more successful than me? If we live a good spiritual life, believe we can accomplish anything, visualize successes, and develop strong and healthy relationships we will not go where taboo behavior lives. We are a gift from God, so use our positive words and actions as models for others.

TRIUMPH

Every country has a national anthem explaining the story of their proud history. Each school, university or professional sports team has a fight song instilling pride and cheering them on to victory. Every person needs a personal strategy that generates triumph and accomplishment on a daily basis. This feeling of triumph in whatever is our endeavor should make our heart burst with excitement and adoration! There should be no better feeling in the world driving our energy and emotions. Compare this positive energy to competing on a championship sports team, accomplishing a self-created goal, or overcoming an incredible adversity. George C. Scott, who played the role of United States Army General George S. Patton in the movie *Patton*, addressed his troops prior to battle in World War II this way. "Americans love a winner and will not tolerate a loser. Americans play to win all the time. I wouldn't give a hooting hell for a man who lost and laughed. That is why America has never lost and will never lose a war because the very thought of losing is hateful to Americans." This is what triumph feels like.

Triumph is learned by mistakes we have made and correcting them the next time. Triumph comes through setting goals with positive emotions such as love, joy and excitement. Use these positive emotions to visualize accomplishing our goals and keep our focus. Whatever we imagine, we can make happen! Believe and speak positive words about ourselves and our goals to maximize our experience. Consistently ask God to help give us clarity in our vision and direct us in the right direction. 1 John 5:4 states, "For whoever is begotten by God conquers the world. And the victory that conquers the world is our faith." Most importantly, be thankful for all we have and the ability to use our feelings and emotions leading us to a triumphant path.

Individuals who have been dealt a less than positive life and struggle with everyday existence must ask help from God and start with small goals. Through positive words and actions, they can change their lives to start feeling better about themselves. They must change the negative images and emotions instilled and generate positive ones. In turn, they will see differences in themselves and the abilities to grow and help others. Spread the infectious feeling of triumph to everyone so they can use their positive energies to be on top of the world. Life should be lived to the fullest, and this triumph should make them jump for joy. Don't let anyone or anything stand in the way of our success story. Focus on positive words and goals, visualize achieving them, and light a flame inside that will never burn out until the triumph is in hand.

THINK

Life is a fast-paced, get-it-done-yesterday proposition where if we slow down, we are left in the dust. As we go from one task to another, we think, but not deeply and passionately. As more jobs and responsibilities clutter our mind, a time comes when we must slow ourselves down for clarity. Naturally, as our day goes is how our emotions flow. We must learn to capture the moment and learn to rethink our way through the day. This will allow the universe to align with our thoughts because everything is connected.

Take time each day to restock our mental shelf with positive words and thoughts. Do not let the day spiral out of control. Good, creative and healthy thinking should feel effortless. When we are thinking of a goal or answer to a problem, only think of the end positive result. Do not make rules or think of all the steps because it will clutter the attraction coming to our mind. As we think and visualize daily, the process will magically unwind, and the answers will appear. This sounds too easy, but when the mind is clear, ideas and energy will flow pointing us to success.

I had a five-acre piece of land listed with a real estate company. I kept wondering why I had not had a bite on the property. I thought the listing was close to being expired, so I called the real estate agent. I learned the listing had expired from the agent, who, frankly, was not going to make a large profit and had put no effort into the business transaction. Instead of getting mad and letting my emotions take over, I told myself I was going to sell it myself. I cleared my mind, declared to the universe, and God, my land was sold, and magically, the land sold quicker than I ever could have imagined. I made one phone call, and from there, I received an e-mail from someone I did not know, asking how much I wanted. The deal was done within two hours of declaring to the universe and God my intentions. Incredible! Demand what we want from the universe, stay focused and visualize the end result.

Romans 12:2–3 says, "Do not conform yourself to this age but be transformed by the renewal of your mind, that you may discern what is the will of God, what is good and pleasing and perfect. For by the grace given to me, I tell everyone among you not to think, but think soberly, each according to the measure of faith that God has apportioned." Slow down and think clearly. Use the law of attraction for focus and do not let emotions get in the way. Put our thoughts in God's hands, and our answers will magically arrive.

THOROUGH

"Oh, that is good enough." "Well, it is better than it was." "We will get to it later." These statements reflect an "Okay to be average" mentality about life. This attitude seems to have crept into every aspect of our world we live today. Apathy has been accepted as the normal standard, and now when someone chooses to be thorough, mustering greatness in their works, attitudes, and beliefs, they are looked upon with contempt. We keep lowering our standards and letting those who cannot or will not be in charge making the rules. This is a complete devaluation of social norms. Choose to be the thorough one, the higher standard, the one who makes the difference in the world. Be a thorough leader and not a follower of mediocrity. Philippians 2:12–13 talks about the ethical implications in daily life. "So then, my beloved, obedient as you have always been, not only when I am present but all the more now when I am absent, work out your salvation with fear and trembling. For God is the one who, for his good purpose, works in you both to desire and to work."

My mother always said, "Good, better, best," when working on a project, demanding we put in our best efforts. Say positive words inspiring ourselves and others. Set creative, fun goals and carry them out with pride and passion. This starts the process, and when our actions are joyful, thoroughness blends into our works effortlessly. In my years spent in law enforcement, my thoroughness displayed taking the extra time with people, writing reports for court purposes, and working within department policy and court decisions establishing my professionalism. An immediate respect was earned as the citizens and my peers always counted on me to leave no stone unturned. Using this thorough standard always gave me a measuring bar for success. This solid foundation learned early in life should be used in our personal, professional, and spiritual life daily.

As a mentor, thoroughness is an important tool to recognize a person's abilities and inabilities. Teaching and showing the differences in a loving and understanding way is the key. We all have worked with bosses who were micromanagers. This type of thoroughness felt like two hands around our throat. Know the difference between these types of thoroughness. A thorough, hardworking person may make the same mistake as a one who is a lazy, mediocre coworker. The difference is the thorough person will receive the benefit of the doubt. The thorough person they will say probably just forgot because he was busy; whereas the lazy, mediocre employee they will say was probably just trying to get out of work.

Establish a thorough mind-set from an early age in ourselves, families and life. We will be the one thought well of, looked up to, given the job, and assigned the responsibilities to make decisions and care for others. Thoroughness in the mental, physical, and spiritual realm will reap life's rewards tenfold. Lastly, act grateful for our thoroughness and use it with the law of attraction to help the world.

TEAMWORK

Teamwork is intertwined every day into all aspects of our lives. A family is a team, a workplace or organization is a team, a church is a team, and our country and its leaders must be a team. Teamwork comes with a cost by sacrificing self and nurturing integrity, trust, character and service. No one, person or idea, should loom larger than the team concept. How we achieve this plateau takes collective thoughts, inspirational words, visualization, organization, and everyone sacrificing for the good of all. As the old adage says, we are only as strong as our weakest link referring to a chain and comparing it to a team.

Motivation positively communicated is the most influential ingredient for success. There are many ways to go this route, and it is not about being the loudest, strongest, or adding adjectives to nouns. It is leading with a loving, teaching manner with gratitude in the heart. We all have experienced good and bad examples immersed in teamwork leading to scattered results. Use the good examples for our reference and discard the bad ones. Lou Holtz was quoted as saying, "We want to impart work habits that will lead them throughout their lives. Most of all, we want to teach them the value of loyalty, integrity and teamwork." Once you learn to work with people, you can accomplish anything. To do this, you must subvert your ego in the service of a higher cause. You must never forget there is no "I" in the word "team." We can never tolerate words or actions that are detrimental to the team.

In my years as a police officer, I took my oath seriously being a part of a law enforcement team, upholding the laws and never compromising the trust of the citizens. When another officer on the team displayed wrong words, actions, or questionable decision making, they were called onto the carpet either by discipline or termination. When the teamwork concept is no longer the priority and needs a directional change, new positive energy should be implemented. This is why corporations fire their CEOs, teams change coaches, and families have disagreements. These changes should be made to uphold the teamwork foundation keeping it solid as a rock. Gratitude should be instilled for those team leaders who passionately uplift, motivate, teach and sacrifice for the greater good. Ask ourselves, how do we make our team better every day? Are we inviting God into our decision process? Are we using positive words and actions as an example to move forward? Do our teammates believe in us and trust us to make sound decisions for the group? If we are doing this, we understand teamwork and are guiding our team in the right direction to achieve success. Proverbs 27:17 says, "As iron sharpens iron, so man sharpens his fellow man."

TRAIN

Training the body and mind to succeed requires maximum effort, discipline, and a can-do, grateful attitude. People who seriously train want consistently to acquire an edge over their situation or an opponent. They make and take the extra effort for preparedness of what life throws their way. If we fail to train the body and mind properly and consistently, situations will arise where the unexpected flourishes instead of being easily handled. Proficiency in any skill takes extensive training. The words and gestures used in training can result in life or death in some situations. An example would be a hostage negotiator using improper verbal techniques and not recognizing the person's behavioral modes. Training with proper words, speech, and positive persuasion will save one or many people's lives.

Training in any team setting takes hours of practice and repetition for success. Communication among members is paramount for winning the battle. A tactical response team works and trains together with words and hand signals before they take action. Miscommunication during this training or a live event will result in serious mistakes made or the possibility of death. Training in every activity, career and sport is imperative for a positive outcome. A motto I learned while working in law enforcement says, "When you choose law enforcement, you lose the right to be unfit." This means there are no excuses but to train each and every day and be physically and mentally prepared at all times. Always think and train outside the box. This allows avoidance of mental and physical stagnation and pushes our limits. When we do reach our mental and physical limits and think we can go no further, ask God for help and visualize achieving our goal. Jeremiah 16:21 says, "Look then; I will give them knowledge, this time I will leave them in no doubt of my strength and my power: They shall know that my name is Lord."

Training with others brings new ideas, builds esprit de corps, and nurtures leadership. Training weeds out those unfit for the skill set needed to accomplish the task. Training can perpetuate timing down to a fraction of a second, movement with military precision, and earn respect in an instance. When we fail to train, it is like someone asking us what time of day it is and looking at the back of the clock instead of its face. No answer can be given with any certainty. Our training must lead to skilled behaviors and routines. Strive to be the best using our training as it hones our skills and sharpens our mental acuity. Be grateful and seek training that teaches and builds a stronger and better us.

TRANSFORM

In the course of our daily lives, we all have said and done something to someone at the inappropriate time, place, or in a manner that was ugly. This response came from our troubled heart, which was probably triggered by negative feelings and emotions. Bottled up feelings and emotions are dangerous, and the words used can be poisonous if not channeled and managed properly. We must transform our words and actions for the good of everyone. Transformation must come from the body, mind, and spirit with love and passion. We are in control to build people up with a positive attitude because whatever we think about, we should thank about. We can turn lives around when we reach out instead of lash out. Romans 12:2 says, "Do not conform yourself to this age but be transformed by the renewal of your mind, that you may discern what is the will of God, what is good and pleasing and perfect."

As we transform our words and actions, the results will be positive for ourselves and others. We talk about the adage, "Hindsight is twenty-twenty." People always say if we would have known now what we knew back then, things would be different. That was what our current situation was when we made that decision, and we cannot go back. Do not think about would have, could have or should have. Look at it in a positive way instead of a negative one. The knowledge gained was inspirational because we could learn by our past decisions and mistakes and take a new path. Life is about peaks and valleys as God throws life's tests at us. God never gives us more than we can handle. Learning from mistakes, handling situations more positively and powerfully, and passing on good is grace in our heart and mind for transformation.

A transformer provides power to energize an entire city. We must act like a transformer with positive energy flow to encourage people to follow our lead instead. A transformer causes people to think about the consequences of their words and actions. The transformer brings light, love, compassion and new ideas to help those who are troubled, frightened, and in need of a positive influence in their lives. The body, mind and spirit are the most powerful tools on our belt to build and mentor other transformers. When we lead by example showing our insights of the world and teaching by the mistakes we have made, people will see us as genuine. There has only been one perfect person created, Jesus. Act grateful for this positive knowledge hundreds of times daily, and we will see a transformation in ourselves to inspire and energize the world around us. Thank you, Jesus, for being my greatest transformer.

THOUGHTFUL

The law of attraction talks about what we think about most are the results we achieve. So we must get our heads on straight and get rid of negative, angry, dysfunctional thinking and actions. Replace the negativity with joyful, loving, constructive ways that will lift us and our brothers to an abundant life. Speak and act courteously to our neighbor with thoughtful intention. Think how it would be to walk in others' shoes and be grateful for all we have. Colossians 4:5–6 says, "Conduct yourself wisely toward outsiders, making the most of the opportunity. Let your speech always be gracious, seasoned with salt, so that you know how you should respond to each other."

Always acting thoughtful to others is easy to proclaim, but how do we live thoughtfully when life's events are not going well? This is the true mark of a champion how to react when the chips are down. Clear our mind, take a deep breath and say thank you. This will create a time delay to reacquire positive feelings and emotions. What can we do for others to feel this thoughtful feeling? Go outside our comfort zone and volunteer to help others. The help we give will bring a satisfying feeling unmatched by any other accomplishment. Learning not to dwell on our own concerns open the doors to thoughtful actions. Compassionate, happy feelings will overflow when we see others smile and tell us thank you for our kindness.

Thoughtfulness is not necessarily bred into our DNA. Thoughtfulness is taught and should be a resolution instilled from the time we were a child. We must continually work hard and think how others will benefit from our actions. Nurturing thoughtful words, actions, and a heart filled with gratitude blooms like a bouquet of flowers. It looks beautiful, smells fragrantly, and is for a special occasion celebrating a loving and happy event. Always act and speak thoughtful language in a sincere manner and not for ulterior motives. We all know people who act and speak thoughtfully, but their mind is focusing on self-indulgence. These people are easily swayed how the wind blows. They are only being thoughtful for their own benefit. This behavior is two-faced and lacks sincerity. These people are dangerous to any cause, organization or team. Their actions will generate thoughtless emotions and feelings that are destructive.

Thoughtful equals genuine in the mind, body, heart and spirit. The good deeds we complete for others with a positive, genuine, and thoughtful spirit will be rewarded many times over on earth and in heaven. Think how our thoughts, actions, and words affect others. When we have mastered thoughtfulness, our inner self will beam with enthusiasm how and what we can do for the world.

TALENT

Some people are born with natural, incredible, God-given abilities. Others have bits and pieces of talent in their toolbox but must work hard to develop their skill set. Some are given the gift of fantastic talents but fail to develop or use it to their potential. No matter which category we fall into, these things are for certain. We must be grateful for our talents, work hard to stay sharp, visualize successes, and pass the information on to others. Most importantly, whatever talents we have been blessed with, they should be used to teach, mentor, and benefit others in a positive way making the world a better place. 1 Peter 4:10 says, "As each one has received a gift, use it to serve one another as good stewards of God's varied grace."

Essential cornerstones of talent require mental, physical, spiritual, and emotional preparation for the task at hand. We need to know what our talents are and how they are going to fit into the situation we are currently living. The goal is to build talent with positive core values and pass it forward for the enrichment of others. Talent is meaningless unless we can have a great attitude and work with others for a common goal. I remember playing on the most talented high school baseball team. Each one of us had remarkable skills to bring to the team. Unfortunately, all the individual talents could not be meshed into a great team with a common goal of winning. We were weak minded only thinking about our individual needs. Talent cannot be selfish, and sacrifice for the better good is required to achieve success. We cannot take our talents for granted because the abilities to use this talent to the fullest may only come once in a lifetime.

Using our talents to mentor others is a tremendous responsibility. Each word or explanation of our abilities or skill set is digested by others and used to grow. It is imperative to show patience while teaching our talent and always uplifting with positive words and examples. The person with the most talent is not always the best life coach or mentor. This is because talent may have come easy to them. They may not have had to work as hard or be the one who had to sacrifice for the good of others. Talented builders who sacrifice are thankful for their abilities, and use positive mentoring skills to uplift usually are the most successful. They look outside of themselves to get the most talent out of others. They use positive words for reinforcement, always talking of the upside. Talent is a gift that has been given to us or developed through an outstanding work ethic. Use our talent considerately for the growth of all.

TACIT

There is nothing more satisfying as silent approval that we read from another person's body language. A smile viewed across the room, a nod signifying happy agreement, a glance that conveys I understand and care. These learned behaviors say we are with you without saying a word. The tacit bond between people is calming when many times chaos surrounds the moment. Using positive energy tacitly applauds good behavior and thought. People feel approval through their senses, which draws them a picture of happiness and success. We are always drawn to tacit leaders. Ones who do not speak loudly or often, but when they do are received with silent credibility. Like Teddy Roosevelt said, "Walk softly and carry a big stick."

Peculiar behaviors arise when people or situations are not managed tacitly. Their words and actions are not loving and kind. Their thoughts are clogged with informational overload. They stop focusing on helping others. Their negative, stirred up thinking takes over, and confusion becomes rampant. Too often, chaotic situations could have been calmed if only someone took control in a tacit manner showing restraint, delegation and leadership. Learn to quiet our language and deeds. Take control of our emotions. My mother always explained to repeat this prayer whenever negative feelings and emotions lurked. "The light of God surrounds me, the love of God enfolds me, the power of God protects me, the presence of God watches over me. Wherever I am, God is." Learn a positive word or phrase to uplift our mind when negativity creeps up on us. Change this image in our mind before it works on our heart. Do it silently with no fanfare.

Tacit people just get it done! Their thinking is perceptive, full of energy and filled with answers instead of excuses. They don't wait for others to solve their problems. They are the first to arrive and the last to leave. They work hard, think success, visualize accomplishing it, and take tacit time each day for reflection. Quiet time is a must for people, so they use loving, helpful and healing words when needed. Tacit leaders bring humility and humbleness to any conversation or situation. The strong tacit ones always earn their respect instantly because of their emotional self-control and monitoring their tongue. Act like the tacit leader so everyone can confide in us daily for support. Do not hesitate to step into a situation and take control because people will listen to us when we are tacit.

TWO-FACED

Our word is everything: A measure of our integrity, honesty, loyalty and credibility. A price which no one can afford to pay when lost. People judge and accept us on our word. They flock to us or scurry away when they see us because of our words. When we talk out of both sides of our mouth, it is like the devil with a pitch-forked tongue. We never want to speak or act two-faced because all the respect we have earned will be destroyed. Two-faced people end up disrespected, alone, and others are unwilling to take a chance with their reputation they have built. Once our word has been soiled, we are done. Rebuilding the two-faced image will take years to repair, and even speaking in good faith people will doubt the turn around. Do not speak or act two-faced; instead, be true to our word.

We all have encountered two-faced people in our careers, in social functions, and everyday life. The first time we realize someone is two-faced, it puts a lump in our throat and makes us feel dejected. It conjures negative feelings and emotions like anger, fear, and mis-trust. We ask, why do these individuals speak and act this way? People are two-faced for many reasons. Francois de La Rochefoucauld, a nineteenth-century French spy, said, "Sincerity is found in very few men and is often the cleverest of rouses—one is sincere in order to plan out the confidence and secrets of the other." They may feel com-pletely inadequate inside and put others down to feel better about themselves. Two-faced people tend to tell others what they want to hear to avoid making honest and difficult decisions. These people also deliberately talk out of both sides of their mouth to get ahead in a career or stir the pot. Two-faced people usually have an evil agenda and conceal their intentions. Regardless, two-faced speech and actions are ugly and unacceptable.

Never speak or act two-faced because it destroys credibility, and people will resent us. Say encouraging words and do not be afraid to choose a side or be completely forthright. Instead of taking the easy way out, visualize our situation and think it through with a positive outcome. Our words and actions will gracefully come from the heart to encourage instead of discourage. Do not be afraid to call someone out who is speaking or acting two-faced. This earns instant credibility and lets the two-faced person know their words and actions will not be tolerated. Never promise anything we are unwilling to deliver. This gives people false hopes. Always be truthful because it will set us and others free for a more peaceful life. Positive, flowing dialogue done in a loving, truthful manner will keep us from acting two-faced and hurting others.

TRAILBLAZER

When we think of a trailblazer, we visualize pioneers, Lewis and Clark, navigating through the wilderness of North America and mapping the land to the Pacific Ocean. Their ingenuity, hard work, sacrifice and perseverance found an avenue for worldly advancement. We must be the one who is the trailblazer in our family's life to chart a course of action with positive words, thereby breaking generations of negative layers. So many individuals carry negative burdens from their upbringing, which they hold inside themselves. These negative feelings, emotions, and scars continue because negative words have been ingrained. In childhood, kids are mean, calling each other names many times degrading a self-feature. There are unsupportive parents who used inappropriate communication tactics to belittle rather than to inspire. Most of the time, their actions were learned behaviors that are now passed on to the next generation. These negative behaviors continue to cause pain and damage that lead to self-esteem issues. Remember, we are in charge of ourselves! Act and speak like a trailblazer to lead ourselves and others to an incredible journey.

Our words and actions say a lot about us and the persona we carry. Set positive goals, always speak loving and caring words, and choose fun, uplifting people to surround us. Trailblazers know how to be positive all the time to everyone because like attracts like. The trailblazer gets the most out of their abilities and makes everyone around them better. A trailblazer assertively motivates with a positive can-do attitude to help achieve a goal. The trailblazer has a giant heart filled with gratitude for all they have and all they will accomplish. A trailblazer always keeps their eyes on the prize and never loses focus even among the chaos which may surround them. The trailblazer always takes on whatever comes their way, never complains, and gets the job done. If everyone lived this way, life would be simple, but we know not everyone wants this responsibility.

Trailblazers constantly are self-motivated to keep the flame burning brightly developing their words and actions to inspire others. When our mind, body and spirit are involved in healthy creative activities, we grow. We then can pass this great knowledge to others. Think before we speak to deliver an encouraging and loving message. Act and work for the good of humanity. Learn to be quiet learning from others. Know when to step forward taking the lead whenever others are unwilling or incapable. Incorporate God into our life daily for answers and guidance. When we choose to do all these things, we are on the right path to be a great and motivating trailblazer.

TREASURE

Treasures represent something valued by someone. They cherish it more than all other items, features, places or things. This treasure creates positive feelings and an emotional glow on the inside and outside. Treasures are physical, mental and spiritual affecting our emotions deeply. Treasures can be buried deeply or openly apparent. What may be a precious treasure to one may mean nothing to another. Our personal goals, values, views and situations alters what we hold dear. In Exodus 19:5, the Lord talks to Moses at Mt. Sinai about treasure this way. "Therefore, if you hearken to my voice and keep my covenant, you shall be my special possession, dearer to me than all other people, though all the earth is mine." This powerful story reminds us to treasure the Lord, act grateful and true to be able to enjoy the treasures in the kingdom of heaven. The words we speak to others, the way we communicate with them, and how we share all our treasures is important.

Physical treasures can be anything we desire. We watch documentaries of people looking for lost or buried treasures from years past. The thrill of the adventure raising emotions of hope and joy. What a fun experience searching for the unknown with a goal in place. Most of the time, the physical treasures we see on a daily basis are right in front of our noses. The spouse we love and courted, our children we conceived and raised, the home we dreamed of and built, and the accolades we earned and achieved. We worked hard, set our mind to it, and put positive energized focus to make it happen. Some treasures are inherited ones such as an heirloom from a grandparent who has passed. These items bring us joy and remind us every time we see or touch it the love and goodness we remember about them. These treasures also bring back powerful words and phrases during the process.

Sometimes, treasures are signs; seen and unseen, learned behaviors, and joy discovered through subtle actions. We may treasure someone's smile, their brilliance in thought, or patience when working with others. These small treasures are most frequent and important, touching our lives daily. These treasures make us laugh, and we appreciate the great, loving qualities that bring us happiness. Life is about finding our treasures and developing them to their fullest. No matter how big or small, treasures make us smile. We have to remember to use our treasures in positive ways, using encouraging words, and not for self-centered, greedy indulgences. Whether spiritually, mentally, or physically, use our treasures intentionally for the good of everyone. Give our treasures unselfishly, lovingly, and have no strings attached. The more generous we are with our treasures, greater gifts will grace us as the reward.

TACKLE

The incredible feeling from head to toe when a daunting task has been tackled inspires us with great pride. All the hard work, hours of preparation, and positive mentoring helped us tackle our goals. These powerful emotions, mental strength, and physical actions encourage us to inspire momentum in others. Encouraging them to tackle their dilemmas and yearning growth from us is a fantastic motivator. The only way to solve a problem is to hit it head-on with all our mental, physical, emotional and spiritual savvy using encouraging words.

Football was a tremendous positive environment developing life skills for years to come. We learned the difference between an "ouch" and a "hurt." We ingrained the mental game plan each week versus our opponent. We physically trained putting the whole package together to compete. The coaches used words and phrases, some repeatable and some not to get their inspirational message to our heart. All of this was to tackle our rival. Finally, saying the Lord's Prayer as a team prior to taking the field was incredibly powerful. Teaching the perfect form tackle we can compare to tackling life. Our head needs to be up; our body needs to be square and in balance as we uplift our opponent and life's obstacles bringing them to the ground conquering our goals. Tackling was practiced and repeated until correct. The powerful, motivating words spoken by the coaches, we still can recite and smile about as if it were yesterday. These examples helped us through life, and we are truly thankful for these men.

Everyone should have their tackle box full for catching life's treasures. We need to have all the tools available to be prepared for the big catch. We cast out our life's skills into the unknown waters of life, and sometimes, the water is calm; and sometimes, it is tumultuous. We troll through life trying to land the great prize. When we reel it in, we understand all the work which was put into the effort. As we go and tackle life, the lessons learned are profound. Personalities are all different as well as life's experiences. The words and actions that motivate us may have a different effect on others. It is important to know the personality when choosing what and how to say our motivating words. Those who have not had positive mentors do not know how to tackle problems. It is our job as a positive, loving, and caring role model to lead by example and give those in need this valuable life skill. Our gift and words will inspire others to tackle life and all that goes with it. Thank your coaches, teachers, and mentors for helping prepare us to tackle life.

TAILOR

A tailor is an artisan whose skill set separates them from anyone else. We were all tailored by God to live, love, and cherish life. Each of us have been given the gift of life to seek happiness and help others flourish. God tailored our special features as a masterpiece. We grow and realize what special areas we have been gifted through our experiences. Our DNA makeup, feelings, and experiences create our future. We can tailor our life and circumstances by positive thinking and surrounding ourselves with uplifting people. Good thoughts equal feeling better about ourselves, and when these images are tailored positively, great things will happen.

When we want something bad enough, we will concentrate wholeheartedly on the wish. We must tailor our mind, body, and spirit in the direction we want to go. Have faith, and our wants and dreams will come true. Think about what we want and visualize us having it. Do whatever it takes to make our possibility a reality. This thought will be effortless, and we will attract all that we need. Mental thought will come to fruition. Believe in greatness and never settle for anything less. Tailor our thoughts around gratitude and build our body, heart and mind soundly with this principle. Tailor our day and never let anyone lead us off course. Remember, we are in charge of our lives every day. The way we think and feel will put ourselves in the right position, and we will accomplish our tasks. Everyone knows what is best for them. Use our gifts every day with commitment to tailor what we want out of life.

It is OK to dream big, challenge ourselves and others, and dare to accomplish the best. Achieve our goals and be aggressive; otherwise, we will be left behind. Use positive words, act as a mentor, and direct others with inspired direction. Our thoughts and actions must be tailored together to get what we want out of life. Always use positive words and actions combined. Tailor our life with all positives. Rid ourselves of all negative feelings, emotions, activities and people who get in the way of tailored success. Get out of our own way. Treat ourselves like a king and return the gesture to others. Tailor our image like an arrow. In the *48 Laws of Power*, Robert Greene suggests, "The arrow cannot hit two targets with one arrow. If your thoughts stray, you miss the enemy's heart. Mind and arrow must become one. Only with such concentration of mental and physical power can your arrow hit the target and pierce the heart." Use our words to inspire and tailor our drive in the direction of our choice. Tailor our life how we want it and achieve all we deserve.

TIDY

We all have seen disorganized people, places, and projects. Their functionality and appearances leave much to be desired. Abnormalities arise, raising questions of moving forward with progress and accomplishment. We were not born with tidy or untidy traits. These are learned behaviors from parents, friends, and mentors. God wants everyone to live tidy mental, physical, and spiritual lives. Without tidiness, chaos reigns in every aspect of our lives and spirals out of control. My parents always instilled the advice of being neat and clean from the time we were little. "Please go and tidy up your room," my mother would announce. It is a positive process and habitually can be introduced to every area of our life. This small word pays huge dividends personally and worldly.

Tidiness begins with the vocabulary we hear and the examples we are shown. Our hygiene must be tidy. As a child, a clean, fresh appearance will keep us from being the one joked about. As we grow older, our tidy appearance will get us noticed by college recruiters, employers or even our future love. People with a tidy, neat appearance tend to make the extra effort for themselves and others. Tidy people notice the little details for success and are given an advantage in life. Tidy does not mean affluent. There have been many success stories of families who had little financial means but were tidy, clean and organized. They were noticed because they worked harder and gained more for themselves and their families. It is our job as a tidy person to inspire and uplift those who have not been shown proper life skills in this area. Whether a friend, colleague, or a stranger, we must teach tidiness with loving, kind words and explain the benefits.

Throughout the Bible, there are examples of those who washed feet. Be the one who is willing to do this for others.

Untidy people, as they grow older, suffer terrible and real consequences. The "do not get the benefit of the doubt for good" jobs. Their mental and physical health is affected. Their children suffer from the inability to have a positive role model and care for themselves. In my many years of law enforcement, untidy people have neglected themselves and their kids which led social services taking the children into protective custody. These extreme examples of untidiness occur on a daily basis and should have been avoided. God does not want anyone to suffer. It is important for someone to take notice and change these untidy behaviors. Take the extra effort and be the one who steps forward, volunteers to make a difference, and encourages the untidy with positive reinforcement. Tidiness can be taught, monitored and learned to change someone's life forever.

TEST

Life every day is full of challenges. We are mentally, physically, and spiritually tested. Our growth and reaction to life's obstacles sets our course for living, learning and mentoring. Testing peaks our intellectual curiosity, readies us for our physical confrontations, and strengthens our spiritual faith. The words heard and used in the testing process play a vital role in motivating or cowering in self-pity. Positive words uplift, give hope and inspire. We may have to repetitively test over and over again on the same scenario, but our fortitude to keep going and overcome is the key. When we physically anguish taking another step, painstakingly think through another problem, and believe in our loving faith, this is where our hard work and testing pays off. James 1:2–4 offers us this view of testing. "Consider it all joy, my brothers, when you encounter various trials, for you know that the testing of your faith produces perseverance. And let perseverance be perfect, so that you may be perfect and complete, lacking in nothing."

Testing builds character, pushes our limits and keeps our integrity unimpeachable. Testing holds us to higher standards. The qualifications earned in our fields gives us authority, allows others to trust us in their time of need, and protects the sanctity of processes endured. Testing is what separates those who are willing to take on more responsibility versus those who do not want the extra work. We all remember good instructors, methods, and words. We also despise ones who did a poor job. Thorough testing hopefully keeps those who should not be qualified out of their area of expertise. We have come to a point in our kinder, gentler society where everyone gets a trophy or the standards have been lowered to make the numbers work. This completely dissolves the testing process and the standards needed. Imagine doctors not qualified to practice medicine, police officers not proficient in marksmanship, or teachers incapable of teaching children subject matter. This is unacceptable and should not happen.

Decide we are the one who will test ourselves and push for excellence in our mental, physical and spiritual life. Develop positive, new ways to inspire and motivate. Choose to lead by example and do not be afraid to test the old guard. Testing gives society faith in themselves and others. Testing also teaches us what areas we need to improve to reach our goals. Life throws us challenges, and sometimes, we are ready, and others it happens in God's time. Remember, the battery of tests that come our way in our lifetime are never more than we can handle. Failed testing many times is a blessing in disguise reminding us to work harder, love deeper, care more, act more responsibly, and be grateful for all we have.

TANGIBLE

The beautiful landscape beaming with vivid colors of the spectrum. The heavenly sweet scent of honeysuckles in bloom. Birds singing and chirping as the wind whispers a tune. The soft, silky skin of a baby in our arms. Our taste buds watering anticipating the rich piece of double chocolate cake. All these are pleasant tangible examples of the five senses we experience daily. God made all these tangible treasures and billions more. Physically, we can touch and enjoy them. Mentally, we can picture them and think of new creations. Spiritually, we can pray for positive guidance for the results from the physical and mental. What is in front of us we cherish, but as Hebrews 11:3 says, "By faith, we understand that the universe was ordered by the word of God, so that what is visible came into being through the invisible." Thank you for all these terrific tangible things.

What happens when we take for granted all the positive, tangible treasures we enjoy? Imagine being disabled and asking someone to see, hear, smell, taste, and touch something. We would rely on their description to explain and paint the canvas. Spiritually, we pray to God for great outcomes, mental courage, and answers to physical problems. All the help we need comes from a positive attitude, kind, gentle, loving, helpful words and actions. Having blind faith is what allows the tangible to exist. Everything is connected in the universe, so tangible does not outshine intangible. We can have all the tangible riches in the world but be mentally and spiritually broken. We can have nothing tangible and be mentally and spiritually strong. The key is a healthy balance.

Adventure out, open our eyes to new tangible opportunities which bring out all our best qualities. Teach and coach the tangible skills needed to succeed. Use positive words to say we deserve all good things. The more tangible things we think, visualize and focus on the better opportunity, we will receive it. We have to believe good things will come our way. Create our life on a vision board and watch one by one all the tangible items we can acquire and goals we want to achieve when we put our mental, physical, and spiritual abilities into it. The fun part is having all the tangible items we want and reaping the mental and spiritual balance. Start thinking, talking and believing in a positive life, and all our words will flow encouraging growth. Remember, tangible is within intangible where all our faithful thinking occurs. Rid ourselves of all negative thinking and words. Start believing we can achieve anything. When the tangible is accomplished, be grateful for all our gifts and share with others.

TESTAMENT

We have read books, watched movies, listened to individuals tell their stories about the past, lived a life, then shared it. There are so many reasons why this is done. Many want to show the depths where they came from to teach others. Some want to tell their stories to get it off their chest, and there are those who want to learn from their situations, teach a better way, and inspire a positive path. Whatever the motivator, we all have a story to tell, the skills to reach out to others, and the compassion to deliver the message. There is enough misery in the world. Speak out and be the one to make a difference for mankind.

Learn about our past, understand and take charge of our emotions, and focus on good, loving and kind words. Our mouth is the window to our heart and mind. No one wants to be gashed by broken glass. Monitor our thoughts before we speak, and as the old saying goes, if we have nothing good to say, say nothing at all. It takes courage and honesty for someone to put themselves out there to give their testament. Do not be afraid because we will be looked up to whenever we take the steps for encouragement and self-fulfillment. We trained ourselves to be mentally, physically, emotionally, and spiritually healthy so we could deliver our inspiring message. This is not an easy task but one appreciated later due to all the hard work and dedication. Carry the torch of light to make everyone better to reach.

Testaments are not easy. They are ebbs and flows of experiences surrounded with emotions, people, and differing opinions of life's work. Negative thoughts, actions, and words do not work for growth. Learn from mistakes and look at the bright side of all situations. Stumbling and falling, later realized, showed us we were not ready for a wanted outcome. Only with mental strength, hard work and persistence did we reach our goal. Our loving, positive words will build trust and mold great self-esteem. This in turn motivates others to fix their current situation and move forward. The universe moves quickly, and in our short life on earth, we must charge other's batteries to encourage and lead. As we live a healthy, well-rounded lifestyle, we will know the time when to step forward and give our testament. When calmness flows over every portion of our life, and we are willing to give it all to God, it is time. John 3:17 says, "For God did not send his Son into the world to condemn the world, but that the world might be saved through him." Give our testament and help the world.

THERAPY

The body is not in balance unless we are mentally, physically, emotionally, and spiritually right. Every family has some type of dysfunction because no one is perfect. Reminder, most people or families suffer from some disorder affecting a healthy lifestyle. Break the bad habits and lifestyles and try to heal the disorder. When the word therapy arises in conversations, no matter in what area of our lives, people become squeamish. Therapy is for everyone else. Relationships and marriages erode because one or both people are unwilling to hear a mediator. People become dependent on alcohol and drugs to heal their pain. People are unable to admit to their faults. Bad behavior is blamed on past events and circumstances. At some point, the wheel has to stop spinning and a loving, kind word of therapy must arise. Never be afraid or intimidated by therapy. Those helping us many times have been in our place and can give positive advice. It is okay to say we need help and do not know what to do. We are recognizing a problem and are not denying it any longer.

Therapy does not have to be a clinical diagnosis or a trip to the mad house. Break the negative stereotype about therapy. We all will need some therapy in our lifetime. It may be as simple as phoning a friend for advice or meeting with them for some needed support. It could be joining a group for loss incurred because of a death. It could be changing our life and stopping the negative actions derailing our life such as chronic gambling, drug use, or sexual disorders. Speaking our mind to others in a therapeutic manner hopefully will guide us and empower us. Ultimately, we have to make the decision to want therapy for ourselves. We can change our current situation with positive, nurturing words. Words that make us be truthful to ourselves and others. Therapy comes in all areas, but the most important therapy is our relationship with God.

Take time every day to fill our cup to the brim with loving, caring, devotional therapy. There are no stronger words to inspire, teach, and build healthy lifestyles. A life to be proud of where like attracts like. Think of a therapy where we are never alone, calm any fear and conquer anything from the world. We will feel an inner fire burning within. In turn, this positive feeling will help us help others who are struggling to survive life's battles. Never look or think of therapy again in a negative way. Live bigger and better recognizing therapy and using it to enlighten ourselves and others. Proverbs 17:22 states, "A joyful heart is the health of the body, but a depressed spirit dries up the bones." Always be grateful for avenues of therapy.

HONOR

Honor represents so many great things because the meaning runs so deep. It is special esteem with respect, integrity, and reverence. Honor is recognition for outstanding achievements, historically, all the way back to knighthood. Honor also depicts the ultimate authority such as a judge's title calling them Your Honor. This powerful word says we are the best at what we do. When we are born, we are given an honorable name to keep unsoiled. Honor is heartfelt and causes us to stand silently with all our attention. Living right with all the distractions of the world is difficult. Circumstances, choices and learned behaviors make or break us as an honorable human being. Create a future of honor by working longer and harder than anyone else. Strive for excellence in everything we do. United States President Calvin Coolidge declared, "No person was ever honored for what he received. Honor has been the reward for what he gave." Establish credibility by our words and actions. God wants us to be happy and thankful for accomplishments and serving others.

Staying on top and pushing ourselves for excellence is not easy. Keeping our edge and staying sharp takes dedication to push ourselves mentally, physically, emotionally, and spiritually every day. The honor of serving others and the world always takes precedent in honorable people. This learned behavior is usually established at an early age. Mentors and positive people push us to greatness. Think of what honor means to us and ask ourselves, are we living up to our end of the bargain? God made us special with purposeful gifts. Decide to do the right thing every day as an example. There will always be someone out there who does things better than us. Seek their knowledge for growth. Set the bar high where others ask, how can we do that? A truly honorable person will always find a way to get things accomplished.

Focus on what we want in life and go after it 100 percent in an honorable manner. Anyone can be average, take shortcuts or even cheat to get what they want. An honorable individual never takes the easy way out for personal gain. Do not let our commitment become stained because of lost focus. The ultimate compliment anyone can pay us is if we act and speak with honor. Horace says, "It is of no consequence of what parents a man is born, as long as he is a man of merit." This incredible word is the ultimate, and no negative feelings or emotions should accompany it. There is not a "but..." included in an honorable person's reputation and accomplishments. Close our eyes and visualize our life of honor. We will be graded by God when we take our last breath, so make every life decision an honorable one.

HUMOR

Life is for enjoyment. Humor brings joy and makes us laugh and smile. Laughter cohesively brings people together for a humorous moment or event. We have to incorporate humor into our life on a daily basis to see the funny side of the world. We have to see humor in ourselves to not take everything so seriously. Humor cures many negative problems temporarily or even permanently. Emotions change with humor and brightens a day. The mental, physical, emotional, and psychological psyche is uplifted with humor. Laughter among others brings out more fun and relaxation, like a domino effect. H. Jackson Brown in his book called *A Book of Love for My Son*, says, "Laugh a lot. A good sense of humor cures almost all of life's ills." God wants us to be full of light and happiness. Humor allows us to go toward the light. Use humor for positive life experiences.

Humor is time stopping and should only be used in uplifting ways. No one likes to be the butt end of a joke when it hurts or demeans. Every person remembers going through school, and a certain kid in the class was repeatedly made the joke. Unfortunately, whether they were made fun of because of physical appearance, personality, disorders or hygiene it stung. We all remember that person or were that person. Those memories and negative humor hurt them mentally, emotionally and psychologically. Today, this ill humor is called bullying. Humor turned ugly against a person, race, religion, creed or disorder is wrong and unacceptable in today's world. These humorous words are discriminatory and degrading. If we do not know three clean jokes to tell on a daily basis, then we should not tell jokes at all. Know our audience, use good judgement, and be respectful toward people before using humor.

Humor brings a positive attitude, and laughter makes us thankful we are alive. In the history of the world, we are only here for a minute period of time. The joy we have and the humor we pass along will be remembered for years to come. We all cherish humorous situations growing up in families. We laugh until we cry because it brings out our childlike qualities. As adults, and our "busy" schedules, we forget how to laugh. We talk about getting our mind right with positive words and actions. Take time out every day to laugh just as we would with praying, eating, sleeping and working. When we incorporate humor into our everyday life routine, it will break up the monotony, and people will look forward to seeing us. Hopefully, we will brighten someone's day. Humor stops tension and negative feelings. A suggestion our family initiates is finding a giant mud puddle or creating one with a hose. Wear old clothes and slide through it. It not only generates humor, but memories captured with pictures and videos of the fun and spontaneity. Laugh loud and long until our stomach hurts and tears appear. We will feel good, and the rest of life's factors will improve too!

HEALTHY

Our body, mind, and soul are our temple. The life we choose to live dictates health, wealth and happiness. So we need to do all we can to live a healthy lifestyle. A healthy mind, body and soul can be developed and nurtured with commitment. Listen to the successful word of the mentors who are living right by their actions. Many at one time were worse off than us. Exercise and diet consistently checked will fuel a healthy body. Reading and learning develops a healthy mind keeping us from becoming stagnant. This leads to healthy, interesting ideas, which are positive. Rid ourselves of negative words and actions. Developing us is not easy, but many times the road to healthy success is in networking with other like-minded people. A study group or exercise buddy pushes us on the difficult days. Our grateful attitude, positive outlook, and self-motivation, which we bring to the table, charges ourselves and helps others reach a healthy lifestyle.

Our spiritual health is imperative for success. God wants what is best for all his children. 3 John 2–4 says, "Beloved, I hope you are prospering in every respect and are in good health, just as your soul is prospering. I rejoiced greatly when some of your brothers came and testified to how truly you walk in the truth. Nothing gives me greater joy than to hear my children are walking in the truth." Pleasing the Lord with a healthy life is the most important piece to the puzzle. We are to live a powerful, healthy life and teach others our success story. Seek a healthy balance spiritually, and when we do, our physical and mental health will come together as they are all connected. Our healthy body, mind, and soul tailors our success, and the pieces of the puzzle fall into place.

It is no secret healthy people take care of their bodies better, work harder, and succeed more because of the work they put into themselves. They live longer because of their strong will and get the benefit of the doubt in everyday decisions because they chose to live right. Healthy people are sick less and can be depended on to get the job done. Live our life like tomorrow is Judgement Day. Our decisions we make depend on a healthy mind. Only God can make it happen for us! Don't get caught up constantly making decisions our way. God has a healthy plan for us, and it is in his time not ours. Seek out a church and start praying. Guaranteed, when our spiritual health is strong, the rest of our health will fall into place clearly. Ask for help, and we will be given total health. Get rid of people in our life who do not live a healthy lifestyle because they will only hold us back. When we decide to make these changes, our life will become universally healthy.

HOPE

Dream big because no one will do it for us. Positive words and encouragement jump-start our day to make it happen. Don't wait for someone to help us out or a miracle cure. Dig down inside, striving for excellence, and do not let anyone stand in our way of success. Hope means always having the possibility of a better outcome. No matter what we have or what we are hoping for, give it all to God to live and demonstrate a positive attitude of gratitude. Hope is a battle of the mind and body to achieve what we want out of life. Those who cannot find hope in themselves or the world end up lonely and alone. Hope requires heart-felt dedication to envision what we want and to work through the dilemma. Hope never closes the door on anyone or anything. It delivers us to a calm environment where plans fall into place with ease and candor. Hebrews 6:18 states, "So, that by two immutable things, in which it was impossible for God to lie, we who have taken refuge might be strongly encouraged to hold fast to the hope that lies before us."

Healing takes place in all forms and having different options for our problem is hope. Knowing where to turn is important to get our life on track. Everything requires hope, from God inflicted, natural disasters, to how to trim the hangnail. When we feel trapped in the dark, downtrodden, or in turmoil, look to the light where hope is right in front of our nose. We all want answers to our situations. The problem is the last person we talk to about our mess is God. Why do we forget God is right with us all the time to lovingly take charge of our problem and offer hope? We are used to doing it our own way instead of allowing hope to flourish in God's time. Never give up because mental, physical, emotional and spiritual healing starts with hope.

Hope makes us think of the impossible, live life to the fullest, and pick others up in need of guidance. Offer hope with our words to encourage. Do not discourage with our tongue. People will look to us for hope because they see us as a positive role model who conquers their problems effortlessly. Looks may be deceiving on how we are handling our scenario. Hope brings grace, and even though we may be suffering on the inside, a steady of calm is displayed. Hope paints a bright, cheery picture when all we see are clouds. Anticipate and take the extra time daily to offer hope, letting everyone know that everything will be all right.

HUMBLE

Accomplishments are important because active actions have to take place to reach our goals. Positive words and attitudes push us forward while we work. Some people will do anything or step on anyone to get what they want, and this is wrong. We all want the best out of life, but we have to act humbly doing it. When we are thankful and grateful for our accomplishments, a built-in humbleness grows because we do not take anyone or anything for granted. Many times, learning to be humble takes time and maturity. Some people are naturally gifted or skilled in their areas of expertise. It is how we react with our successes and weaknesses when humbleness goes and grows. It is okay to know we are good at something and show our talents while performing the task. It is another thing to brag incessantly how great we are and appear boastful. This is not humble!

How do we go about our day when we know we are truly talented? Are our reasons to teach and help others flourish, or is it all about us? Our words and actions speak volumes about how humble we are. Our words and actions must help us grow mentally, physically, emotionally and spiritually. No matter how talented we are in something, there is always someone who is better. Humbleness keeps us on an even keel, helping us to avoid the huge peaks and valleys. We all remember a boss, an athlete, or individual on the fast track to success. They move quickly rolling over everyone or thing in their path. Suddenly, the carpet is yanked out from under them, and a big fall ensues. Compare it to the story of the tortoise and the hare. The tortoise always wins because he plans, acts humbly, and is respected for showing class. This is a great reflection how to handle life's situations.

Proverbs 3:7–8 says, "Be not wise in your own eyes, fear the Lord and turn away from evil; this will mean health for your flesh and vigor for your bones." Taking the higher road sometimes means saying nothing at all. Our humbleness grows in these circumstances when our emotions are running high, and we feel like saying something we should not say. Just because we know we are right does not mean we have to tell everyone how right we are. Our words have to match our actions for developing humbleness. One inappropriate word at the wrong time can destroy all the hard work and accomplishment worked on for years. Monitor our words and actions all the time, use them to uplift others, and be thankful to God for all his gifts. When we reach this pinnacle, we understand humbleness.

HAPPY

Happiness is not just an emotion, it is an attitude! Our life depends on knowing where to find it, how to sustain it, and willingness to share it. Norman Vincent Peale, in his book, *The Power of Positive Thinking*, explains, "It's just as plain as the nose on your face. When I get up in the morning, I have two choices. Either to be happy or unhappy, and what do you think I choose to do? I just choose to be happy, and that is all there is to it." The words we heard, the lessons we learned, and the actions we took were shaped from parents or mentors. Nobody grew up in a perfect world, so many times, negativity was emulated and carried forward. Happiness requires positive hope in every situation, so the glass is always half-full. We have to consistently strive to lift ourselves and others. When we are happy in ourselves with God first, our mental, physical, and emotional well-being will beam.

We have to work on ourselves every day and even sometimes trick ourselves into being happy. Turn our negative situation into a positive one. It may simply be as easy as an encouraging word or song that brings back powerful, happy memories from a great time in our life. Think of others, do for others, and give others an outlet they can find happiness. Lead by example and encourage those who are not in a happy place right now. Make a list of positive things in our world and about life, which make us happy. Surround ourselves with happy people who do not dwell on negativity. Set encouraging and attainable goals to find our benchmarks. When we succeed, reward ourselves. Happiness is a state of mind, so if our thinking is not happy, our efforts won't matter. Visualize success, practice our happy dance, display a grateful attitude, and proclaim it repeatedly. We are happy!

When we feel happy inside, we are energized, and this is when creativity explodes. The time to reach out to others is now. Use our God-given abilities to get the ball rolling. Everyone is different, so find a way to reach out to that person. Put a smile on someone's face, share a laugh with them, and listen to them break out in song. How blissful it is when we spread happiness. Mentally, physically, emotionally and spiritually when we see someone make a breakthrough, it is the best gift delivered. It is our job as a human being to spread happiness in any positive way to help the world. When we make this conscious and honest effort, good thrives, and evil will disappear. Challenge ourselves and others to spread happy, good news.

HONESTY

Honesty is a character trait that we struggle with today in society. Honesty should mean the same thing as it did when American Patriot and United States President Thomas Jefferson said, "I love to see honest and honorable men at the helm, men who will not bend their politics to their purses nor pursue measures by which they may profit and then profit by their measures." This statement reflects one of the finest and truest character qualities a person is bestowed. How honest are our leaders leading the political realms, the self-made businessman, our neighbors or our own family? Many people become nervous when they want to speak just how honest they are in their endeavors. The stigma attached to the word downright affects emotions. We have to be honest with ourselves with everything we do because in the end, God judges us as he has seen beginning to end. That alone should strike fear into a normal person. Unfortunately, society is not wired that way anymore, and we see degraded degrees of honesty from people.

We all want to know words people speak are genuine. We all have been lied to whether a little white lie or a whopper. When we know we have been betrayed, it hurts, which results in anger and other negative emotions. Societal standards in education, governmental decisions and everyday life have become clouded and not cut and dry. Challenge ourselves and set an example to be the honest man, the one who has scruples to do the job right. Step up and right the wrongs that have slid through the cracks because no one wants the responsibility. Propel ourselves with honesty and integrity for the good of all. The price a person pays for being honest is high, but well worth it. Our honesty serves as the backbone to lead society out of averageness. Our honest words and actions have the abilities to change others for the better and want to make the world a better place.

We must be grateful for the honest person who does their job every day and the overflowing positive feelings they give. Honest people attract other honest people because they cannot stand the thought of betrayal. Positive words and emotions stemming from honest behavior makes everyone around them comfortable. When we make it our duty to hold people accountable, honesty means something. Honesty does not want to keep up with the Joneses. Honesty looks us in the face and tells us the truth even when it hurts. Honesty with positive reinforcement done in a loving way is forgiving and teaches. We have all made mistakes, some which are honest mistakes, some which are not. In the end, when we can look ourselves in the mirror and say we honestly did our best for everyone involved, we are that honest person.

HEART

The heart is the center of our body, nucleus of a transportation network, core of our emotions, and affects every aspect of everyone's life. The symbol it represents everyone understands and uses to show emphatically what or who they love. The words spoken with love, compassion, and warm feelings come from the heart. We remember being told we are loved by family, friends, and others who genuinely care. The heart can also be broken and stressed by hard-hearted people using nasty words and actions. These hurtful words and events trigger uncomfortable thoughts for years causing people pain and suffering. How we use our heart and words is the key to mental, physical, emotional and spiritual growth. The heart unchecked is dangerous because all life flows through it. Take time daily to see where our heart is in our life, relationships, projects, and make sure what comes out of our mouth is truly heartfelt with gratitude.

The building blocks to a strong, healthy, loving heart are the decisions we decide to make every day. Are these resolutions made for loving growth for ourselves and others, or are ulterior motives present? Proverbs 4:23 says, "With closest custody, guard your heart, for in it are the sources of life." This says it all because our whole being runs from the source. Attached are all our emotions, physical attributes, mental preparations, psychological dilemmas and spiritual thought. All this opens the floodgates to love or hurt. We have to choose good, heartfelt words and actions to stem positive growth and a loving spirit. Listen to the words that come out of our mouth. Learn from mistakes we have endured or caused from the past and make good changes. Our heart and body run with what we put inside it. Encase it with a solid base, which does not fail. Mentally, be prepared for what comes our way. Physically, diet and exercise to strengthen our core. Spiritually, surround ourselves with God each day and be thankful.

Our heart is now a solid foundation built by us with the love pouring out touching others. Monitor our heart daily and cherish our genuineness. Reach to others who are growing and lifting up those hurting. The heartfelt warm feelings we give are the most valuable accolades anyone can achieve in their life. People are willing to follow those who take the extra moment to listen to a problem and genuinely care. People also recognize those who say they care but are only giving them lip service. There is nothing wrong with wearing our heart on our sleeve. In this world we live, it is more important than any time in history to nurture and have a grateful heart.

HOME

The environment most people are the most comfortable in is their home. They have their own set of rules, live the way they choose, decorate it in their own taste, and put their pride into it. Memories are made with stories which last a lifetime. A home is a safe haven from all the world's troubles where we can unwind and take a deep breath. If we were lucky enough to grow up in a home, big or small, we now remember the colors, smells and intricate details as vividly as if it were yesterday. A home also tells stories that affect emotions deeply. A happy home where everything seems right or a dysfunctional home filled with daily problems. However we grew up, our home said a lot about us. The goal is for a loving, caring, positive home filled with words of wisdom and inspiration. It is up to us to create our home. It takes hard work and dedication.

Choose or build our home with thought and care for our family's needs. Proverbs 24:3–4 says, "By wisdom is a house built, by understanding it is made firm; and by knowledge are its rooms filled with every precious and pleasing possession." What a wonderful way to look at starting a home. This positive outlook makes us think of all the good things to come and to stay focused on what we want. We can put all the wonderful items in our home and fill it up, but the most important things to put in our home are love and commitment to our family. When each family member is on the same page about their responsibilities, the home front flows nicely. When communication is lacking and a head of the household is not there to take the lead, this is where the home falls apart. Fill our home with spiritual wisdom and follow through on being the leader in troubled times. A home without a direction and someone acting as the leader will falter.

The head of the household needs to prepare themselves in every way, so their home will not fail. Look to those positive, successful families for guidance and see what has helped them. Seek God every day for spiritual advice, decide to find the best job to support family and do not settle for less. Our family is our home, and our home is our family. All are connected, and we have to decide a strong home filled with joy, hope, love, care and understanding is the only way. Our home filled with family is the greatest possession we can own. Home is where the heart is, so be creative and give this solid foundation to our family.

HELP

Too many times our own stubbornness and vanity stand in the way of getting the help we need. Always saying we can do it ourselves does not work. We all need help sometimes. It is one thing to think and act independently, and another to climb the mountain of life alone. The words we choose to use and hear over the course of time can make or break us. The law of attraction tells us like attracts like, so if we are not around positive people and lifestyles, we are looking for help in the wrong places. Living a positive and meaningful life full of abundance takes help. Daily, we must work to find the balance in our mental, physical, emotional and spiritual lives. We must seek worldly help with people but cannot rely on them solely. When we rely on humans too much, we become disappointed and negative. We may think they are not giving or helping enough for the moment. We should be grateful for any help provided but ultimately must ask God for help and guidance.

Birth to death, there can be small amounts of time or over one hundred years of living. Only God knows his plan for us. Handling life's situations on earth require good people, healthy knowledge, and a willingness to pass on help for success. It is important to know who we can depend on for help or where to find it. Many times, we have to struggle and work out problems for ourselves because it equals positive growth. Unfortunately, in serious situations, people have waited too long and are past the point of no return. We have to know when it is time to get help with an illness, relationship, or other important situation affecting our life. In the end, when seeking help, sometimes we forget God is with us every day. Anthony J. Paone, S.J. in *The Daily Bread* says, "Above all the persons and things that satisfy your needs each day, put your main trust in me [God]." We have to remember, help will come in God's time.

Help should always be given with an open heart and received with gratitude. Simply taking an extra moment and talking with someone or listening can be extremely helpful. Our positive encouragement or willingness to hear a problem connect us emotionally. This may make the difference in a life. We never know when God thrusts us into situations and uses us. A man walked up to me at a trucking company where I was teaching Illinois vehicle laws to new drivers. He asked if I remembered him. He told me I arrested him for drugs six years earlier, and I had changed his life. He thanked me for the help. This was an encounter I could not have planned. We all can think of personal events when we were at the right place at the right time or changed our mind unknowingly avoiding a bad event. Help many times comes without notice and is unforeseeable. The assistance we give or receive may come from many places. Grateful thoughts, actions, and words with the primary focus on God will give us all the help we need.

HABITS

We form our habits from what we see, hear, believe and think. Habits can be good or bad, depending on positive or negative influences. They can take only a minute or a lifetime to form. Building positive habits for strong personal growth will help individually and others societally. The words we hear pave our road to success or failure. It is easy to pump someone up with positive words celebrating a good habit. No one wants to hear negative things about themselves. Sometimes, the heartfelt truth needs to be said to change negative habits. Positive habits last a lifetime and teach valuable life lessons aimed at success. Everything we do as an adult is emulated by children. The examples they see and hear many times are carried forward to the next generation. Many times, we only have one chance to get it right. We must be grateful for all our positive habits we formed and be glad God has mercy on us for bad habits we have created.

We are creatures of habit. We do and say what has brought success from past practices. Mentally, physically, emotionally, and spiritually, we know what habits make us feel right. Going to morning mass or making spiritual time starts our day with God's blessings. Many successful athletes eat the same meals, dress methodically, or do the same routines before each contest to get to their comfortable mental state. The same habits do not work for everyone. Developing positive habits takes discipline, hard work and leadership. We must look and search for positive examples to build us up daily developing solid habits. A father must exemplify and demonstrate a strong base of habits to help his family grow. We must monitor our habits and ask ourselves, are we acting and mentoring the way God would want me to? Pray continually just like the Bible tells us. It is a great habit.

Keep our habits in check by practice and accountability from friends and mentors. Like-minded people hold us to a positive standard. Avoid people and circumstances who exhibit negative attitudes, actions and words. These habits pull us down in all directions. The consequences to these bad habits can hurt us for life. Author Jim George says, "Eventually, your little choices are going to become habits that affect the bigger decisions you make in life." Our habits should be beyond reproach, and if we have developed bad habits, only we can make the changes. Sharing our successes with others molds a positive future so they can build their dreams. It is our job as a human being to be the best we can be, and it starts with learning and building positive habits. Help others develop a plan leading to more responsibility with their habits. Emphasize positive reinforcement to achieve their goals and always show them the benefits from good habits.

HYPOCRITE

A person true to their word is not a hypocrite. We all know someone who promised us something and did not follow through with action. It may have hurt us mentally such as a relationship ending. Physically, it may have hurt us when someone was supposed to protect our back and didn't. Emotionally, we may have been scarred by a friend with their untruthful words. Spiritually, people practice religion and turn around and act like heathens. Hypocrisy causes pain, anxiety, and mistrust. No one likes feeling this way, but when dealing with earthly beings, we experience this daily. Job 6:15–17 says, "My brethren, are undependable as a brook, as watercourse that run dry in the wadies; though they may be black with ice, and with snow heaped upon them, yet once they flow, the cease to be, in the heat, they disappear from their place." It is a fact, at some point, we will be hurt by hypocritical words or actions.

Our words and actions must have integrity so others know we are trustworthy and not hypocritical. Telling others to call us if they need something and meaning it. Keeping our engagement when we would rather be somewhere else. Doing the right thing for the right reason and not worrying what people think. When we do these things, it gives us the credibility to restore feelings. These positive actions help others believe there is still good out in the world. Not only will others believe in us, the great feeling we receive from following through delivers accomplishment. We all have felt and dealt disappointment through hypocrisy. The pain caused or received should be enough to say we never want to feel that way again. Everyone makes hypocritical mistakes in their lifetime. The work we put in with sincerity will minimize hypocritical dialogue and behavior.

Accountability is the key to beating hypocrisy. Challenge ourselves in every facet of our life. Are we spiritually saying and behaving how God would want us? Do we treat our body and others with respect by diet, exercise, and actions? Are we showing genuine compassion and interest in others when they are opening up to us? Find others who share this passion to be non-hypocritical and hold one another to it. The look of sorrow and disappointment on someone's face because of hypocritical words or actions should be felt in the pit of our stomach. Decide, we do not want to hurt anyone by not fulfilling a promise. When we work on ourselves deliberately with help from others, we will grow. Remove the hypocrite from within and see the beauty, and trust work wonders. Declare to the world, we will be a hypocrite no more!

HUMANE

Humane words go a long way when dealing with others on a day-by-day basis. Our thoughtful and kind interaction will go far when people see we have compassion. Each situation we encounter can have a different outcome, depending on whether or not we are humane in our words and actions. Holding our tongue and not allowing our feelings to come forth is a way God tests us. John 14:30–31 proclaims, "I will no longer speak much with you, for the ruler of the world is coming. He has no power over me, but the world must know that I love the Father and that I do just as the Father has commanded me. Get up let us go." This powerful verse explains not giving Satan a place to interrupt God's plan. We receive mercy from God because we choose good words or silence over nasty, hateful ones.

Humane actions show strength of character and positive examples for others to follow. Too many times, people walk by someone who is dirty, does not fit in, or is asking for help. A small, positive gesture may make the difference between success and failure for this person. Always make time even if we feel we have none for those in need. We never know when God is testing us to see how humane we are. Humane people normally are well-rounded in the mind, body and soul. While on patrol one evening, I picked up a hitchhiker who was trying to get to a hospital to see his mother before she died. I drove the man forty-five miles where he was able to communicate with his mother before she passed. I could have called a cab or another means of transportation, but I took the extra effort to be humane. I will never forget this man, and he will always feel gratitude toward me.

The best way to focus on kindness and compassion is to volunteer. We live in a world where organizations are begging for help. The Salvation Army has to ask for volunteers each year to ring bells. The Red Cross always is in need of blood resources. Libraries are constantly seeking someone to read to children. These are programs that help all races, colors and creeds across the board. Show leadership and humane behavior by sharing our God-given talents with those less fortunate. Instead of waiting for others to ask for help, step forward and ask if they need it. If the world focused on humane words and behavior, so many problems would disappear. All it takes is some time out of our day. On our day of reckoning, God has a score card on us. Hopefully, he will recognize our humane words and actions instead of idle time and selfish endeavors.

HOLISTIC

The words we hear and speak shape our lives interdependently. Everything is connected and affects us from head to toe, inward to outward. A positive balance is where we want to land. It is difficult to always have every area of our life on track at the same time. We are always a work in progress to grow and help others. We want a healthy, positive body, mind, and soul. Since most families suffer from some form of dysfunction many ways to a positive lifestyle may have been neglected. Families who do not attend church regularly or seek God have missed out on spiritual growth. Overweight families may have skipped building a strong body with exercise. Some may have been taught the importance of education and how it builds our future, while others were not fortunate enough to stay away from vices and damaging behaviors that affect every aspect of their lives. No one is perfect! We have to learn how our words and actions can dramatically change our lives to build a holistic body.

Building a holistic, positive us takes practice and a willingness to always try to be better. Look and see where we can achieve more or fill in the holes. It starts with God and asking for help with whatever area we need improvement. Number one, we have to have blind faith in him and be grateful to him before we start. We will not see results in any area we are building or struggling until we give it all to him. We have to stop trying to do everything ourselves! We do not build a house without a strong foundation. Surround ourselves with uplifting people full of good words and examples. Luke 11:36 says, "If your whole body is filled with light, and no part of it is in darkness, then it will be as full of light as a lamp illuminating you with brightness."

As we learn how to build a holistic balance in our life, we move forward and mentor others. No one is ever too old or young to learn. It takes years of practice, and when we see breakthroughs, it energizes us to spread positive words to others. Ask for God's love and guidance every day with excitement of life. Fill others who may be struggling in an area with positive encouragement and show them how when we bring God into our life a transformation takes place. Open the gates for someone to a flowing life filled with passion. Give others the answers where to find the holistic equilibrium to make their bodies healthy and strong.

HASTE

Hasty words and actions can be perceived positively or negatively. A situation may dictate swift resolution when a dangerous, deadly scenario exists. Haste can be bad though when we do not think through the situation or use inappropriate words and tactics based on emotions. When this occurs, it causes us to go too fast. Haste affects us mentally, physically, emotionally and spiritually. We have to recognize haste while speaking and acting for the big picture.

The law of attraction likes speed, and sometimes, we become too eager. This causes us to make verbal and mental mistakes. Training with our thoughts and words can make haste manageable. We need to think through our words and actions with God's help daily. His guidance will prevent haste popping up and creating negative consequences. Hasty words and actions create manufactured stress, which is not productive for anyone and is not healthy for the body.

We all want an answer to a question now and forget it will happen in God's time, not ours. Isaiah 5:18–19 says, "Woe to those who tug at guilt with cords of perversity, and at sin as if with cart ropes! To those who say, let him make haste and speed his work; that we may see it, on with the plan of the Holy One of Israel! Let it come to pass, that we may know it." God does not give us more than we are ready. Physically, we work to make our goals. Mentally, we prepare and think critically. Emotionally, haste can put undue stress on us allowing unsound speech and thought. Spiritually, we have to fight these battles keeping haste in check asking for patience.

Ask God for help daily with our words, thoughts and actions so we do not appear hasty. He will give us answers before we think of them planting positive seeds. A clear conscience and mind giving him the credit will keep us from haste. We all struggle with haste, so pray throughout the day. This will help us with known and unknown scenarios, which will cross our path. The peace and confidence we feel inside will allow us not to overreact. Haste has to be consistently worked on and will never be completely mastered. Do not be too quick to condemn others and look at the entire story. Slowing down and actively listening to others will keep us from haste. Sharpen all our God-given skills to think logically, speak kindly, and act appropriately for the setting. Most importantly, be grateful, not full of haste.

HALLOW

Honoring our words and actions, making them positive, is important. What we hallow is just as purposeful. When we hold something dear to our heart and are grateful for it, joy is fulfilled. Make sure we are hallowing the right priorities, which God would agree. Make the extra time and effort to look at the big picture to see if hallowing something is right. Hindsight is always twenty-twenty, but are we in it for the long haul, or are we satisfying a want-it-now attitude? We must be willing to put in hard work to see if what we are hallowing is positive and strengthening, or will it eventually wear us down. Always check to see if the benefits outweigh the hindrances.

It is alright to have treasures that we worked hard for as long as we can afford it and appreciate it. We see too many times today when as parents, we want to give our children more than we had, but it is not hallowed. We caused this dilemma and need to ask God for guidance. Matthew 23:16–17 says, "Woe to you blind guides, who say, 'if one swears by the temple, it means nothing, but if one swears by the gold of the temple, one is obligated.' Blind fools, which one is greater, the gold, or the temple that made the gold sacred?" Monitor first if people are ready for hallowed gifts by their speech and deeds before delivering. Readiness is the key because if we deliver too soon, feelings of disappointment and lack of appreciation can ensue. Make sure everyone is on the same page and explain positively why before moving forward or taking a step back.

A hallowed leader is respected by their vocabulary and demeanor. They know the right thing to say at the right time always being able to explain their pursuits. Belief and spreading positive reinforcement for everyone every day make us revered. Following through with our word is just as important because it builds trust and integrity. When people believe in a cause and are inspired to action, a hallowed feeling comes to life. An example would be the servicemen and women who put their lives on the line to make America and the rest of the world free. The most hallowed and moving ceremony I have ever seen with its words and actions is the changing of the guard at Arlington National Cemetery. Every feeling, emotion, word and motion burns an indelible image into our brain. When we witness a hallow display such as this, it changes our lives. Every day, we must check and see if we are edifying our ideas and works positively toward hallowed beliefs. Seek God daily to see if we are hallowing the right way.

HARVEST

Words used thoughtfully, lovingly and positively will bring an abundant harvest to our lives. The dialogue we use daily reflects a lot about our relationship with God and our earthly interactions with others. As we harvest our words and deeds, are we getting what we verbally conveyed? Did we choose to honor God with our tongue or spew negativity and filth? We all have had a slip of the tongue, but when it becomes a continual habit, a way of life, or an ungrateful attitude, we should not be surprised of the unhealthy harvest. Job 4:8–9 explains, "As I see it, those who plow for mischief, and sow trouble, reap the same. By the breath of God they perish, and by the blast of wrath they are consumed." Our words if not channeled positively will eventually come back to haunt us when we say the wrong things to the wrong people at the wrong time.

We tend to harvest the people, language and actions from being around the same type. Our words and actions may be learned behaviors. When we speak, it comes out positive and negative. If we have always been put down, told we were worthless, and will not amount to anything, eventually we will suffer emotionally and start believing this barrage of lies. If we have always spoken harsh, abusive, profane language usually that is what we harvest in return. When we use the Lord's name in vain or obscene words, it hurts God and is a sin. Today, because it has become so commonplace to swear and use obscene phrases, people forget and underestimate their words. The Ten Commandments all have the same value. If you use the Lord's name in vain in God's ear, it is no different to him than stealing, cheating or killing. We must monitor our words and actions; otherwise, we may be getting a harvest we do not want.

Cultivate a positive harvest by hanging out with good people. Speak uplifting, appropriate words, and honor God daily with our habits. We must work at it and make it a lifestyle choice. A grateful attitude toward God will change our harvest. What is in our hearts is what comes out of our mouths. We acquire this through practice, patience, and a cognitive effort to better ourselves and others. We do not plant a garden without the proper tools. If we are having difficulty finding a better way for improvement, then turn to the Bible and God for help. Our words can get us into a lot of trouble, but they can also give us peace. When we see change in ourselves and can help others, this is the most fulfilling and abundant harvest a person can achieve.

HEED

Some people don't get it, don't care and cannot recognize how their words and actions damage others to the core. Heed the powerful responsibility of speaking positively, developing a mindful dialogue to uplift others, and pay attention to reflecting a grateful attitude. We have to deliberately monitor how we are reacting toward others daily. Heed how words and actions damage mentally, physically, emotionally and spiritually. Our vocabulary, habits how we handle confrontation, and negligent behavior are factors how we heed what comes out of our mouths. Stop a second and think what we are going to say before we speak or do something we can't take back. Listen what others are saying to us and think through it because if we feel we are being attacked, we stop the hearing process. Curtail the urge from always having the last word. Many times, people are only trying to tell us something for our own good, so heed their advice.

Are we heeding our words and actions for the right reasons, or are we just saying and doing for others to get us noticed? If we are doing this, it only hurts ourselves and others more deeply. Our words and actions must be affirmed with integrity. When teaching about almsgiving, Matthew 6:1 says, "But take care not to perform righteous deeds in order that people may see them; otherwise, you will have no recompense from your heavenly Father." Heed spiritual guidance when we are troubled how to say something or deal with a difficult or uncomfortable situation. Many times, it is merely an oversight how we used a word that can change the environment. As long as we are heeding in a positive direction with good intentions and people know that, our transgressions are usually forgiven.

Always heed someone else's shoes before we speak and act. We all have our own opinion on every subject and need to learn only to give it when asked. Control our tongue with educated words instead of mean, vulgar ones. The Bible, a dictionary and thesaurus not only give us better word choices to use in situations, it cleans up our tongue. Many times, we can heed the same message with educated meaningful words and get a better outcome. Notice how when we were younger, we thought we knew how to handle everything; but as we matured, we realized we needed our elders to give us guidance? Consulting with experience always helps, so heed this opportunity to absorb all we can to win the battles with our tongue. When we reflect on positive words and choose definite actions, it makes us feel better, and we can spread this joyous feeling to others. We are responsible to heed our words and actions.

HAUGHTY

We all have seen and heard people by their words and actions, who think rules do not apply to them or are bigger than the world around them. Their haughty attitude, gestures, and language make others loathe them. They are ungrateful, selfish people incapable to notice how their words and actions hurt those around them. They surround themselves with people who are similar. What we are seeing and hearing on the outside is covering up all the inadequacies on the inside. These haughty people have either been raised the same way and do not know any different or are asking for help as they hurt on the inside. 2 Samuel 22:27–28 says, "Toward the sincere you are sincere; but toward the crooked you are astute. You save lowly people, though on the lofty your eyes look down." God puts in the maximum effort toward us, and we must give him the same. Make a commitment to the world based on God's love.

Haughtiness is a sign of immaturity mentally, physically, emotionally and spiritually. Many times, the only way to reach these people is to let them hit rock bottom. We all have heard testimonies from others saying they never thought it would happen to them. Well, welcome to the real world, my friends. We need to reach out to the haughty in a sincere, loving manner to help them find their way. Confidence in anything we do is important, but when arrogance rears its ugly head, the lines have been crossed. What we say, how we say it, and the way we carry it out says a lot about us. Many times, haughty people have acted this way for so long they do not hear themselves. Instead of being mad or alienating them, take the time to get to know them. We might find they have no friends or anyone they can confide. Everyone can be haughty at times and stay in their own small social circles. It is important to branch out and include everyone. It is amazing to learn why haughty people talk and act the way they do.

A haughty person can change and make amends. Most of the time, a spiritual side is missing. They either never were introduced to spirituality or did not see a need until they hit bottom. Everyone needs people from all walks of life to keep a steady balance. Hearing different people speak and react to different circumstances helps us see what is healthy. When we hear people speak God's word and how meaningful it was to their life, it is positive and magical. A successful life is not based on what we have, but how we apply what we have to make others better. Speak loving and kind words, get out of our comfort zones, and reach out to everyone to avoid becoming haughty.

HEAVEN

Everyone talks, dreams, and thinks about their picture of heaven. All our senses enlightened with no more troubles, and everyone speaking and acting kindly toward others. Wouldn't it be transcending to have heaven on earth where people spoke and acted this way? Our words, gestures and actions are the reason for an unheavenly world. What has happened to good, clean living which was the norm? Our words and actions whether learned or ingrained has brought our society to this point. Everyone talks and acts for shock value, portrays themselves as the toughest creature ever made and is disrespectful toward authority. It is time to clean up our words and actions, bringing respect and kindness back to society. It would be nice to walk down the street again in safety and not have to listen to vulgar, repulsive dialogue. It is possible when we take control of our words and actions and stand up for common decency.

We complain about others how they talk and act, but we must be the one to set the standards. If our words and actions hurt our heavenly Father, it should sound an alarm. If our actions are not heavenly on earth, and we are putting our efforts into personal gain, then we will be judged when it is time to meet our maker. We have to stop idolizing things which are anti-good and hurtful. Matthew 6:19–21 says, "Do not store up for yourselves treasures on earth, where moth and decay store, and thieves break in and steal. But store up treasures in heaven, where neither moth nor decay destroys, nor thieves break in and steal. For where your treasure is, then also will your heart be." This does not mean we cannot have nice things but realize the big picture is our life in heaven.

Challenge ourselves and others to be the best we can be every day. Take notice of immoral, disrespectful and exhausting phrases and deeds and say enough. Our balance toward a heavenly norm must be satisfied. When we are mentally, physically, emotionally and spiritually strong and stand up for clean living, we can be unstoppable. Pull others with us to take back bad behavior and words. Teach and explain how heavenly words and actions make the world a better place. Do not be afraid to do and say what is right. When we lead in this direction, good will follow and chase evil away. Heaven on earth is possible again when we make it a societal priority, condemn wrong behavior and make decisions based on God's love. Stop focusing on negative words, behaviors and manners. Live our life with positive zest and help others reclaim heaven on earth, so we may be reunited forever in heaven.

HERITAGE

It is important to know our heritage so we understand where we came from, what gene makeup we inherited, and how to cope with what we have been given. Each person's DNA is different along with how we were raised and in what type of environment. Our heritage plays a vital role in the words we use and the actions we display. Heritage affects us mentally, physically, emotionally and spiritually. Heritage answers many questions we have about ourselves and how we react to circumstances. If we learn our heritage early, it can keep us from making many of the same mistakes our ancestors made. Knowing our heritage and developing a healthy lifestyle from our past can be important to pass onto others. Our heritage can be bright and proud, or dark and unhealthy. How we handle our heritage will make a big impact on the world.

We see folks who cannot get out of their own way and blame it on their past. Our heritage is important, so we understand it and make positive attempts to better ourselves. The difference is whether we have a grateful, can-do attitude or wallow in self-pity. The words we heard from parents or mentors hopefully were positive and helpful. If they were negative, we definitely learned what we did not want in our lives. A sound heritage filled with spiritual guidance plays a huge role in moving forward. 1 Corinthians 3:10–11 says, "According to the grace of God given to me, like a wise master builder I laid a foundation, and another is building upon it. But each one must be careful how we build upon it, for no one can lay a foundation other than the one that is there, namely Jesus Christ." Powerful words with no higher authority exemplify how to proceed with life.

As we know our heritage and pour all our efforts into positive endeavors for others, we grow. We challenge ourselves mentally to learn as much as possible and know where we get our knowledge. Physically, we build a healthy body and know our limitations. Emotionally, we study our feelings and monitor how to handle ourselves. Spiritually, we pray for the best for ourselves and others in every circumstance. Heritage is important to learn about our families from the past, so we build a bright future. We cannot change our mother and father. We cannot change where we were born. We can change our attitude based on our heritage. History will repeat itself if we let it. The outstanding leaders and mentors do not take no for an answer and keep pressing for new innovations. Make our heritage one of greatness by encouragement and optimism. Let no one stand in the way of leaving a proud legacy.

HARMONY

Harmony: The beauty when we see and feel our whole situation falling into place perfectly. Harmony starts with our words and actions as we communicate with others. Harmony also can be body language that says we are on the same page. Here are some examples when harmony was working in my life. Mentally, the feeling of studying for a big exam and knowing all the answers at test time. Physically, pitching a no-hitter where my catcher and I were in perfect sync. Emotionally, handling an upsetting situation with compassion, ease, and grace by saying the right words. Spiritually, when I prayed or dreamed something and God brought it to fruition. Too many times we reap havoc on situations that could have a harmonious outcome, but we open our mouths stopping the smooth flow. Using the law of attraction when something is working well we should not interrupt the course of action.

Harmony should be positive and feel supportive. Too often today, harmony is broken because of negative language and pursuits stemming from an all-about-me attitude. Harmony should say we care about you and what you are trying to tell us. Harmony gets out of whack because people decide it is more about winning an argument. Harmony should bring joy and happiness to life. Some people thrive on causing chaos and living in drama draining all our harmony. We have to decide we are not going to let anyone steal our joy and ruin our peace. James 3:18 says, "And the fruit of righteousness is sown in peace for those who cultivate peace." This is why it is imperative to join people who bring light and carry a harmonious tune. We all know people who could stop a train with their words and attitude. Once we learn this about them, we must distance ourselves. Whether it is a friend, coworker or a relationship when we feel there is no harmony, it is time to go.

Each day starts new with life's events. How we handle them is important for harmony. Every morning when our feet hit the floor, say thank you for this gift. Smile big and confirm God will not give us more than we can handle. Count our blessings about all the great things in our life. Recognize no matter what our situation may be, someone else is worse off than us. Make a concerted effort to compliment others even on small things. Choose to do a good deed for someone even if we do not know them. Pause a moment before we comment back to someone during a conversation. When we check ourselves and learn to appreciate, our words and actions will automatically flow harmoniously.

HEROES

The term hero is bestowed on someone who accomplishes great feats, displays incredible bravery, or thinks quickly to take control of a situation. We all know someone in our mind who represents this stature. Without their daring and determination, many circumstances may have changed drastically. Their actions and words were positive saving someone's day or life. These stories are widespread and sensationalized by media outlets for everyone to see and hear. The most important heroes are everyday ones that work in our life. John 7:4 says, "No one works in secret if he wants to be known publicly. If you do these things, manifest yourself to the world." Put ourselves out there to make a difference in someone's life and be their hero. We never know when the smallest good deed or positive word will inspire someone or change a negative way. This is why Jesus Christ suffered and died for us so we would do good works for others.

Positive praise, caring, and teaching right from wrong come from heroes who stand up for others daily. Whether we had good parents, siblings, friends, teachers or neighbors, we all remember who was a hero in our life. We know what they did for us mentally, physically, emotionally or spiritually. The gratitude we felt for them is priceless, and we learned from their mentoring. Our hero would want us to pass on these valuable lessons and positive feelings to others. Speak and act positively and tirelessly to spread our message. We can never do enough good deeds in the world. Society has so many organizations and causes to help be someone's hero. The everyday hero should act spontaneously with great intentions. They should bring people along for the cause and be infectious.

Heroes recognize other's needs and step forward without asking. Giving needs to come from the heart whether it is time, effort or money. A hero is grateful for all they have and are willing to share it. Heroes' actions are unselfish and cause others to want to do more. We may see ourselves and say how can we be a hero to anyone? Just showing we care about someone in God's eyes makes us a candidate. When we reach out to others, we learn valuable information and life lessons about ourselves. Whenever we think we have no more room to give, we are only being tested by God to pick it up a notch. Heroes set the bar high and rise to whatever challenge is facing them. Look at our life and ask ourselves are we doing enough for the world?

Amazingly, our hero will rise up and answer the call for duty and humanity.

HARDSHIP

We sometimes feel depressed and confused about life. We cannot take any more negative incidents coming our way. We ask, why do all these things keep happening? Hardship affects people differently and how we react to it comes from learned behaviors and words. Some people overreact to hardship and make the situation worse. Hardships can be mental, physical, emotional or spiritual challenges. During these low points, we must dig down deep inside ourselves and conquer hardships. God is testing us, and 2 Corinthians 1:5–6 states, "For as Christ's sufferings overflow to us, so through Christ does our encouragement also overflow. If we are afflicted, it is for your encouragement and salvation; if we are encouraged, it is for your encouragement, which enables you to endure the same sufferings that we suffer." How positive and powerful to know God is always at our side guiding us through all the rough times!

Are our words and actions creating the hardships in our lives? We have to take an honest look at ourselves. We attract things to us by our words and actions. Many times, we have to change our thoughts from negative to positive. Occasionally, we need to look at the people around us and decide if they are part of the created hardship. When we realize our hardships are self-inflicted, we can choose to roll in the same direction or change paths. Only we can decide to change our ways. When we make uplifting changes to improve our hardships, it is magical for our whole being. Learning positive improvements and living by our changes takes courage. Once we master our hardships, it is imperative to share our successes with others to lift them out of the dark. Solid leaders are able to change paths when hardships are thrown their way.

Unfortunately, many people suffer through hardships that were unforeseen and no-fault of their own language and deeds. A family member born with mental or physical disabilities. Losing a job because a company chooses to down size their workforce. An assailant terrorizing a shopping mall killing innocent victims. In these often difficult and tragic situations, we question everything, including God, asking why? Life is not fair, and frequently, these terrible things happen to those God knows will persevere. Hardships bring people together as a strong reminder to always strive for a positive and loving disposition toward others. In circumstances like these, no matter how bad it appears, apply gratitude toward a positive outcome. Say thank you for the good which is still surrounding us. Focus on righting the hardship with all our abilities and develop a plan. This plan should entail dialogue and means emitting a positive frequency for a new beginning.

ABLE

Situations arise in life when we are called upon because we have the skilled abilities to succeed. People rely on us to get the job done. Whatever the event we are immersed, we have trained mentally, physically, emotionally and spiritually. We work efficiently to accomplish the task and use positive experiences and words from the past. Franklin D. Roosevelt said, "The ablest man I ever met is the man you think you are." Confidence is built from positive experiences and learned from defeat challenging us to do better the next time. Everyone has the ability to win; it is what they do with their talents that counts. When we are able, be grateful for our God-given abilities. An acronym to remember when thinking of able is, Always Believe Life's Exhilarating. Those who are able add an always moving positive energy toward life. They lead, direct, teach and pass it on to others enriching the world.

When we know we are able, treat it as a gift from God. Feel grateful for our qualified power to discern. Work positively and recognize the magnitude of what we can help others to accomplish. When we are able, our own priorities should be last. Able people have the spark to action, magical look in their eyes, and a spring in their step. How joyous and heartfelt to watch the ablest coming to those in need. How inspirational to see when we have uplifted someone and the excitement on their faces when we have made a difference. The exhilaration on the faces of those who were liberated from Axis powers by the Allied forces in World War II is a dramatic picture of the able helping the weak. There is no better feeling knowing our abilities gave someone another chance at life. So hone our able skills and pay it forward.

Staying able takes dedication, hard work and humility. Always remember we can learn anything from anyone. Present an open mind and listen to keep our skills sharp. Do not rest on our laurels and accomplishments. There are so many people who were once able, who have let their abilities dwindle. Many never used their talents to their capacities. Life happens, and positive words and encouragement are the keys. Think of those who have never had a positive mentor to show them the way. As an able individual, this should keep the flame lit to help others mentally, physically, emotionally and spiritually. Our abilities and devotion to others is what able is all about. When we recognize people saying and acting negatively toward others, it is our duty to step in and make a difference. People are a product of what they know. If they do not know a better, positive way, it is up to the able to intervene. Remember, Always Believe Life's Exhilarating.

AIM

The ever-changing world today raises questions what direction society is headed. Instability and indecision causes confusion which does not drive toward a positive aim. When committing to life's challenges, we shall only go at them in positive, constructive ways using encouraging words and actions. Dwight D. Eisenhower said, "When you are in any contest, you should work as if there were to the very last minute a chance to lose it. This is battle, this is politics, this is anything." Always aim for high standards and understand what it takes to reach an objective. When we take aim, it should be for unselfish reasons with a grateful attitude. Our aim needs a positive purpose for the good of mankind. Aim is not only an idea, but requires hard work, discipline, dedication and knowledgeable information. Aim is what we focus on and stems from learned behaviors from the past. Aim is achieved many times by previous failed attempts.

Our aim may be fueled by many reasons and emotions depending on the circumstances. Remember, aim needs to be directed in a positive direction; and unfortunately, doubters, pessimists and jealous people try to steal our joy. Our aim is what we say it is, and no one can take that away from us. Stay focused because when we are good, everyone wants to take a shot at us. Aim must not be half-hearted and insincere. Prior to each season, a manager or coach is asked about the expectations of their ball club. The standard aim is to win a championship. A follow-up question would be do we really believe in our aim? We have to ask ourselves the same question when working toward an aim. Aim requires mental, physical, emotional and spiritual discipline and toughness. All these areas must be strong to achieve a successful aim. When working with others for a purpose, our aim should not be bigger than the project. When many people are focusing on an aim, it is difficult to stop the positive momentum.

Momentum pushes our aim forward with the law of attraction. We may know what we want the end result to be, but there may be many steps in between to achieve the result. Do not question the process because many of our steps will open up with people, ideas, books or other resources. Keep a strong focus on our aim because many times the answers will come from unlikely sources. As the energy for our aim is strong, it will attract everything we need to succeed. There is not always a timetable when aiming for a goal. Patience is important and putting our mind, body and soul into our aim will bring it all to fruition.

ADORE

When we speak from the heart, people revere our words as they burn an indelible image. Positive adoration lights a fire, creates positive memories, builds a commanding trust, and opens up a path to love deeply. Think of the loved one in our life where all our words, actions and emotions cannot adore them enough. Whether it is our spouse, family member or friend, this adoration makes us thankful each day delivering constant joy. Adoring words are strong, meaningful and divine. Our relationship with Jesus should feel this way. His love for us is unmatched, adoring and awe inspired, which requires the utmost respect. Malachi 2:4–5 talks about living right with God's commandments. "Then you will know that I sent you this commandment because I have a covenant with Levi, says the Lord of hosts. My covenant with him was one of life and peace; fear I put in him, and he feared me, and stood in awe of my name."

Adoration is a mutual trust that is earned, and the thought of losing it is devastating. No one wants to lose the soft, safety blanket feeling we had as a child. Sometimes, we take for granted the adoration earned by our words and actions. When this happens, it feels devastating. Losing a dear friend over an unintelligent argument is hurtful. Betraying a loved one by straying from the relationship defies trust. Turning away from God and only listening to our selfish temptations pushes us away from adoration. We have to guard our heart, cleanse our mind against impure thoughts, and filter our words against negative dialogue. The positive feelings when we adore someone must be protected above all costs. As we surround ourselves with people, we adore our outlook on life changes for the better. Words are kinder, love is sweeter, and our actions are heartfelt. Learn and live how adoration changes our perspective body, mind and soul.

Turn to God to guide us through our everyday decisions. God adores us and wants the best for us when we are at a crossroads. God adores us enough to occasionally make us feel the pains of life so we know the difference. Start every day with an adoring and grateful attitude. Stop ourselves from saying or doing negative things. Draw a line forming a boundary, so we never lose the adoration of others by poor decision making. Adoration is kind language and intelligent knowledge of the subject we are adoring. Adoration makes us mentally, physically, emotionally and spiritually refreshed. Our great experiences will make us adored and push us to help others. Always remind ourselves why we adore someone or something as it will bring a warm, cozy smile to our face.

ABHOR

What we have seen, heard, and experienced growing up plays a vital role shaping our core values. We learn what we like or what we abhor. The thoughts, actions and emotions that are learned instill our reactions toward mental, physical, emotional, and spiritual growth. We can choose positive or abhorring words and actions based on what we know and feel. When we reject something vehemently or loathe an activity, it creates negative energy. It is important to differentiate between like versus dislike about certain topics. Do not dwell on them in abhorring ways where it consumes us. Act and speak gratefully for knowing the difference and thank God for granting us this emergency brake. When we do not use this mechanism to channel our thoughts, words and actions, it can damage us in abhorring ways. Abhorred behavior when it affects us or our family directly is when it is time to get involved.

In Leviticus, chapter 26:14–17, God talks to Moses at Mt. Sinai about the Israelites and their rewards for obeying him as well as the punishments for disobeying him and his established commandments with abhorrence. "But if you do not heed me and do not keep all the commandments, if you reject my precepts and spurn my decrees, refusing to obey all my commandments and breaking my covenant, then, I in turn will give you your deserts. I will punish with terrible woes—with wasting and fever to dim the eyes and sap the life. You will sow your seed in vain, for your enemies will consume the crop. I will turn against you, till you are beaten down before your enemies and lorded over by your foes. You will take to flight though no one pursues you." What a powerful and deeply emotional look when we abhor what God has created. Sometimes, it is best to pick our battles in life.

Control our abhorring attitude and be grateful for all the good in our life. Say thank you for controlling our tongue, not walking down the wrong path, or breaking God's commandments. No one is perfect, but learn and share with others how not to become abhorring in the mind, body, and soul. Challenge ourselves daily with devotional time to recharge our spiritual batteries. Channel our energy toward positive people and outcomes. We are in control of us, and sometimes, we ask why did we deserve this? We attract into our life all the things whether we believe it or not. Gratitude versus abhorring behavior is easily recognizable and changeable. Make ourselves healthy and help others along the way. Positive words and encouraging actions takes dedication and practice. Master our thoughts, so the only thing we abhor is not getting the most out of life and being the best person we can be.

ABSTAIN

Making worldly choices versus godly decisions challenges people every minute of the day. Thinking and acting out because it makes them feel good for the moment. Whether it is peer pressure, status or pure selfishness many times we need to abstain from making these choices. We must look at the big picture and decide if mentally, physically, emotionally and spiritually, if this behavior is healthy. We must abstain from dialogues that degrade or ridicule. Refrain from kicking someone when they are down. The opposite should occur using our words and actions to uplift and encourage. 1 Thessalonians 5:22 states, "Refrain from every kind of evil." Our stability and strength depends on abstaining from worldly choices that do not honor God. Jesus bled for us to take away the sins of the world and put the Ten Commandments in place as a guide to follow. When we ask God for his guidance and abstain from making decisions based on what others think or say, we are on track to a healthy life.

We can honor God and act as a positive example by abstaining. Make the assertive choice to not use negative or foul language. Fast one day a week, and during the Lenten season, pay tribute to Jesus. Make decisions about family, money and social interactions based on abstaining from evil. Tithe by doing good deeds for someone daily and abstain concentrating only on self. What sacrifices can we make on a daily basis to honor God and improve and develop a healthy mind and body? Abstain from making poor dietary choices, refrain from joining in negative talk and worldly chaos. In today's world, it amounts to turning off the TV and electronic devices and spend time with God daily. It is amazing how wrapped around the axle people get from watching and listening to all the negativity in the world. A quiet environment and spending time with God is essential to abstain from getting consumed by dark thoughts.

Abstain from acting as a follower and avoidance of getting involved. God made us with light with the idea of spreading love and kindness. Help others with a grateful attitude and abstain from becoming full of ourselves. A humble heart and mind will deliver precious gifts to the world. Abstain from keeping track of our good deeds and mistakes. It is not a contest whoever does the most gets an award. As our daily life unfolds, it should be a surprise when someone approaches us and says, do we remember when we did this good deed? God knows the score, and the bottom line, he wants us as an asset to the world. Abstain from evildoing and self-righteousness. Abstinence builds character.

APOLOGIZE

Our humbleness how we react to apologetic circumstances stems from what words we heard and what actions we were shown. We can apologize for every little thing even when it is not our fault and be overapologetic. We can be like The Fonz character from the show *Happy Days*, and even when it is our fault say, "Wwrrrrrrong," like pulling teeth. How and when we say we are sorry says so much about our character and emotional state. Overapologetic shows someone constantly beat down and wanting peace at all cost. Apologizing only when being ordered to shows arrogance and insecurity. When apologizing, take the responsibility to admit when we are wrong, act humbly toward the person hurt from our actions, and move forward so we can continue to interact together. Bury the hatchet and do not hold a grudge.

People we have insulted feel when our apology is genuine or curt. The words we use when we are apologizing can make all the difference. Tell them we are sorry. Explain what we did and why we did it. This is where our communication may solve the problem, so we are on the same page. Listen to them, tell us how our words or actions affected them. Then be sincere; our intentions were never to hurt them. Learning from our mistakes only makes us stronger. Andrew Jackson states, "Any man worth his salt will stick up for what he believes is right, but it takes a slightly better man to acknowledge instantly and without reservation that he is in error." Our apology should have faith behind it. Do not speak before we think or act impulsively. Don't hold on to our mistakes. God wants us to live lovingly and spiritually free.

Many times, the words we hear, the actions we take, stem from the company we keep. We have heard birds of a feather flock together. It is so true watching arrogant, blameless people who are unapologetic and do not think twice about emotions and feelings. It is uncomfortable for everyone near. Running with the pack is Satan guiding the behavior. God knows our words and actions. Be thankful for the ability God gives us to restore a situation and ask for forgiveness. Confess our sin when we are wrong and apologize to those we have harmed. Growth mentally, physically, emotionally, and spiritually will take place and lead to future successes when we are able to humbly say we are sorry and work toward a positive outcome. Always consult with God before stating an apology, make it come from the heart, and constructively move forward taking away any shame or guilt.

APPRECIATION

Appreciate not only the little things but all things because it makes us critically aware of every situation. Our words and actions shape our world the moment we are born. Using appreciative words such as *please* and *thank you* takes us a long way in life. Writing a simple thank-you note because someone remembered us shows appreciation, respect, and class. Countless times our kind word or deed will come back to us tenfold. Our positive and appreciative words to others sets a standard for mentoring. Most importantly, show appreciation to Jesus each day for all the special gifts he made for us. Colossians 2:6–7 says, "So as you received Jesus Christ the Lord, walk in him, rooted in him and built upon him and established in the faith as you were taught, abounding in thanksgiving." As we recognize and treasure this value, our life will unfold magically with unwavering faith and appreciation.

Appreciation of physical skills helps us accomplish tasks, work diligently to attain difficult goals and recognize abilities for leadership and mentoring. Mentally, when we appreciate knowledge, it sharpens cognitive abilities and allows us to think through any situation bestowing confidence. When we appreciate emotional stability, it leads us through ups and downs of life. It allows us to handle adverse incidents with a calming presence leading others to safety. Spiritually, God knows how much we love and appreciate him. He rewards us for our good deeds on earth. God instills wisdom and grace in us to teach, help and work with others daily. Each of us have unique qualities God gave us so we can appreciate life. Appreciate our vigor to serve and walk in his path. Pass on this appreciation God has shown us by sharing our stories.

Instant gratifications devalue appreciation. In a world where everyone wants the newest, fastest, latest and greatest improvement, we tend to forget the rabbit never won the race with the turtle. Appreciation equals work, thought, patience and manners. Appreciation without these pillars in place leads to entitlement. We are all guilty of providing more for our children than we had. Unfortunately, our output does not always equal appreciation. Newer does not always mean better. Appreciate basic necessities we have but do not take them for granted. It is our responsibility to bring back an appreciative attitude toward people, language and actions. We must do it through God and his works. Without God, there would be nothing to appreciate or celebrate. Remember, appreciation should be perpetual motion. The more we appreciate good words and works, the more we receive and are able to give others. Thank you, Lord, for all you have given us!

ACCOUNTABLE

Saying what is right and acting accordingly even when no one can hear or see us is the mark of accountability. We choose to be accountable or unaccountable for our words and actions. People act and react to the accountability of laws, morals, values, and circumstances. How people speak and carry themselves comes down to what they have heard and seen. If they have not been surrounded with positive, disciplined families and outstanding guidance, they will not know what it means to be accountable. Accountable people take words seriously and do not go against the grain for self-indulgences. They stay their ground to see a job through and believe in a system. Accountable people recognize the big picture and see all the parts making the whole. Accountability must be taught mentally, physically, emotionally and spiritually. The importance of this gift leads us through life and teaches us belief and gratitude.

Building confidence through accountability takes teamwork. A mentor or teammate keeps core principles intact and holds us responsible. Every moment be accountable to God. Ezekiel 18:20 says, "Only the one who sins shall die. The son shall not be charged with the guilt of his father, nor shall the father be charged with the guilt of his son. The virtuous man's virtue shall be his own, as the wicked man's wickedness shall be his." So even if we were not spoken to and taught well, we have a choice to better ourselves and be accountable. It is not a blame game. Accountability starts with us, and once our words and actions follow, a foundation is raised. Hold ourselves in high esteem to do the best we can in every venture. Our life depends on our words and actions to make our life a success story.

There are many ways to keep ourselves accountable in all areas of our life. Do not do anything that we would not ask others to do. Have a friend or mentor to share our concerns and keep each other on track. Set goals for ourselves and withhold small pleasures to keep us accountable. Take time each day and pray about decisions we will be making before we have to initiate ones affecting ourselves or others. Plan ahead for life's unexpected occurrences with a life insurance policy so we create a legacy for our loved ones. Help and share our successes with others for growth. Our rhetoric and actions are the most powerful attributes we can have to build character. Our accountable speech and actions build a reputation which will last a lifetime. Never defame our name to undue our accountability. Priority number one, be accountable to God, family, ourselves and others.

ACCEPT

Acceptance is one of the most difficult yet fulfilling concepts to grasp. When we learn to accept ourselves, others and the world the way they were naturally intended, positive, happiness occurs. Accepting words and actions point us in the right direction. Acceptance means no longer tearing others down for their looks, beliefs and qualities. When we learn to accept, we grow mentally, physically, emotionally and spiritually. Acceptance starts with thanking God for all his gifts. Romans 15:7 states, "Welcome one another, then as Christ welcomed you, for the glory of God." Acceptance takes work and an honest look at how we see ourselves, others and life's anomalies. No matter how hard we try, sometimes life is not fair. We either can accept it with grace or become bitter. The true warrior accepts his circumstances with a happy heart and stays upbeat. Our words and actions are a reflection how we are accepting life.

Acceptance pulls everything together harmoniously while unacceptance tears things apart. Our words and actions are the same way. Our emotions, feelings and reactions are either positive or negative. When others say, here he comes, hopefully they are commenting on an accepting, caring and loving person. Coach Britton used to say, "If, ifs, ands and buts were hickory nuts it would be Christmas every day." It was his way of telling us no excuses and accept the circumstances we were handed. Only we can make it better. Only we can make positive changes. Do not accept anything but our best effort. In every circumstance, we need to accept and realize others are worse off than us. Accept our talents humbly, use positive and encouraging words, and give all we can to enrich others. Accept and recognize everyone has faults. Acceptance should be used in positive fulfillment, not negative banter or dysfunctional circumstances.

Acceptance should not stunt our growth as a person. It is okay to notice different people, but when their negative attitudes or harmful ways stop positive growth, it is time to distance ourselves from their unhealthy and unacceptable ways. Positive words and a healthy lifestyle help us discern what types of acceptance we can coexist. Never accept unhealthy words and circumstances tearing people apart.

Our attitude and gratitude needs to be checked daily for acceptance to work. Pray the Serenity Prayer daily to put us in the acceptance mode. Accept ourselves and others working meticulously to help and nurture. Lead the way to show a better outcome and mentor an accepting life full of greatness. Followers accept less of all circumstances and stop positive progress. Accept only things in our life that will enrich. Our powerful and positive demeanor will enlighten the world and show different types of acceptance.

ACCOMPLISH

Motivation whether self-generated or mentored allows us to accomplish the daily grind, life's challenges, or attain personal goals. We have the power to accomplish anything we want if we use positive words and actions. Choose what we want and go after it. Mentally, prepare and visualize accomplishing our goal. Physically, work tirelessly honing our skills. Emotionally, understand our feelings and recognize battles we will incur while accomplishing our goal. Spiritually, examine ourselves so we do not deceive ourselves. We must compare ourselves before, during and after the process giving God all the glory and thanks. It is important to understand this balance as we proceed toward accomplishing our goals. The law of attraction shows us all these are interconnected for accomplishment.

In the process of accomplishing more, we have to remember not to step on others while attaining the prize. We can get tunnel vision solely focusing on our route to accomplishment. It is important to monitor our own conduct so we do not burden others with our process. We must not forget others who sacrificed their time, effort, or money to help us accomplish our feat. The parent who travelled and attended all our games. The teacher who spent extra time with us learning a subject. The mentor or coach who built us up and developed our skills. All these people deserve gratitude from us. There can never be enough thanks in the accomplishing process. Each day as all our battles are won, we feel this support pushing us forward. Accomplishment and reaching the summit only last a short period of time. When we are no longer on top and on the way down, how we treated others will help us through life. These positive ties along with kind words and actions can steer us toward other accomplishments.

Accomplishments must be self-examined for accuracy, so we are not living off other's laurels or creating a false picture. Galatians 6:4 says, "Each one must examine his own work, and then he will have reason to boast with regard to himself alone, and not with regard to someone else, for each will bear his own load." It is important we do our own work because it will give us a sense of pride. We can cherish the thought of honestly accomplishing our goal during a certain period of time. God knows our accomplishments and how we obtained them. The positive, exhilarating feelings when we accomplish an individual or team feat last a lifetime. Mentor and challenge others to complete their accomplishments. We know the incredible feelings of accomplishment, so give it back for all who helped us. Develop a positive mind, body and soul to accomplish everything we deserve out of life.

AMICABLE

An amicable outcome should be the intention for resolving all disagreements. Amicable words and actions need to be expressed focusing on friendly solutions. Arguing for the sake of righteousness is counterproductive. Mental, physical, emotional and spiritual strife dominate without well-thought amicable mitigation. There are amicable answers to all life's challenges. Work toward speaking and acting amicably every day. This will present levelheadedness, and our amicable demeanor will bring people together. The world is filled with turmoil. C. S. Lewis said, "Has the world been so kind that you should leave the world with regret? There are better things ahead than we leave behind." Amicable people must move forward, think ahead, and look at the bigger picture of our heavenly Father when creating solutions.

Amicable people are fair and willing to make positive sacrifices for others' lives. It is easy to listen to others and hear their words and see if their actions are amicable. Positive people, who are good natured, initiate conflict resolution and words of encouragement. Any self-centered, small-minded, negative person can throw fuel on the fire when trying to resolve differences. We can choose to act as a conflict starter or an amicable imparter. How we react when decisions do not go our way reflect our maturity and growth. Whether the outcome was for or against us, we have to realize life is not always fair. God has a plan for each one of us, and only he knows why. Do not let feelings or emotions take the reins. Many times, we are tested by those around us to see how we handle adversity. Sometimes, our words and actions are inappropriate, so be thankful amicable people point it out.

Teaching and mentoring amicable decisions is a life-long process. We are not always right. Amicable solutions are good for the whole. It is important to be ourselves when making amicable decisions because if it is not well-thought-out, a domino effect can occur. Whether good or bad, the law of attraction picks up momentum with the decisions we make. Learn to take our time when we can. Amicable decisions must be strong, positive examples based on successful principles. Consult with God prior to making amicable decisions. Learn to become still and calm before we speak or act.

Some life-changing, amicable decisions must be made in a split second. In my years in law enforcement, amicable decisions were made quickly for officer and public safety. Hindsight is always twenty-twenty, and we must learn to live with it. In a life-threatening situation, it is much better to be judged by twelve than carried out by six. When making amicable decisions, the bottom line is doing it for the right reason, for the good of the whole, and with the guidance of God. If we follow those virtues, we will live amicably.

ADJUST

Words and actions need flexibility, understanding, and adaptability to adjust to every situation. Stubbornness in language and mind-set cause emotional stress, which has negative consequences.

We all have been in situations where our words or actions, because of our inability to adjust, have caused disagreements. This does not have to happen if we adjust what we are saying and listen to how we are saying it. Life happens fast, and we all like saying and doing things our own ways. Adjusting is looking at the other spectrum first and adapting when necessary. We should never adjust if the decision creates dangerous consequences or compromises moral and godly virtues. Positive words and actions should be used when adjusting to any situation, so a successful outcome can be reached. Each party when adjusting should not feel any remorse or hurt. The goal of adjusting is for a healthy compromise solving the issue at hand.

Some people are not capable of adjusting their words or actions. It is important to recognize these negative and selfish ones. It is not worth arguing with someone who is unwilling to make a positive change. We have to accept their unwillingness to adjust and know it is their choice to speak and act the way they do. We have to protect our body, mind and soul from these people. They enjoy running others down because they are unwilling to adjust and feel so bad about their own image. It is important to try and listen to these people and offer them some sort of assistance for positive living. If they are unwilling to listen, then it is time to adjust our focus and go help others who would want some help.

Adjustment is important for the body from head to toe. We can monitor our words and actions, so we do not cause arguments and hurt feelings. We can adjust our body, so we feel strong and healthy instead of worn. Don't let our mind and body get so out of adjustment; it takes a miracle for healthy communication and living. People, when they feel physically out of adjustment, see a chiropractor for spinal alignment. We have to learn about our body to know all the signs of mental, physical, psychological and spiritual fatigue. We must know how to fix ourselves and help others feel better about themselves. Taking the extra time to pray for adjustment will help us get through daily battles. Matthew 12:33 says, "Either make the tree good, and his fruit good; or else make the tree corrupt, and his fruit corrupt; for the tree is known by his fruit." Change is important for growth, and we should be thankful for the abilities to make these adjustments.

AMAZE

Words and actions affect us in every endeavor and truly amaze us when they hit home. It is an amazing experience when we come across someone with a healthy mind, body and spirit intent on spreading joy to others. On the other hand, when we encounter someone with negative, unhealthy habits, we think it is amazing how they've become so lost. What makes the difference is their amazing abilities to separate earthly and spiritual mind-set. Positive words create incredible wonder of the possibilities of greatness. Positive actions take hard work and creativeness for accomplishing our goal. Together, positive words and circumstances when in conjunction will aspire amazing results. We immediately notice someone who appears to have everything together and also the one who needs serious help. As we learn to critically think and act positively separating the earthly and spiritual world, we will truly amaze others by our wisdom what to do when things do not go our way.

Learn to love, work, play, and help others with a positive passion for life built with the amazing love of God. Astonish others by living by example in our words and actions. Then go deeper by using the Holy Spirit to take us where we need to go. Zechariah 4:6 says, "Not by might, nor by power, but by my spirit says the Lord." In order to keep the body, mind and soul healthy, we have to rely on the amazing love of the Holy Spirit. When we consistently follow this path, amazing results will occur in our life, and we will give energy to others. Our positive words and actions will have greater credibility. Amaze others with our passion and vision. Help others with our strength and caring. Do this while being thankful, giving the credit to God.

No one is perfect, and we learn by our mistakes. Our life's experiences prepare us for success or failure. Some people had everything and eventually have nothing. Others had nothing and now have everything. Amazingly, how we got there is not important. What is important is to have a consistent, positive lifestyle with healthy choices. Anyone can follow the crowd, but those who tell themselves we can do better by depending on God are amazing. Our answers will feel amazing with the decisions we make. When the Holy Spirt is inside us, there is always something there to reach back to in times of trouble. Amaze others with our positive attitude and uncanny knack to do for others. Amaze others with our abilities to remain calm during the storms. Amaze others with our love of God and show them how his love for us has granted peace in our life. Thank you, amazing God!

AMBITIOUS

Watching and listening to people, we can quickly recognize ambition by their words, actions, attitudes, and body language. What motivates them is their story and God's plan. Work ethic is also tied directly into ambitious people. How we were raised either with encouragement or discouragement makes the difference. Positive, self-motivated individuals want to achieve more and have a guided direction. A can-do, thankful attitude for our God-given talents should push us toward greatness. A strong self-esteem and a willingness to succeed creates self-confidence. Recognizing we have the tangible life skills is a true gift from God, and we need to use them ambitiously. Ambitious people use positive words, project a beaming smile, walk with a purpose and have a zest for life. Listening to an ambitious person, we learn what they want to accomplish as they design a plan of action that excites. When the challenge has been met and the glory has been given to God, ambition has arrived.

Ambition comes from remembering our roots and wanting to do the best. Humble beginnings and recognizing those who inspired us will always keep the fire burning. Those positive people mentoring and helping us through difficult situations always left us with a successful message. Ambitious people are never satisfied with their accomplishments and want to do more. These same people volunteer to help others in need. They try to figure out solutions that would make someone's life easier. Ambitious people want to take others by the hand showing them the way to success. Ambitious individuals also teach and discuss mistakes they have made along the way for improvement. Ambition should always be filled with gratitude surrounding ourselves with positive people. Proverbs 16:1 says, "Man may make plans in his heart, but what the tongue utters is from the Lord." Sometimes, our words and actions often produce results different from what was originally planned. An ambitious person accepts this challenge and moves forward toward the new goal.

Life's law of attraction is momentum, and sometimes, things do not always go our way. The difference is the ambitious person always finds a way to turn the negative circumstance into a positive one. Ambitious individuals find different outlets that get them going again. Prayer, positive thinking and surrounding ourselves with great people are the motivators. Ambitious individuals work with positive people, and when this group sets its sights on good things, nothing can stand in the way. This is why a team achieves more. Ambitious people always reach out to God and give him the glory with every accomplishment. An ambitious person is always hungry to learn from others, find inspiring wisdom through literature, and listen to upbeat music with a positive message. Ambition comes from many positive forms; find the ones that continue to inspire us.

ASPIRE

We all aspire to say and do good things. Aspiration is a state of body, mind, and soul; and when directed through God's word is the most powerful. Finding the right word or way sometimes is difficult, but when we use God's aspiration, we do the best for the most. We know when we see someone filled with God's word, they are following the path of love and devotion. Psalm 119:1–2 says, "Happy those whose way is blameless, who walk by the teaching of the Lord. Happy those who observe God's decrees, who seek the Lord with all their heart." When we are young, we aspire to be anything we want and dream big. Hopefully, we have positive words and actions moving us. Life happens as we grow, and through trial and tribulations aspiring slows or stops. Never let life's exchanges stop creative aspirations. Never give up and always aspire to do and be the best.

Challenging ourselves to always be in a healthy, aspiring mindset takes discipline and practice. Thinking in the moment does not keep up with life's obstacles. Teach ourselves to think and act ahead of the curve always aspiring to have a plan B. Life is short and fast, and in order to successfully aspire anywhere, we must think and act creatively. Aspiring creativity comes out of the necessity of not being left behind. Positive words, actions, and mentorship propel us to the top. Anyone can say we can't do it, life is hard, or this is too stressful. Every we can't or can is a new creation. It is what direction we take it that counts. Aspiration never takes a day off or allows us to settle for less. Aspiration must be solid, uncompromising, and done with bravado. Celebrate our creative aspirations.

Positive people develop positive aspirations for a complete and successful life. We think we can, we think we can, we think we can builds momentum. Mentally, physically, emotionally and spiritually live like the well-oiled machine in perfect rhythm. Prepare to go after our aspiring dreams with a passion. Aspiring people think beyond the box and outside their comfort level. Learn to get comfortable and poised where others cannot handle the heat. Rid ourselves of negative vocabulary, poor decision making and a defeatist attitude. Aspire greatness and lead others to life's victories. Make the decision we are the best and will not settle for less. While aspiring for excellence, a thankful heart pulls God's love into the equation. When God is on our side, creative aspiration comes from places least expected. Aspire to say and act with thoughtful intentions. Aspire to grow as a better person each day. Aspire to do for those who cannot do for themselves.

APPEASE

Words and actions can cause appeasement or incense others stirring up their thoughts and emotions. We do not always have to agree with a view, but we need to speak and act with restraint. Our words and actions do not always have to be blunt or right. We must make people feel they are part of the process for appeasement to work. We must appease to calm the storm, so intelligent and not overemotional conversation takes place. Positive words, a composed demeanor, and direction from above bring appeasement. Mental, physical, emotional, and spiritual debates can quickly inflame events into chaos. A leader needs appeasement skills to tranquilize any situation with positive dialogue and loyal actions. A good appeaser, people trust, and know his motives are pure. When avenues of appeasement are exhausted, turn to God for help. Through scripture, positive stories, and prophetic outcomes, they pave the way to appease life's challenges.

In Galatians 1:9–10, Paul talks about people not following the biblical teachings this way. "As we have said before, and now I say again, if anyone preaches to you a gospel other than the one that you received, let that be accursed! Am I now currying favor with human beings or God? Or am I seeking to please people? If I were still trying to please people, I would not be a slave to Christ." Stay the course with the solid foundation of God and do not appease others who cannot follow a path of righteousness. It is not always that cut and dry. In a perfect, positive world, everything falls into place. When someone has been beaten down verbally, mentally and physically with negativity, it takes great work, healing and positive mentors to restore order for appeasement. God gave each one of us gifts to use toward appeasing others with kind words and actions for a healthy and happy life.

Everyone can tell us where the most tranquil place they go in times of trouble. It may be different for each of us, but we all know where our appeasement exists. The law of attraction shows like going toward like. Loving, positivity and kindness go a long way toward appeasement. Run from negative situations and find our safe haven.

Surround ourselves with positive, driven people who speak intelligently and can find appeasement in life's situations. Learn from their valuable experience how to handle rough situations and turn them into appeasing outcomes. We will feel deep gratitude for our mentors who show us how to turn precarious situations into appeasing ones. Thank God for giving us the verbal and life skills to help others intelligently. Appeasement is one of the most tangible skills a person can learn as they live around others daily.

ASSURANCE

Speaking and doing things with assurance builds our reputation. This self-confidence draws people and inspiration to us. Positive verbiage and actions show conviction in our mind and manners. Many people struggle with assurance because they question their abilities. A solid foundation of God, family and work support us in times of trouble, but provide the guidance to success. Learn reliance on these to overcome any obstacle for assurance. It sounds easier said than done because many times, one or all of these ingredients are missing for the path of success. If our family is not the positive outlet, find people who are. If our work does not bring assurance for happiness, find and work toward a better living. If we are not visiting and sharing our life with God daily, negativity prevails instead of assurance. Growth mentally, physically, emotionally, and spiritually occur when our mind and body work hand in hand creating assurance.

Assurance is built and not given. Decide to be the person others can count on because they trust our words and actions for assurance. Use positive words to uplift others and help them believe in themselves. Explain our passion by our experiences and tell them everything will be alright. Do not listen to or take negativity to heart. Remember as Isaiah 51:6 says, "Raise your eyes to the heavens, and look at the earth below; though the heavens grow thin like smoke, the earth wears out like a garment and its inhabitants die like flies, my salvation shall remain forever and my justice shall never be dismayed." When we believe in God's assurance, everything else is trivialized. Even when times are tough, and we cannot comprehend why, it is time for gratitude. Gratitude reminds us to count our blessings for assurance. When we recall this, things are not as bad as they seem.

Having assurance allows us to take a deep breath, reflect on our situation and think clearly about our next move. If we do not believe or always try to do things alone, we can quickly become misguided. Do not speak and act obtusely. Assurance is nurtured with the help of others and God. Do not be prideful because it will not give us confidence in the mind and body. An open ear will many times soothe the sound of a full mouth. We all have been around those who carry themselves with assurance and those who bring chaos. Positive versus negative any day of the week helps assurance grow. Decide today to be the inspiring one, the person we can count on, and lead the way to assurance. As our confidence grows, our successes will peak too. Assurance, when multiplied like the law of attraction, will be fruitful to all we mentor.

ARTICULATE

Meaningful words, conversations, and actions with positive direction shows maturity and character. Too often, people express themselves in unintelligent speech surrounded with negative emotion. This results in inarticulate behavior saying and doing things that are purposefully hurtful. When we hear and see this, it should make us cringe. God did not make us to destroy one another with vial vocabulary and unreserved actions. Articulate people think before they speak, use positive and kind words, and intelligently communicate even when in disagreement. Articulate people are easy to spot because they are good speakers, lead with intelligence over emotion, and use spiritual guidance in every day matters. Articulate people understand to be in control of themselves mentally, physically, emotionally, and spiritually, they must systematically work with a positive attitude and gratitude. If we talk and act articulately, the right words and actions will naturally flow. Articulation takes commitment and practice. Eventually, people surrounding us will recognize our articulate gift.

Articulate speech and intelligent behavior take a lifetime to master. Encouragement with positive words and examples from the time we were young is the beginning. Education and learning shape our vocabulary and social interaction. Articulate people challenge themselves by reading frequently on different topics. Another idea is meeting with others discussing topics with differing points of view. A speech course or debating team are excellent avenues toward articulate growth. When we are chosen to speak to a group, deliver a eulogy for a family funeral or guide others in an emergency situation, our preparation and articulate response will shine. Our articulate words and thoughtful actions will provide calm, direction, and confidence for others. We all have experienced situations where the leader was unprepared and exhibited poor verbal skills. We also have witnessed articulate leadership, and the difference is night and day. Aspire to be the articulate one people emulate.

Articulate individuals tend to surround themselves with others of similar caliber. They have a spirit to teach those in need as a positive mentor. Titus 2:1 states, "You, however, must teach what is appropriate to sound doctrine." Articulate people must speak and act correctly so others believe and respect their reputation. Articulate leaders must walk the walk and talk the talk with a grateful heart. So many people depend on articulate leaders, and when they fall from grace, hearts and beliefs are shattered. Live above board mentally, physically, emotionally, and spiritually. Decide we will intelligently articulate any matter that comes our way. Avoid going with the crowd when negative talk or bad gossip cause harm. Remember, articulate people should help themselves and others go places for the societal good. Negative, inarticulate individuals wallow in the quicksand they create, going nowhere. When we choose to be articulate, we are consummate.

APPLAUSE

Life is full of challenges, struggles, disappointments, successes, and thankfully, accomplishments. All of us have experienced each of these at some point in our lives. Positive words of praise push us along, and hard work leads us to the applause earned from a job well done. The goal should not be about hearing the accolades. Sir Edmund Burke, an eighteenth-century Irish philosopher, said, "Applause is the spur of noble minds, the end and aim of weak ones." Our body, mind and soul should be free of negativity to open all avenues of creativity. Truly great work naturally flows when positive words, thoughts, and actions are behind the creator. When our work benefits the greater cause of others and is selfless, that is when applause should be recognizable. When we add God behind our endeavors for guidance, this is an equation toward success. Make our life have meaning whatever direction we go, and applause will follow.

Applause should be appropriate for the occasion and not cheapened. Today, where accolades are handed out for just belonging, it is important to recognize legitimate and positive efforts. We acknowledge the best with applause, we clap for a wounded warrior, and honor a hero for saving a life. Legitimate and well-earned praise deserves applause. Applause is also used demonstratively to show contempt. When a referee is having an off night and makes the right call. Applause can be used scornfully by a dullard when someone does something embarrassing. It is mean spirited to cheer when someone trips, breaks something, or is made to look foolish. Unfortunately, this type of applause has become forefront in a cynical world. Police ourselves and recognize if we are applauding the right efforts. A rule of thumb should be, are we applauding positively for someone who truly deserves the accolades due to their accomplishment?

Applause is uplifting, inspiring and makes us on fire to do more good for others. Live our life positively and to the fullest each day. Surround ourselves with positive people who want to make a difference. When we are solid mentally, physically, emotionally and spiritually, good works will follow. Cheer others onto success, and their efforts will invigorate. Could we imagine hearing the thunderous applause and feeling the adoration when listening to Lou Gehrig give his farewell speech at Yankee Stadium, learning the polio virus was cured or watching Neil Armstrong walk on the moon? These examples send chills down our spine as if we were there. We are capable of unlimited successes, and when people reach these great heights, applause should be deafening. Think and react gratefully when positive accomplishments deserve applause. The world is full of good people who have accomplished great things. Applaud them appropriately and cut loose with loud gratitude.

ADMIT

Always take ownership of transgressions and admit our faults. Accountability is important for everyone and everything for growth and relationships to flourish. Whether in our personal life, community setting or business world, we need to admit mistakes and move forward before larger results appear from a minor miscue. When we do not admit our mistakes, eventually our mind, body and soul are ready to blow like a tea kettle. The pressure from not admitting our mistakes, moving forward, and asking for forgiveness will destroy any chance of resolution. Admission equals penance, and we all need to be thankful for the ability to say we are sorry. Admission is positive words and actions, and we must truly want to come clean. People half-heartedly apologize every day for things they have done wrong. We can see through these negative statements and mannerisms. Admitting we are wrong with sincerity gives us a fresh start like taking a deep breath.

Admitting we are wrong heals mentally, physically, emotionally and spiritually. Mentally, our mind does not shut off, and we have to keep covering one lie with another. Physically, we are beaten down when we do not admit guilt because our body starts to suffer with illness from the stress. Emotionally, when we do not admit to wrong, we sail from one end of the spectrum to the other. Happiness turns to sadness, anger to suffering, and stability to depression. Admitting wrong will keep us off this reckless roller coaster. Spiritually, we have to answer to God for all our wrongs, and there is no hiding. God knows what we are going to do before we do it. Psalms 25:11 says, "For the sake of your name, Lord, pardon my guilt, though it is great." Admit when we are wrong and get back to a positive, healthy life filled with honesty.

Admitting we are wrong takes courage because it will lead to embarrassment. Admitting we are wrong builds character as we choose between right and wrong. Admitting when we are wrong helps instill trust that may have been lost if we have lied. When people know we will not cover up the truth, we are recognized for our candor. Positive energy will flow when we admit to our mistakes. It will lead us in new directions for our good. The law of attraction talks about everything being connected, and when we choose the right path, good things will happen. If we admit our guilt and are truly sorry, God forgives. Once we are there, it doesn't matter if others will not forgive us. It is a burden they have to carry. When there is any doubt, admit it and shake it off.

ACQUIRE

It is important to acquire wisdom, knowledge, positive direction, and work ethic in order to build ourselves into a strong person mentally, physically, emotionally and spiritually. Life brings opportunities to learn and create our own universe. The playing field is not always equal for everyone trying to acquire all the great things life has to offer. It is up to the person to choose how they can even out their chances by the choices they make. God created us, gave us the parents we have, and put a blank slate before us. It is up to us to acquire the good, loving lifestyle filled with earthly and heavenly treasures. Colossians 3:16, explains, "Let the word of Christ dwell in you richly, as in all wisdom you teach and admonish one another, singing psalms, hymns, and spiritual songs with gratitude in your hearts to God." Remember, give all the glory to God as the most important thing we can acquire.

Building this unselfish view takes extreme patience, searching our souls, and looking at all we have acquired. Acquire positive experiences with grateful people who have accomplished goals for the good of the world. This positive outlook helps us become unselfish and God oriented. Opportunities we created were only granted because of the love God bestowed on us. This does not say we cannot acquire nice things of our own accord. It conveys if we are fortunate enough to have plenty, we should share it with others who are less fortunate. Sharing our earthly and spiritual riches is important to help others succeed. We live in a time which is the most information-friendly era ever recorded. There is no excuse but to acquire the most positive things imaginable. Set our standards higher than anyone will ever give us credit for and acquire more.

Focus on positive words and actions. Concentrate all our efforts with spiritual guidance. Blend the two together and enrich our mental, physical, emotional and spiritual being. When we do all this, a powerful union is made where we can acquire anything. There is power in numbers, and when we master our life and pass on this valuable information, we build incredible bonds. Amazing work gets accomplished when we put all our acquired efforts together. It is interesting to think what the most important thing we acquired will be when we meet Jesus, and he asks us this question. Never stop acquiring wisdom and knowledge from God's word. It enlightens us, gives answers to many yet to be asked questions, and fills our heart with love and kindness. Acquire all our knowledge from the best people, with the greatest intentions, and do this with a grateful heart and attitude.

ADVICE

Advice comes in different forms by many people and is supposed to be positive. In a perfect world, our advice angel would sit atop our shoulder and help us make every decision correctly. We all have been raised in different situations, so the advice we have received may not have always been positive. We learn by the environment we have been thrust in, so going forward can sometimes be confusing. Positive words, actions, and people surrounding us make the difference. Over the years, we will need advice mentally, physically, emotionally and spiritually. Hopefully, our mentors are giving sound advice when needed. It is important to seek God when we are pondering what to do. Proverbs 6:24–25 says, "A wise man is more powerful than a strong man, and a man of knowledge than a man of might; for it is by the wise guidance that you wage your war, and the victory is due to a wealth of counselors."

How do we know if the advice given is right or it should be taken with a grain of salt? We have to start believing in ourselves and using our positive words and experiences to guide us in making our decisions what to do. Through the years, we will grow, and some decisions will become routine. More serious decisions will take extra time and soul searching. When making our decisions, try to leave emotional energies out of the process. Emotions can entangle us when seeking advice. Sometimes, the best advice given or received is none at all. Occasionally, too many people get involved in our decision-making process, or they want to steer us in their direction. When seeking advice, logically think through how the decision will affect us and others. Advice should point us to what is the healthiest and prudent choice for our life.

The difference between success and failure can teeter on the advice given or received. Advice needs to be positively constructed and come from a loving and caring angle. Parents sometimes need to step back and let their children make decisions on their own. This is for their own good even if it means mistakes. This tough love will help our child grow and think through things on their own. Consider who we are giving or getting our advice. Hopefully, a strong parent, teacher, mentor or friend can help us through rough times. As we get older, we all can reflect on those special people who gave us advice for growth. We all remember good advice we received and bad advice too. As we establish ourselves in a positive light, be willing to help those who need guidance. Also, be thankful to know when we should keep quiet and not offer advice.

ATTACK

If we want the most and best out of life, it is up to us to attack the competition. Words and actions must push us forward with positive motivation. We must be willing to mentally, physically, emotionally, and spiritually put it on the line. Attack mode comes with controlled aggression. Mentors and coaches try to get the most out of us with their verbiage and examples. Self-motivation must come with passion striving for our goal. Attack our personal life with vigor. Better ourselves with the most knowledge we can find on our areas of concern. Attack any bad habits we have and strive to live a healthier life. Attack our career with fullness and attention. Give more when our coworkers strive to be average. Some people do not understand attack if they were lit on fire. Have a belief no one can work as long and hard as us. This is attack mode.

Settling is not a choice for people who understand attack mode. They have a visionary purpose and know if there is a will, there is a way. People who live in attack mode do not only have one plan for their goal, day and life. They have multiple options for when one does not work. Their ferocious determination won't allow an obstacle to stop them. Look at people who lose limbs and then continue a positive and motivational life with their prosthesis. They understand attack mode, and most of all are truly thankful. Attacking life is a confidence knowing everything will turn out fine. We may not always know how, but we keep working, and eventually, it will fall into place. Excuses are not acceptable to people who live their life to the fullest. When people continually say they were busy when something does not get done, they do not understand attacking life.

Surround ourselves with people who get it, hold us accountable, and work with us to attack obstacles. Negative people with their excuses and poor-me attitude will never go far in this world. People come in and out of our life for a reason. When we are attacking our life's goals, they help us keep our focus and differentiate those who are holding us back. Proverbs 27:10 states, "Your own friend, and your father's friend forsake not; but if run befalls you, enter not a kinsman's house. Better is a neighbor near at hand than a brother far away." Attacking life makes us realize we need every type of person to help keep our perspective and come away victorious. When attacking life, give it all to God. We will always have a partner who never leaves our side, guides us through decision making and growth, and teaches us self-control and accountability. Life is great when we attack it with a loaded tool belt.

ACKNOWLEDGE

Understanding the world and how our life fits in takes years of acknowledgement, patience, and perseverance. Each of us acknowledge ourselves in different ways depending on positive or negative encounters. We also acknowledge others in the same way by what we have heard and seen. Positive acknowledgement for a job well done, purposeful motivation for times of encouragement, and passionate direction are what we hope for to live our lives to the fullest. Acknowledge great thinkers and learn from their works. Acknowledge healthy eating and exercise habits to fuel and shape the body. Acknowledge all our emotions separating the good from the bad and learn how to live with them. Acknowledge God is in charge and helps us work through life's challenges. Daniel 2:46–47 talks about King Nebuchadnezzar at Babylon acknowledging God. "Truly your God of gods, and Lord of the Kings, and a revealer of mysteries; that is why you were able to reveal this mystery."

Living together we must acknowledge right from wrong for civil obedience. We must acknowledge when we are wrong in our thoughts, words, and actions. Acknowledge others have value in their life and can enrich ours if we are willing to listen. Turbulence in life stems from failing to acknowledge a relevant fact out of stubbornness. We must acknowledge positive words and behaviors for the good of others. We should not acknowledge negative words and actions that cause harm. Like it or not, we must acknowledge there is a pecking order in the world. Military and paramilitary organizations have a chain of command, and it is imperative to acknowledge this direction. We must also acknowledge our family positions. Dad and

Mom are the boss, and the kids should not be the tail wagging the dog. Acknowledge our current circumstance and realize others have dilemmas too.

Acknowledge we were made for a purpose to do the most good for others. We must acknowledge the truth will set us free. It is important our words and actions acknowledge who we are and why we stand. Learning who we are sets the tone for our direction and accomplishments. Do not be afraid to speak up when situations are unjust as long as we are acting within the laws and acknowledge authority. Acknowledging nature is stronger than man, so act prudently. Life is not perfect, and it has its ups and downs. To make the rough times smoother, we cannot do it alone and forget about God. Acknowledge our creation as a blank slate. Go about each day and acknowledge the special gifts he gave us. Acknowledge all these positive emotions such as joy, happiness, gratitude and faith to enrich our lives and others. Believe in ourselves because there is only one you.

ABIDE

There have been laws since the beginning of time. Governments, communities, and businesses have laws, ordinances and policies they want people to abide. The thirty-first governor of Illinois, Adlai E. Stevenson II, said, "As citizens of this democracy, you are the rulers, and the ruled, the law givers and the law abiding, the beginning and the end." Conforming to all these life rules can be chaotic. Usually though, they are put in place to protect people from themselves. If there is a rule to obey, it is because someone has done something to make people put this law into action. We have rules we need to abide within our own lives. Personal rules that make us comfortable, family rules that help us reside with our loved ones, and public rules that help us get along in the community. It is important to abide by these laws and norms to help the world run smoothly.

Abiding to laws is important mentally, physically, emotionally, and spiritually. Mental toughness is important to obey for our own personal path, whether it is for a diet, studying, or planning for a future. Physically, abiding to exercise and fitness keeps the body in good shape. Emotionally, keeping our feelings under control is important for a calm demeanor. Spiritually, keeping our word with God and his laws decides whether we see heaven. Abiding to laws, norms, and social rules is a huge challenge because everyone has grown up in different settings. Abiding to a set of rules is different from one person to the next, depending if our experiences were positive or negative. Following the rules in life can be difficult but is really best for everyone. Anarchy would rule the world if it were not for people abiding to everyday rules.

The most important thing we can abide by is the Golden Rule, "Do unto others as we would want done to us." Positive words, pleasing attitudes, and a grateful heart should be what we abide. Abiding takes discipline, encouragement and an unselfish attitude. Too many people do what they want, whenever they want, without regard toward others. When we abide by our personal rules, community ordinances or written laws, we are doing what is good for the whole. We must also be thankful and grateful for lawmakers who do it for the good of others. They want to make a difference in the world. People complain about too many laws, but when asked, they would not want to put themselves out there to do the demanding work. Abiding in God's word will make all our decisions to conform much easier as we can follow the Ten Commandments and live for eternity.

NOW

Ready, action! Life is a stage where our performance is live. Our words, decisions, and actions are seen by everyone in a split second with social media, Internet, and people's reactions are instant as they respond. We always want to do, be, look, and feel the best at all times. Mentally, physically, emotionally and spiritually, it is not always possible, but the show must go on with speed. The law of attraction talks about moving fast where one action is connected to the next through energy. Positive vocabulary, thought, emotion, relations, and a partnership with God prepare us for now. Now equals joy, love, passion and happiness living for today. Psalm 118:24 says, "This is the day the Lord has made; let us rejoice in it and be glad." Now is the time to shift our life in gear setting our goals, conquering personal battles and building our dreams. Now is how; and when we want something bad enough, our life will turn to wow!

Dedication to now is important because we have to put our body, mind, and soul in a positive state. Visualize now, write it down, do whatever it takes to keep ourselves in the motivational spirit. Everybody loves a winner, and we must remember not to let anyone try and tear us down. The trek to now takes hard work, perseverance, and a grateful attitude. The world is filled with detractors, and we must say to them, not me, not now. Now is excitement, saying thank you for our special gifts and knowing we are never alone on our now journey. Believe in ourselves and our now process. Surround ourselves with positive people who root for us. Read positive literature keeping our now line going. Ask God for guidance daily and talk with him about our now. It will be truly amazing when we hear our positive answers to now in situations we were not planning. Make now feel like bliss.

Now is living with a purpose and not depending on others to get us motivated. Our fire must be lit from within counting our blessings saying life is easy. Act grateful for our ability to not let others steer us down a negative lane. Focus on only positive results, and when any negative thought, feeling or action presents itself, flush it. Our now will benefit ourselves and others for a more rewarding life.

Commitment to excellence is now, and mentoring others will give them confidence to fulfill their dreams. Now keeps our body, mind and soul fresh and young at heart. Feel negativity and stress disappear as we are filled with positive. Reach out to others as a servant, Jesus did. When he lived on earth, he was a man and took all our pains and negative things away so we could live for now. When we reach someone, feel their excitement, and see their elation, now really works! There is no limit to now! Each person's dream, goal or situation is different, so new and refreshing is now!

NICHE

Some people are born with a God-given niche, most people prepare and work hard to find theirs, and unfortunately, there are those who never find one. Everyone has some great quality about themselves to positively refine and develop into their niche. Positive words, traits and life experiences must be turned into skills that specifically suit our abilities. Jeremiah 29:11–12 says, "For I know the thoughts that I think about you, says the Lord, thoughts of peace and not evil, to give you a future and a hope. Then you will call upon me, and go and pray to me, and I will listen to you." So when we are searching for our niche, God will guide us in the right direction. Our niche portrays and explains us. Exemplify our niche with a positive and grateful attitude. Make our niche one of pure enjoyment that fills our heart with joy and happiness.

Life is a full-time examination of our skill sets. Finding a steady and comfortable niche takes time and effort. Even if we have a God-given niche, like having a ninety-nine-mile per hour fastball that comes out of our hand like a thunderbolt, we still have to work at it. Write out a list of all the positive qualities we have. Take our best qualities and tailor them to our needs mentally, physically, emotionally, and spiritually. We will learn what areas we can succeed and ones we may need some improvement. We hear testimonials of people who say they never thought they would be doing this job or reach this goal. The difference was they believed in their niche, crafted it, and powered through. We can be sure they did it with the help of positive mentors who gave uplifting and inspirational advice. Our niche can be a gift or a choice. Either way, do not forget about God in the equation.

Make our niche one which is positive, helpful to others, and honors God. People find all kinds of niches they perfect, but doing it degrades themselves, others and turns out to be negative societally. They might get rich and famous for something which is immoral, impure, or just flat outrageous. Avoid these niches because if this is the type of niche we want for success, we would be better off not finding one at all. Our niche should be remembered as one of respect, devotion to others, and fun-loving. We all know and remember people who helped us succeed. They had special niches we thoroughly enjoyed, and their caring spirit passed it on to us. We added these joyous experiences in shaping our niche because good qualities and stories need to be shared. Find our positive niche, dedicate ourselves to it, and ask God to help us along the way.

NEGOTIABLE

Everything in life is negotiable. No is not an acceptable answer unless we allow it. The art of negotiation comes from the words we know and use. Negotiations can become emotionally charged if we do not use positive dialogue and keep our senses calm. When negotiating, our goal is to get more than the other is willing to give. Negotiations can be about anything and affect everything. Everything in our life we have brought into it, and whether we like it or not, the law of attraction says we did. We can negotiate every topic, choose every side, confer, discuss, sell, discount, or reach agreement. Our words are important, and we must not be afraid to speak to them to have a friendly negotiation. John F. Kennedy said, "Let us never negotiate out of fear. But let us never fear to negotiate." Whatever the topic, know we can have what we want through our positive verbal skills.

We learn what to say, how to say it, and when to close the deal through our trials and listening to others. A crafty negotiator already has a second plan ready to strike if the first does not do the trick. It is like a beautiful song flowing melodically, and hitting each note perfectly. People negotiate with their families, friends, coworkers, and others to get the deal of a lifetime. Just like a fair fight, it should be one-on-one matching verbal and nonverbal skills. A solid negotiator brings all his tools to the table. They may involve playing on emotions, working a crowd, or even fibbing a little to get what we want. Negotiations are a learned behavior since we were a child. Begging to stay out later, requesting a different option, or trying to stay out of trouble stating we will never do it again; these are learned negotiations. Ask God to help us think and speak clearly when handling negotiations.

People build their careers around negotiations. Attorneys negotiate their client's freedom. A hostage negotiator uses all his verbal skills trying to save lives. A debt collector gets as much money out of a person as he can. A judge and arbitrator listen to each side and render a fair decision. This is negotiation. When we negotiate, we create an information highway that carries important talk back and forth building a bridge. We should be thankful to learn such an important art as negotiation. Negotiation gets us through life and into a better place. Never quit when negotiating because the other person is hoping we say, alright, we give up. Act and talk with confidence believing in ourselves. Work hard at it and negotiate even more fiercely. We know when we have won our negotiation because the other person says we have a deal. Mastering the art of negotiation is a thing of beauty. Our strong words and confident actions will be what make it possible for everything in life to be negotiable.

NUCLEUS

Our nucleus reflects our body, mind, soul, beliefs and feelings. Our words tell a story how we were raised. Positive words tell of happiness and joy, while negative words express pain and suffering. A strong nucleus comes from all our experiences and how they shaped us. The heart, brain and central nervous system delivers our core to the surface. Mentally, physically, emotionally and spiritually, we figure it out with the help of God. Our nucleus, when energized with positive words, drive us to do good things for the world and achieve success. When our nucleus is happy, healthy and full of vigor, we generate creativity. A strong nucleus gives us confidence and direction. When we connect positive words and actions into our everyday thinking, our nucleus feeds the fire to share our great works with others. Mentoring and nurturing all these positive elements demonstrate when the nucleus is strong, everything else is too.

Channeling positive values, emotions, and information toward success we need to keep the ball rolling with momentum. Our nucleus cannot be compromised. We have to protect it at all costs from negativity. Small bumps in the road cannot penetrate our nucleus. Our strong core has been built to uphold all that is sacred to us. If we allow a bad day, negative words, behaviors, or events to cloud our focus, then it is time to readjust. Adjustment helps keep our nucleus evenly balanced. Psalm 26:2–3 states, "Test me, Lord, and try me; search my heart and mind. Your love is before my eyes; I walked guided by your faithfulness." We must trust the seen and unseen to keep our nucleus intact with blind faith in God. Talk to him daily while going through our processes. We must remember to refuel ourselves each day with thanks. Nothing can touch our nucleus unless we let it.

Power, strength and leadership come from our nucleus. We choose what is good and cast away what is negative to build our power plant. Maintaining the nucleus takes time and effort. Never stop learning about new ways to better ourselves. Innovations, research and development keep us on the cutting edge to strengthen our nucleus. When we do all we can to keep our nucleus strong, more pathways to positive success open. We can teach an old dog new tricks developing growth mentally, physically, emotionally and spiritually. Get rid of the expression, "because that's how we have always done it." Our nucleus can be altered some when the knowledge we have received gives us better results in our daily lives. Pray for positive change, and if it feeds our nucleus with more meaningful and healthy outcomes, then do not be afraid to change.

NURTURE

Nurturing others is a skill not everyone is qualified, and it takes hard work, patience, and positive influence. The other end of the spectrum are those who enable instead of nurture. It is a fine line, but we want to see learned verbal and cognitive skills where someone can eventually function on their own. We are all guilty of wanting to give more to our next generation than we had, but the kinder gentler way is not healthy for growth. Mentally, physically, emotionally, and spiritually, we need to give our all to shape and nurture. Positive words and examples help nurture through difficult or growing times. Nurturing someone and energizing them with good, loving direction is a gratifying experience. We all remember who was a positive nurturer and those who should not be in that field. Thank God for those who instilled quality nurturing. A nurturer gives and receives more in return.

Nurturing is tough love, and sometimes, we have to allow struggle to ensue. There are bumps in the roadway, but how people handle the rough spots show their maturity and how they were nurtured. It is not easy to watch someone filled with negative emotions and anxieties. Many times, they did not receive positive how's or what's to navigate through. Nurturers teach others to believe in themselves and trust their own intuitions. Nurturing builds confidence for better decision making, fortitude, and handling our emotions. Psalm 144:12 says, "Then our sons in their youth will be like well-nurtured plants, and our daughters will be like pillars carved to adorn a palace." When articulated in this perspective, God truly loves his children, and he has a plan for them. When we give the gift of nurturing, we empower not only one generation but many to come. Nurturing allows us to make the world a better place before transcending into heaven. Always do our best to nurture the rest.

Positive nurturing adds value to everything it touches. As we get on a roll, never forget our base that begins with God's brilliant plan. Nurture our solid base for all the great qualities we represent. When we nurture this with maximum effort, our positive life will unfold in front of our eyes. Set our sights on whatever we want and nurture it until it becomes fruition. Visualize our nurturing turning out brilliantly as we better everyone around us. Use our five senses to measure success. The nurturing trained us for success, and we followed through. Thank God daily for nurturing us and giving us all the power to do the same. Nurturers do not allow negative people, words, or events to ruin the moment. Challenge ourselves to help someone every day by nurturing. There is not a prouder endeavor than nurturing someone and watching them make it on their own.

NAVIGATE

There are those who are navigators, and there are those who are followers. Navigating through life and propelling ourselves to success depends on us! No matter where we came from and what circumstances we inherited, we have what it takes if we get our body, mind and soul right. Positive thinking and rolling up our sleeves to do the work will allow God to navigate us toward success. Look around and be grateful even for the smallest detail. Pat ourselves on the back and give all the glory to God saying thank you with every step. Do things new and true to our heart to find direction. Isaiah 43:19–20 states, "See, I am doing something new! Now it springs forth, do you not perceive it? In the desert I make a way, in the wasteland, rivers." So even in the bleakest conditions, plow through never letting anything stand in our way.

Navigation takes mental, physical, emotional and spiritual toughness. A warrior stands tall until the end, and a captain never abandons his ship. Our job is to let all the distractions bounce off us and handle our business. When difficulty arises have a talk with God to keep navigating us in the right direction. Focusing on our positive way to success will build up our boiler to steam ahead. It is easy for others to criticize because negative people who are jealous want to see us fail. It is important to navigate and gravitate toward others who want to see us win. Find a trusting soul we can share all our vision and navigation. Many times, it is those we thought would give us the least support are the ones who come through for us. Never discount anyone who is willing to help us to the top. If they share our passion and energy, let them help.

Navigation takes control, and while climbing to the top, make sure we acknowledge those who have helped us along the way. Never use anyone for personal gain then discard them. Life is full of people who are self-centered and step on others. The greatest feeling is hitting our plateau with those who helped us navigate the course. Navigation takes a filter for our body, mind, and soul to keep us on an even keel. Successful, positive people are never surprised by detracting words or actions. They have a knack to manage their game and persevere. As we move toward success, look to see how it helps others. Does our navigation enrich others with positive and helpful direction? Navigation is mindful of others and works toward the good of society. Our dream, goal, or invention, when navigated with positive reinforcement and God's guidance, is a recipe for success.

NEIGHBOR

We all remember neighbors for various traits. Hopefully, we lived with good, positive, and kind ones. Our neighborhood was probably known for something that stays with us today. It is important to always be the best neighbor possible. Share with them and be generous. Learn about their families. In our childhood neighborhood, everyone knew everyone by their first names or nicknames, their kids played together, and we reached out to one another for as little as a cup of sugar for cookies. An established neighborhood provided comfortable relationships, families who genuinely cared about others and parents who not only looked after their own children but were eyes and ears for other parents in important times. Our positive words and actions built caring relationships that made conversation not awkward. We helped one another in times of need. We developed trusting relationships and watched families grow and mature. A strong neighbor is important for shaping our character.

Proverbs 3:27–28 talks about acting like a good neighbor in this way. "Refuse no one the good on which he has a claim when it is in your power to do it for him. Say not to your neighbor, "Go, and come again, tomorrow I will give, when you can give at once." A good neighbor is generous with their time, effort and money. Visit our elderly neighbors and check on their needs. Mow our neighbor's lawn who has a bad knee, free of charge. Offer assistance, financial or other, to a neighbor who is down on their luck and don't expect anything in return because we are doing it out of the goodness of our heart. We grow mentally, physically, emotionally, and spiritually when we are a good neighbor who does good deeds. Pray for our neighbors and their families for success and safety.

Life is fast-paced with people running in every direction. A good neighbor has contact with one of theirs every day. It might be as small as getting the mail at our respective mailbox, carpooling children to an event, or having a neighborhood picnic. This keeps the neighborly feeling going and establishes friendships. A neighbor is an extended family, so there will be some ups and downs. Just as important, we must mend our fences with small troubles so they do not turn into something more. Positive talk and genuine interest in their lives usually helps neighbors cohabitate. We do have to be careful with getting over intrusive and realize our family has faults too. Avoid the better-than-thou attitude and do not overexpose our own successes. It is important to recognize our neighbor's successes and act genuinely happy for their gifts. A great neighbor is someone we will cherish for the rest of our life even if we no longer live in that neighborhood.

NOBLE

A noble person is described with positive words such as magnificent, honorable, virtuous, or superior. Attaining this stature hopefully was done with high morals, integrity, hard work, and intelligence. Noble people must take control of themselves mentally, physically, emotionally, and spiritually. Noble people remember and do the small details well. They must spread kindness and act with humbleness in their daily works. A noble person must make sure they do not get too big for their boots. Successes can quickly swell people out of an everyday doing good for others and make it about themselves. Noble people avoid this at all costs and keep their nose to the grindstone for the sake of others. Noble creates goals for societal good and channels their ambitions. When noble people work to their capacity and reach out to God for direction, incredible results occur. Noble people think and act grateful for all they have and all they can give.

People remember noble things that were done for them to keep them afloat. They are grateful for the noble people acting as stewards and servants to make a difference in their lives. Harriet Beecher Stowe, American author and abolitionist said, "To be really great in little things, to be truly noble and heroic in the insipid details of everyday life, is a virtue so rare as to be worthy of canonization." Noble people do not want or demand any type of applause for their actions. They know the work they are doing is God's work coming from the heart. Noble people do not ask how long it is going to take to get a job done. They just roll up their sleeves and start. A noble body, mind, and soul using positive mentoring is unstoppable. Their energy is contagious, and it jump-starts others to join the noble cause.

Noble words, actions, and attitudes must be nurtured to develop others and keep momentum rolling. Everyone has their niche in life, and when we blend many of these noble talents together, we can take on bigger projects. God put us on earth to be grand, not by-stand. Noble people are exalted in the word, great in their actions, and majestic in their vision for success. Noble people charge forward in life. Pick out someone who was noble in our upbringing and share their secrets to others. Demonstrate their great qualities. Emulate their loving and caring characteristics to pass on to others. Noble people are loyal to their works. They keep their eyes on the prize for a better life for themselves and others. Always acknowledge a noble person with a simple thank-you even though it is not expected. Ask God to make every word or action that comes from us a noble one.

NEW

When we think of new, we think positive. A newborn baby, a new family, a new home, a new job, or that new car smell. All represent a fresh start given to us by our outstanding God. New means ready to go with batteries charged. New ideas and inventions spurred on by incredible creativity excite our senses. When we hold something new, we take incredible pride and care. Mentally, physically, emotionally and spiritually, we must look for new positive things to keep us interested and up to date with all the good we can achieve. New breakthroughs in technology can make us healthier in the body, mind and soul. We must be grateful for new things because they give us a positive outlook on life. Spiritually, God shows us new ways and answers our prayers. John 3:3 says, "Amen, amen, I say to you, no one can see the kingdom of God without being born from above."

We cannot confuse new with always being the best way to solve problems. What works best is what needs to be done especially in critical times. When people are terminally ill, sometimes they are introduced to new experimental drugs to see if it will lead to a new breakthrough. Unfortunately, these new, untested treatments can cause other disorders or even death. So new in this case is taking a chance. Sometimes though taking a chance on the new does lead to success. So without new, we will never know unless we try. Everyone deserves something new once in a while to break up the monotony of life. New brings a smile, makes our emotions joyous, and gives some self-pride. Some people confuse brand new, out of the box, as new. We can get used to things that generate just as much happiness because it is new to us.

The law of attraction talks about generating a feeling of having it now, and this is where the creative mind opens to new ideas. When we want something new, we have to visualize getting it. Our words and actions must be positive, firing on all cylinders, to attract the new. New is the extra gear that gets us going and takes us away from everyday challenges. New cleanses us and gives us a clean slate. When searching for a new idea, changing our lifestyle or celebrating a new goal, it all comes from God. We ask him if this new situation is right for us. We ask him to point us in the right direction. We know all which is new and possible comes from him. We know all which is new comes from the faith of the old. New is belief and not taking no for an answer. New is reborn for the good of all.

NOTORIETY

Positive words and actions on a regular basis leads to success when we put everything we have into it, and from this, we will gain notoriety. What our notoriety is for and how we handle the pressure that comes along with it will establish our legacy. Our notoriety may be known on a local, regional, national or international level. Our happy, smart, and positive reputation will light the way for those in need and make the world a better place than before we earned our notoriety. Mentally, physically, emotionally and spiritually, our notoriety will put us in the forefront for others to try and knock us down. How we handle our notoriety with all the instant social media outlets and everyone having access to it will test our persona. Achieving our notoriety, it is important to say and act grateful at all times. A built-in humbleness needs to surface. Matthew 23:12 says, "Whoever exalts himself will be humbled; but whoever humbles himself will be exalted."

Notoriety most times does not reach the famous level for most people, but what we are notorious for with our own family is what is most important. Shaping our children with positive, loving inter-action is what we strive for with our words and actions. Living a God-filled, positive lifestyle with love and passion is the notoriety we want to build. Our emotions and how we learn to react to life's situations, especially in a family, establish our notoriety. When an event happens, which is nonproductive or negative, people around us are going to say, he or she is going to blow a gasket when they find out? Hopefully, that is not our notoriety. To keep from having this type of notoriety, always look for the positive and ask God to guide us through these times. We are in charge of our notoriety.

Our notoriety once established is what people will remember about us for years after our death. Establish ourselves doing good things for others, creating new things that will benefit society, and building a positive resume second to none. Our goal should be to lay the groundwork where once we are gone, people say he or she always spoke and acted positively toward everyone. Visualize all the important and positive things we can do for others. A clean mind, body, and soul with God's guidance will build an impeccable notoriety. Do not give anyone any ammunition to chip away at the notoriety we have created. Awareness of our surroundings that can be uncomfortable or unacceptable is important for protecting our notoriety. Always have a backup plan wherever we go to avoid embarrassing situations out of our control. Our reputation and notoriety is all we have, so keep it safe and positive.

NOSTALGIA

Celebrate positive speech and actions from the past, which are bittersweet. The importance of nostalgia is like going to a spring seeking youth from the cool fresh waters for renewal. Nostalgia is remembering people, places or things that generate positive emotions of joy, happiness and excitement. Take a look at ourselves, and we vividly remember when we were the happiest or felt the best. We are proud of our great accomplishments and cherish the memories that were created. Nostalgia allows us to remember the past and recant it colorfully. Nostalgia allows us to see how far we have come as a person, community, or society. Our words and actions are ones of excitement celebrating life when we take a trip down nostalgia lane. Nostalgia gives us grateful feelings toward family, friends, times and feats accomplished. With God, nostalgia is possible because of the glorious and positive gifts he gave us to succeed.

As much as we want to cherish nostalgia, we have to be careful not to live our lives in the past. Everyone thought their era of music, fashion and memories was the best. Nostalgia is fun to remember, but we must mentally, physically, emotionally, and spiritually change with the times. We have all seen people who are stuck in their nostalgic eras. They never move forward in thought, emotion, or adapting to societal changes. As they fail to move forward, their social thoughts, words, and actions can be unacceptable in today's world. Nostalgia is good as long as there is a positive reason. Nostalgic words and actions that are degrading and hurtful are unexceptionable. Exodus 16:23 said, "Here in the desert the whole Israelite community grumbled against Moses and Aaron. The Israelites said to them, 'Would that we had died at the Lord's hand in the land of Egypt, as we sat by our fleshpots and ate our fill of Bread! But you had to lead us into this desert to make the whole community die of famine.'" The Israelites were nostalgic because they did not believe.

Too many times when we work with people in the community about a cause or project, there are those few ones who cannot escape the nostalgic mind-set. If the setting was to make something look or feel old, they would be on board. Unfortunately, people who choose not to be forward thinking about issues get left behind. New does not always mean better, but when nostalgia stops progress for societal good, this weakens thought. Words and actions always should be positive in every discussion when concerning nostalgia. Nostalgia mixed with fresh thought recognizing the old for its worth is encouraged, but also needs to be shown where improvements can be made for future endeavors.

NORMAL

Normal speech and actions are perceptions of what environment we live and work, where we were raised geographically, and the era we were born. What is normal today would have been abnormal a generation removed. Nearly every family has a computer, tablet, MP3 player, or other communications device they use and participate in social media on a daily basis. This is today's normal. Just thirty years ago, only a small amount of families had a home computer; and fifty years ago, only large corporations or NASA had them. So as technology grows normal changes. What each family considers normal is what they see and hear. Their mental, physical, emotional and spiritual norms come from their environment. Positive words and actions hopefully are the norm, but we know this is not always the case. Normal changes also with race, culture and creed. So to understand normal in the world we live, we must be conscientious and knowledgeable to learn about other people, places, and traditions.

The idea of a normal family does not completely exist because everyone has some form of dysfunction, and no one is perfect. Hopefully, normal in our family starts with love, kindness, trust, sharing and caring for one another. Normal is maintaining a positive attitude and a grateful heart for all the gifts God has bestowed upon us and our family. Normal is listening with eagerness and helping others through their difficult times. Normal is a desire to succeed and always giving our greatest effort. Normal is surrounding ourselves with positive mentors who shape us to want to lift others to a better life. Normal is having integrity and positive values to stand up for what is right and for those who cannot stand alone. Our speech and actions set the tone for normal to exist on a daily basis.

If we have not experienced good, positive norms for whatever reasons, it is up to us to change a negative into a positive. There is a balance we must have for normal to exist in our life. Proverbs 9:6 says, "Forsake foolishness that you may live; advance in the way of understanding." If we think through things before we act and speak, normal should surface. It is when we are out of control with our words, actions, and emotions when abnormal behaviors appear. We are in control of this, and we cannot let other people's words or actions uproot our normal. Whenever abnormal starts creeping into our life, it is time to visit with God for some advice. His guidance will restore normal and keep us well-balanced. Remember to control our normal with all positive words and actions. Look for the good in everyone and realize everyone's normal is different.

NICE

We all have a visualization in our minds of someone or something that is nice. A nice personality, smile, or laugh we embrace. A nice word, deed, or circumstance, we witness and appreciate. Nice comes from the heart and soul. We all recall when someone has done something nice for us, or we have returned this gesture to others. Nice usually starts with family and how we have been shaped. The decision to speak and act nicely to or about others sometimes gets lost in our everyday life. A conscientious effort must be made many times throughout our day as situations evolve, which challenges our niceness. Mentally, physically, emotionally and spiritually, we must control ourselves and learn from mistakes for nice to consistently flourish. Instead of negativity and tearing down, always look for and say good, positive things to others. It may be difficult at times to curb our tongue or not react to someone or something. When in doubt, let nice win out.

Nice moves people to accomplish more together, generates enthusiasm, and solidifies the idea to do for others. Anticipation of nice things coming our way brings joy, happiness and surprise. On a birthday or anniversary, we have someone close their eyes before their gift is given. We can feel the power of nice. Nice is really important and touching when someone is not expecting the gesture. Giving someone help they were not expecting whether it is financial, positive reinforcement, or a deed done is what captures the essence of nice. Luke 6:34 says, "If you lend money to those from who you expect repayment, what credit is that to you? Even sinners lend to sinners and get back the same amount." When we are in doubt what to do, always think, what does God want us to do? A thankful mind, body and soul will help us develop nice.

Life is a work in progress as is nice. Nice does not happen overnight. Accumulation of scenarios whether it happens to us or others shapes us. Saying and acting nice toward others who are not is where we earn our stripes. We have been in awkward moments when we want to speak our mind, and we take the higher road by saying nothing. This takes control of our emotions and growth. When we are nice, we do not burn bridges, which someday we need to cross. We accept people who are not nice for who they are, but remember how they are. There are times when nice is challenged, and someone intentionally hurts someone. This is the time when we either stand up for ourselves or others, but do it in an intelligent and articulate manner. Nice is never a mark of weakness. Instead, nice is a healthy, positive demeanor guiding our life where we give and receive the most blessings.

NAÏVE

Naïve sophistication, perception and judgment in our speech and actions is no way to succeed in the world. Naivety when we are young is good to a point because we have not been exposed to the negative sides of society, such as profanity, sex, or drugs. A child growing up in a positive household should be naïve about certain things, but educated not to participate in these areas. A fine line has to exist between naivety and enablement. As we mentally, physically, emotionally and spiritually mature, our naïve words and actions become learned for the setting. We would not act immature at a job interview, tell inappropriate jokes at church, or ask someone how their family member is doing when we know they died. Life polishes the naive off us as we grow and gain insight about daily situations. We learn how our feelings keep us in check, so we do not say or do naïve things at the wrong time.

Guidance with naivety needs positive mentors and a strong spiritual light. Craig D. Lounsbrough, in the book *An Intimate Collision: Encounters with Life and Jesus,* says, "I pray that I am never so foolishly naïve or roguishly pompous to think that I can be the captain of my own ship, for if God is not at the helm, my ship will soon be at the bottom." This is profound because we cannot speak, act, and think that we can do everything by ourselves. Having great family, friends and prayer will allow us the wisdom and knowledge to fight through naïve. As a preteen, I can remember sitting with peers and was asked, what was sperm? My answer was drugs. I was laughed at uncontrollably because I was naïve. It felt very odd, and I asked my mother. She sheepishly smiled at me and explained it, so I would no longer be naïve. This is why a positive and loving upbringing is critical.

Sometimes, naivety is the hard way when it comes to friends, relationships, and life. Everyone is raised differently, and what is naïve in one household may be the standard in another. We all have our own ideas about what traits make up a friend, love, or worldliness. When others do not live up to our standards, we become hurt. That is okay because we learn not to be naïve. We attract qualities that are like us, but learn everyone is different. Experiencing love, joy, and happiness is why we were created. Naivety keeps us young at heart and reflects clean, honest living. As we grow, we can choose to be naïve about the world, informed and educated, but not participating in negative behaviors. This is not burying our head in the sand, but not getting inundated with negativity. Sometimes, what we do not know does not hurt us; and being the last to know can be a good thing. Speak and act naively about negative endeavors, but not positive ones.

NEAT

Well-spoken people who have control of their actions ordinarily establish themselves as neat and orderly leaders. Their simple, yet systematic approach to situations add neatness and confidence. Their words and actions seem to be handpicked for the moment depicting skill. Neat oratorical preparation opens the eyes and ears when delivered with zest. Language and actions, when presented positively, need to touch the mind, body, and soul. After someone speaks, hopefully, it will always be something to inspire and remember. Neat words and actions are not a mixed message, but resound clearly. Neatness adds a command presence that demonstrates preparedness and thoroughness. Neat and orderly speech and actions have a psychological effect telling others we dare you to challenge our system of success. Recognizing neatness in delivery and actions is a measuring stick whether we have our game together to compete in life's challenges. Show us someone who is neat in speech and actions, and we will show someone we want in our corner.

Neat symbolizes nonchaotic. Positive living starts with cleanliness. Choose to talk and act neatly. A neat bedroom with clean sheets always has provided a great image where and how to start and stop a day. The fresh aroma and feeling of peace as we crawl in or take our morning stretch. Neatness also comes from the heart. How we feel on the inside many times is spoken and portrayed on the outside. Wonderful words express kindness, love and compassion. When negativity creeps in our space, continue to spiritually reflect, so neat returns. If we do not know what to do or say, ask for God's blessings for restoration. When orderly speech and actions come back, we can feel ourselves gain confidence. It feels like a pressure valve releasing steam, restoring neatness. Neatness takes years of preparation, trial and error. Not all words, styles, and actions work well for everyone.

Neat takes mental, physical, emotional and spiritual balance for success. Neatness is a checklist, pros versus cons, and do's and do not scenarios. Order affects our life and everyone in it. Neatness is a positive factor, but when it becomes obsessive-compulsive, it treads on others. Not everyone wants the same amount of neatness in their life. Neat and orderly signifies control, and sometimes, we need to learn to let go and let things happen on their own. Love and spiritual guidance work better when we realize God is in control. We know how neat works for us, but we need to see how it affects others. This is a cause and effect in life and relationships. Moderation with neat and orderly is alright as long as it does not change our core values. Neat is a work in progress that will have an impact in our world and others in it.

NEED

Do not confuse need with greed in our words and actions. Everyone has needs to be filled mentally, physically, emotionally, or spiritually. What we think we need may not always fit into the time or place. Our words and actions are the same way as they contribute to our rise and fall. Having a need to better ourselves and others by our words and actions is an essential characteristic. A need to help others fulfill their lives with positive direction is what we should strive for most in the world. We need to be the best, say the best, and do the best every day. Find something that motivates us to need more. Inspirational need requires big shoulders to carry the load and lean on. Have the courage to challenge and face our needs. Positive needs for ourselves and others should excite and inspire our desires. The need for gratefulness in our words and actions can never be forsaken.

Need may consist of bare essentials for survival or opulence. Each person knows what they need and when they need it. Positive communication by our words and actions is the needed key. When we think of a need for ourselves or others, it should be kind, loving and generous. Our needs should not overshadow the needs of others less fortunate. Balance our needs and expectations. Good health is a need for everyone rich or poor and cannot be taken for granted. Positive energy is an important need motivating others to obtain objectives. Luke 12:15 says, "Take care to guard against all greed, for though one maybe rich, one's life does not consist of possessions." Needs of material goods should never outweigh the love of God and all the treasures he provides. We need to focus on the inner self controlling our words, actions, and emotions. As we develop our positive needs, others will see us as their needed example and follow.

Needs can change for various reasons. What might be a critical need today might be an obscure need tomorrow. We must prioritize our needs for the good of all. We need not to be selfish and sacrifice for others. What others think a need should be in our world they can never judge until they walked in our shoes. We do not know everyone's story or why they needed something when they did. The important thing is to respect other's needs and be willing to listen to them. Whether we need to pick ourselves up and dust ourselves off or continue our need to succeed, it all should be positive interaction. Say and do good things, fulfill needs for others, and act grateful for all the needs God has granted us.

NAG

Repeatedly telling someone over and over about something, constantly projecting actions of ill temper, allowing negative emotions to take over, and criticizing someone habitually with a salty attitude are all examples describing a nag. These are not positive ways to use words and actions. Nagging brings out the worst in people, relationships, and is counterproductive. No one likes nagging and strife involved with everyday activities. People do not become nags immediately. Nagging can be learned from our upbringing, earned through years of practice, or someone who does not have respect for others. Whatever the cause, a nag is no fun to live our life around and drains us mentally, physically, emotionally and spiritually. The nag usually lacks self-confidence in self, so criticizing covers up their wounds. A nag can also constantly spew negativity because they want to be in charge of everyone and everything. Nagging is a sign someone is hurting about something, so speak positively and be ready to listen.

Each of us has had a negative day or experience, but we must bounce back, so nagging and complaining does not become the norm. Nagging makes people want to run away from our presence. We have to channel our words, actions and emotions away from complaining and start looking at the good in everything. Start praying for nags about their negativity. Nagging is not gender specific. Proverbs 27:15 describes nagging this way, "For a persistent leak on a rainy day the match is a quarrelsome woman." All men out there, don't laugh! We can be quite a treat to live with too. Our words must be loving and kind, instead of being right. Nagging how ignorant we are drains us mentally, listening how fat we are scars us physically, hearing how we are out of control drains us emotionally, and the nonsense of there is no God drains us spiritually. Naysayers, stop, please!

Enroll in the course for positive speech, actions and gratitude. We control us, and it is a choice to be positive and not a nag. When we feel negativity coming on, stop, pause and say thank you for the good things surrounding us. Understand most people are trying the best they can to manage whatever is nagging them in their lives.

Encouragement and compliments go a long way for people to succeed. Positive thoughts lead to positive words that extends into positive actions. When nagging begins, whisk it away with light conversation and laughter. Say let's not go that way. Channel our focus on what is good and pray taking away all that is bothering us. Nagging is something if we do not work on can cause serious damage. Count our blessings, be positive and supportive of others, and deliver an attitude of gratitude. This will stop the nagging.

NATURAL

The words and actions representing us do they flow naturally or take time and effort? Do they express love and kindness, or are they irksome to others? Natural words should convey faithfulness and flow freely. Our words and actions many times are naturally related by blood, and we have generations of negativity to conquer. We must challenge ourselves and others where natural positives manifest so that it comes from our lips and bodies. Natural, positive mentoring with our language and actions should be the norm. Natural speech and actions are spontaneous and happy. Natural morals should be certain and with conviction. Mentally, physically, emotionally, and spiritually, our natural life was created by God. He knows when we are acting and speaking natural or are being hindered by something. Gratitude flowing naturally about our circumstances and the world helps our mind, body, and soul get on a positive track. When our words and actions naturally blossom from gratitude and God, our world will shine brightly.

Our bodies have a natural rhythm, and like a precisely tuned engine, we know when we are sputtering. We also need to know how to correct and naturally get ourselves back in focus. Learn to do and say positive things that naturally make us feel good. The law of attraction talks about putting ourselves in places that makes us feel good. Maybe it is watching a beautiful sunset, walking on a beach or listening to a waterfall. The bottom line is everyone needs their positive place to recharge. Timing is everything, so know the natural ebb and draw on great experiences to uplift our world. Our feelings can influence or disrupt our natural state. Controlling and monitoring our emotions are important for our natural health. Healthy bodies and minds cause natural inspiration while negative ones cause desegregation. Know our natural flow and trust how things affect us.

The natural world was created by God for us to enjoy. All the breathtaking images relaxes our mind and body for peace. When we try to think of all the man-made things that coagulate with natural ones, we have to trust the natural. Proverbs 3:5–6 says, "Trust in the Lord with all your heart, on your own intelligence rely not; in all your ways be mindful of him, and he will make straight your paths." Natural has nothing artificial to screw it up. Naturally, our speech and actions are behaviors that we learned many times from those who should not lead. If our words and actions naturally inspire, then we are going in the right direction. Listen and monitor ourselves to make sure only good and natural words flow out of our mouth. Natural is positive and anything else cannot compare.

NETWORKING

One of the most positive, motivational, inspirational, and transcending words is networking. In all walks of life, networking is paramount for getting jobs, getting jobs done, changing thought patterns, creating new inventions, selling goods and mentoring the world. Positive thoughts, words, and actions give networking its status for making life fresh and exciting. Networking keeps our ideas new and stops tunnel vision. Whether mentally, physically, emotionally, or spiritually, networking keeps our speech and actions in focus while others encourage us toward our goals. Together, the world can accomplish more together. Romans 14:19 says, "Let us then pursue what leads to peace and to building up one another." Remember, when we are stuck in life and do not know where to turn, networking gives us the channels to power through the situation. Networking lines of communication picks us up and keeps us positive. Networking also reminds us to have gratitude about everything in our lives.

Networking is a way to meet others who want to inspire and mentor others. There are no boundaries with networking because a group can be a few or as large as they desire. When people get together for a positive cause, the most work is done, the greatest time is spent and the biggest results occur. The networking message should not be fighting against, but being pro a cause. It is all in the wording that gives the powerful message the drive forward. Don't fight against cancer for example, but be pro a cure for it. Positive words and actions draws energy, and networking this model leads to more success. God plays the biggest part in networking because he brings people together at the right place, time, and reason. Too many times in our lives, we meet people and our paths cross. We never planned on it or focused on it, but it happened for networking reasons. God gives us this incredible gift.

A cognitive decision to speak and act better as a person is a challenge. Networking allows us to do this because when we are around other people, we do not want them to see us at our worst. We want to shine, so they see our best side. Networking holds people accountable for their words and actions. This is why when we are in unfamiliar territory to reach out to others for help. Proud people who are unwilling to change usually are not involved in networking and end up alone. Monitor ourselves and our loved ones. When we see them slipping into constant alone behavior, it is time for networking. Positive speech, actions, and works renew the body, mind, and soul. Networking solves problems, has a purpose, and allows us to feel inspired. Reach out to someone or something every day and show them how networking keeps people on a positive track.

NOURISH

Nourishing our body, mind and soul in all phases makes a person strong. Mentally, physically, emotionally and spiritually, growth must take place to handle all life's endeavors. Nourishment comes from many sources and must sustain us. In the beginning, as a child, we nurse from our mother to give us nourishment for survival. Eventually, food nourishes us physically so we can grow healthy. There are millions of people who are not so lucky and do not get enough nourishment. So be grateful having enough to eat! What nourishment we receive also gives us brain power. This develops our speech and actions. It is important our mentors growing up have intellectual nourishment to help us say and do the right things. Emotional nourishment is important because we grow and can keep ourselves together when things around us are out of control. Finally, spiritual nourishment makes us whole. We must hunger for God and all his goodness to keep us balanced.

Good nourishment in all things pushes us to achieve our goals and be better people. Psalm 37:18–19 says, "The Lord watches over the days of the blameless; their heritage lasts forever. They will not be disgraced when times are hard; in days of famine they will have plenty." Gratitude and our relationship with God gives us nourishment in everything we do. We have to always be positive and accept the Lord's nourishment because he died for all our sins. When we are not strong in areas of our lives, God invites us in and gives us his loving nourishment in the Bible. When we look to other avenues of nourishment trying to make ourselves happy, we tend to stumble. How great it is to know the nourishment we receive from God comes from belief. Start this moment building on the nourishment received so we can give freely.

Nourishment comes from our loving and caring heart. When we are generous with our nourishment, we help to carry forward many people who are down. Nourishment goes from head to toe, inside to out. There is no limit to the nourishment people can provide if they only choose to take time and give. Nourish with food, shelter, time, compassion, and God. Combining all these elements, there should not be people in the world suffering. Choose to be the nourishing leader who thinks outside the box to get the job done. Turn the tide and think what if no one ever helped us or our family when in need? Nourishment takes commitment with an attitude of doing more. Whenever we believe we have no more to give, pinch ourselves, be grateful for God and provide more nourishment to others. When we get our mind, body, and soul right, we nourish so others will flourish.

NOVELTY

Say what we mean and follow through with positive actions. New novelties are created each day, and as quick as they come, they also go. Trends, music and language patterns are novelties no matter what decade we lived. Certain words or phrases distinguish themselves from the era they came. People will say those words or novelties were from the fifties, sixties, seventies, eighties, etc. Positive words and actions survive novelty status no matter when we lived. They inspire and invoke positive conversations from the past. We may not remember who invented a certain novelty, but what we do take in is what it did for us, how it made us feel, and if it was positive or negative. Novelties should inspire and make the creative juices flow for the betterment of the world. Mentally, physically, emotionally and spiritually, novelties should help us grow and add a fresh prospective to life. For this, we should be grateful.

Novelties are unique, and when speech and actions are affected by them, it usually is something to cherish. Positive events and words are novelties we should remember, but sometimes, we lose track of them. Ecclesiastes 9:14–15 says, "Against a small city with few men in it advanced a mighty king, who surrounded it and threw up great siege works about it. But in the city lived a man who, though poor, was wise, and he delivered it through his wisdom. Yet no one remembered this poor man." We sometimes forget novelties that were important in the moment, but fade away over time. Positive novelties should stick in our brain and give us a wow factor for recollection. Too many times, great novelties become forgotten, like adults listening to the radio bringing the world to their living rooms. The space shuttle sending astronauts into the galaxy discovering new planets and life. The Internet that has brought our entire world into the palm of our hand. These are all novelties that we take for granted and are part of our everyday life.

Words like fantastic, incredible, best, and great are all positive words that have stood the test of novelty language. New novelty trend words such as sick, bad, radical, and cool had negative connotations but are now considered positive when describing something.

As society moves with the times, words and actions have more meanings because of novelties. Novelties make people think outside the box to get away from the mind-set that's how we have always done something. Novelties need to improve our standards of life. Novelties do not need to interfere with historic traditions, which honor our heroes of the past. The decision to speak and act accordingly should never be shaped by a novelty. When a novelty is positive, embrace it; otherwise, let it fade away for another day.

NEWS

Speech and actions that come from news should be enlightening and positive. No one wants to be the bearer of bad news constantly. There are those who always want to carry on gossip and keep the negativity rolling. Those people are easy to spot, and they wear us out mentally, physically, emotionally, and spiritually. News should not be used for digging up dirt, bringing people to their lowest point, and scattering the world like broken glass. In the world we have become the shock jocks with a microphone and have tossed aside good taste for, we heard the news here first. Where has all the good news gone? Good news is still here; we just have to look for it in our daily lives. The person who helps his neighbor, the funeral celebrating a decorated old soldier, and stories of kindness and compassion. Good news makes us smile and happy instead of aggravated and confrontational.

News should inspire and get into our heart. News should tickle our feelings to go and push a good cause through. Inspiration to action generates positive feelings and makes us want to help this project succeed. Good news lifts people and things up to increasing heights causing a soaring spirit. Proverbs 25:25 says, "Like cool water to one faint from thirst is good news from a far country." All our senses are enriched with what that cool drink of water representing good news can do. Good news refreshes our body, mind and soul. When enough people feel enriched and empowered, anything good is possible. Our motive must be pure and selfless when spreading the good news leading to positive actions. The minute news becomes about us, instead of them, our intentions get spoiled. Always think about the good of others when listening or talking about news. If news is not positive, it is gossip and not worth carrying the tune.

There are times when telling bad news comes with the territory. There are ways to do so without degrading and killing the spirit. My law enforcement career has caused me to make over seventy family death notifications. I sat with each gender, every race, color, and creed. This bad news never was easy to explain, but each time, a delivery of love and compassion was expressed. Not knowing a lot about each person, positive features were always relayed about their loved one. I did not care if I knew "the truth" about them. They were still loved and cherished by someone. This news was usually devastating, but in the end, many families invited me to the funeral, or I received a note from them telling me they were glad it was me who brought them the news. Now, I have realized I was doing God's work bringing news. News, when relayed, most importantly, should be coming with the grace of God. If we are not spreading news with God's intentions, then stop.

NECESSARY

We think and say things every day that have an impact on others, whether it is necessary or not. Some find it necessary to give their opinions on every subject matter. What is not necessary are words and actions that are negative, resulting in damaged self-esteem and unkind stereotypes. What is necessary are words and actions that empower, uplift and motivate others. Our learned behaviors are a pattern, and it is necessary to continually move on a positive path. It is necessary we break down negative words, thoughts and actions and turn them into loving, caring, and helpful resources. Growth can only take place in our lives if we choose to surround ourselves with positive activities, people and dialogue. Mentally, physically, emotionally, and spiritually, it is necessary to fight positive battles with kind words and a grateful heart. We choose the words that come out of our mouth and the actions we take. Make positivity a necessary tool.

It is necessary to not let our emotions control our words and actions. When we allow fear, anger, or any type of dread lead our day, it is necessary to change the channel and listen to God's word. If we focus on all these negative emotions, they will consume every area in our life. It is necessary to not keep reflecting on what is wrong. Using the law of attraction, if we are creating negative circumstances and keep talking about it, they will get the attention. It goes the same way in the other direction looking for the positive in any situation. It is necessary to always focus on happy, joyful things so our heart is filled with bliss. When our heart is filled with good, our words and actions reflect all the necessary steps for happiness. It is necessary to monitor our language and deeds every day and have faith in God's word.

Learn it is not necessary to do everything ourselves. Some people because they have been let down in the past have trust issues, so they want to do it all by themselves! It is necessary to let go and believe it is in God's hands. Matthew 21:21 says, "Amen, I say to you, if you have faith and do not waver, not only will you do what has been done to the fig tree, but even if you say to this mountain, 'Be lifted up and thrown into the sea,' it will be done." The strength to move mountains is necessary when we believe wholeheartedly. This takes patience, which will lead to growth. It is necessary to put belief in the right place and positive, great things will come in time. It is a necessary commitment for positive words and actions to flow on a consistent basis.

NIRVANA

Our words, actions, and mind-set have everything to do with a peaceful, powerful, and positive life. Conditions change, and we must roll with the flow to find nirvana. Nirvana is releasing all negative words and actions for peaceful interactions inside and outside. When things do not go our way, we must let go and give it all to God. Take an honest look at ourselves and decide if we are bringing situations on ourselves creating negativity, or are we seeking nirvana? Controlling our emotions, and our tongue may be difficult at times. Our humility and maturity depend on it. If we are using positive and peaceful methods toward resolution with goodness in our heart, and in a godlike manner, nirvana can be achieved. Romans 12:2 says, "Do not conform yourself to this age but be transformed by the renewal of your mind, that you may discern what is the will of God, what is good and pleasing and perfect." Daily practice of God's word is essential for nirvana to flourish.

We all know people who talk a good game but do not follow through. These people have a difficult time finding nirvana in their lives. They try to do everything themselves and be in control. They are never in control and resist turning it over to God. Nirvana means enlightenment inside and out. We see those who look good on the outside, but their insides are a mess. Nirvana will not flourish everywhere until we gain peace ourselves. We are being tested by earthly things to see if we give it up to God for faith and trust. God never gives us more than we can handle, but he watches if our attitudes and emotions drag us along. Mentally, physically, emotionally, and spiritually, we have to give it all to God for nirvana. When receiving any glory, make sure to recognize God as the reason.

Nirvana heightens our senses and make us more aware of others and the surroundings. Nirvana allows us to put ourselves in others' shoes and be kind, passionate and understanding. The ultimate life goal is to achieve nirvana in heaven gaining serenity and tranquility. We can only do this by living our life with purpose establishing peaceful surroundings while here on earth. Every day should be a self-test to see if we are preparing ourselves by our words and actions creating nirvana. Get rid of negative talk, friends, habits and anything that is not moving us toward nirvana. It is negative and self-destructive to let any earthly things control us. Speak and act grateful for all we have but know with God's glory is what makes nirvana possible. Dedicate our life to God and others to establish nirvana wherever we go.

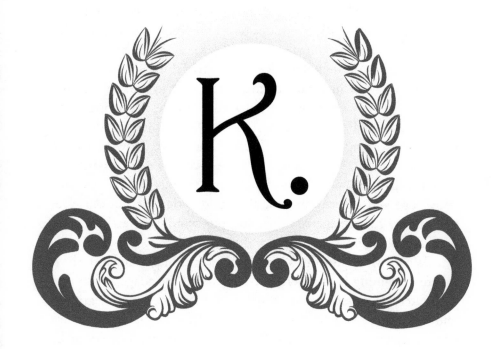

KNOWLEDGE

Knowledge comes our way via words, actions, experiences, education, religion, culture and tradition. Knowledge can be calmly debated in civil manners or destructively leads to war. How we use our knowledge is important to plan and do as much good for others as possible. Knowledge is also dangerous for people with misunderstanding, bad attitudes, intentions or a willingness to use it to harm others. How we use knowledge is a choice, and we have to stand behind those who use knowledge for positive things. 1 Corinthians 8:1–2 says, "Now in regard to meat sacrificed to idols: we realize that all of us have knowledge; knowledge inflates with pride, but love builds up. If anyone supposes knows something, he does not yet know as he ought to know." Even though we know better, we do things anyway. Knowledge is grace given by God to help us grow mentally, physically, emotionally and spiritually. We must take knowledge and use it to mentor and build better lives for ourselves and others. Knowledge is a gift, and our words and actions must present positive imagery continuously.

Where we acquire our knowledge is just as important as the how we are explaining it to others. We have heard the adage, "Consider the source." Reputation and credibility are huge because integrity in knowledge makes or breaks a statement. An example in the police world are confidential sources. Reliability of information can make or break going forward on a case with the knowledge presented. Another important factor when considering the use of knowledge is, what was the agenda of the person presenting it? If it was for teaching positive things, spreading love and joy, or doing something good, then fine. If the knowledge received destroys, tears down or hurts others, then discard that kind of knowledge. Translation is vitally important in how knowledge is understood. Think of all the inventors who, if their work was misinterpreted, could have failed instead of enjoying success. Knowledge should always be clear and concise, so we never have to open Pandora's box.

Act grateful for the knowledge we receive. It is important to learn things to gain knowledge on life matters. Knowledge will help us grow in life, confirms decision making and allows us to keep from making mistakes. Knowledge helps us learn from our past and teach us about a bright future. Knowledge packs a punch to use God's wisdom spreading enlightenment and positive mentoring. Knowledge and a solid understanding of ourselves will bring about fruitful relationships with God and the rest of the world. Always hunger for increased knowledge for ourselves and the surrounding world. Never be afraid of gaining more knowledge. As long as we understand it and use it for positive endeavors, it will not be destructive. We are blessed with knowledge, and when we use it with people who have the proper motif and are helping society, great things will happen.

KUDOS

The recognition of something tremendously accomplished marked by happy words and gestures from others. When someone goes beyond the norm and completes a job well done, they deserve kudos. So many times, people go through the normal grind of life and receive no kudos. It is important to recognize people when they accomplish something great mentally, physically, emotionally or spiritually. Kudos pushes us to maximize our efforts and gives us a euphoric feeling. When receiving kudos, it is important to act grateful and pay respect to the ones applauding us but also to give the glory to God for granting us the talents to succeed. The law of attraction builds on momentum positively motivating others to strive for excellence. Everyone likes to receive kudos for support and thanks. Kudos brings every positive emotion to the forefront and can leave someone literally speechless from complete happiness. Giving and receiving kudos takes humility and humbleness.

We can never measure how much kudos means to someone during certain times in their lives, which makes an incredible difference between success and failure. Inspiration from kudos brings tears of joy to some and lights a fire in their body, mind, and soul. People all start out from various backgrounds and situations. Positive words and actions generating kudos can make all the difference in the world. We hear in testimonies without our support, great feats would not be possible. Think of times when we received kudos or not. Sometimes, it hurts us when we feel deserving but kudos do not come. Kudos unreceived is like finishing in second place, and hopefully, it will make us work harder the next time. Kudos is important celebrating great things, but should be marked for special occasions, not just a participation trophy. We have to learn to do great, positive works because we want to, not just for the kudos.

The biggest kudos we will ever receive is our award from God when we enter heaven. Living the right way, focusing on his glorious words, and giving a loving heart to the world will help us achieve kudos. Uplifting, mentoring, and pushing others to greatness is our gift toward kudos. The happiness we receive watching others succeed shows maturity and growth. When we would rather see someone else win then receive kudos, our cup overflows with joy. Matthew 6:1 says, "But take care not to perform righteous deeds in order that people may see them, otherwise, you will have no recompense from your heavenly Father." Genuine happiness for others in life is a servant's attitude, and this is all the kudos we need. Kudos comes from a kind and loving heart. The kudos, which will result, will be positive words and actions to be remembered for a lifetime.

KIND

Words and actions need to be loving and kind, building others positively. The choice to talk and act kindly is always beneficial. Our mentors shape us from youth, and it is important guidance to kill with kindness. A kind person builds bridges and does not burn them. A kind word, action, heart and soul shapes us mentally, physically, emotionally and spiritually. God made us to speak and act with kindness, love and compassion. Anything else is unacceptable. Letting kindness shine through and not letting negative emotions steer us takes reflection and maturity. It would be easy to let negative words or situations dictate, but it takes patience and faith in God's word to let unkindness roll off like water. Kind living represents gratitude toward others and all our treasures. Ephesians 4:32 says, "And be kind to one another, compassionate, forgiving one another as God has forgiven you in Christ."

Troubled days when kindness does not seem near takes all the strength we can muster. We cannot let negativity and bad attitudes lead the way. On these days, kindness and a positive change is essential. One kind word or action can turn things around. When we are thinking or saying what else can go wrong, kindness has to roll off our tongue and leap from our heart. The law of attraction is about energy toward an outcome. Make kindness the king, and positive energy will flow with answers appearing from places least expected. Find great things in our heart and from the past to lead on those tough days. These kind moments will bring a smile to our face, joy to our heart, and add a spring to our step. A kind, joyous and loving attitude takes constant faith and work daily. Speak and act like a spiritual warrior guiding the way for kindness.

Kindness is not only about saying or doing, it is listening too. Listening to our heart about right and wrong kindness surfaces. Our interactions with others from childhood through adulthood stirs feelings that lead to the golden rule. We can be the outlet others can depend on for kindness. Listening inspires wisdom that leads to kind words, actions and advice. God put us on this earth to be loving and kind to each other. Kind people have vision to see the difference and the humility to set kindness in motion. Kind people recognize peace at all costs. Lessons are most remembered when a word or act of kindness has given us the benefit of the doubt. A decision and a way to kindness can be achieved when mixed with God's word. Kindness cannot be found only in earthly ways, but a strong blend of prayer about every decision will lead to it. Kindness never leaves us behind.

KING

It's great to be the king! The figurehead of a country, the king of rock and roll, and of course, the One and only, the most powerful, our Lord God Almighty. When we speak and do for the King, we are energized with happiness, inventiveness, and recognize power and prestige. It is an honor to work for the King. Greatness and gratitude multiply in the presence of the King. We use positive words and display servantlike qualities toward the King. Psalm 20:6 says, "May we shout for joy at your victory, raise the banner in the name of our God. The Lord grant you every prayer!" Giving glory to the King connects us mentally, physically, emotionally, and spiritually for success. Leading by example and giving it all to the King will reveal gifts through our words and actions. As we focus on our goals with help from the King, we see clearly.

King of our castle means being in charge of us and making positive, healthy, and fulfilling choices. As the King of us, decisions must be positive to grow and mature. Kings must be grateful for their attributes promoting positive words and actions. Kings must mentor others with their successes. A king shares all he has to make others better. Kings must know they are always being observed. Kings must know they are always being watched and need to live at a higher standard. Increased responsibility comes with king territory. Kings have the abilities to change others with their valuable riches. Kings protect, instill power in others, and use inner and outer resources to make a difference. Kings have a duty to others because they have been entrusted with power. Our King, Jesus Christ, is omnipotent and omnipresent. He knows our thoughts, words, and actions before we do. Trust our King and give our life to Him. Our King gives us peace and grace in handling all our situations.

The king is in charge of his kingdom and must understand to have compassion when sharing with others. Absolute power comes with costs, recognizing other's needs must take precedence. Kings must make everything run smoothly. Inspiring words must come from the king to command attention. We must believe in our king to establish a community feeling. A king must have plans for all situations for credibility to be established. Trust in the king comes from positive examples where things are done for the common good. When we reflect on kings of the past usually we can say things good or bad. The king's legacy says a lot about his leading and interacting with others. The most important King of all is God. When we put this King first there is no other search. Amen to the King.

KINDLE

Words and actions can kindle positive or negative experiences. They can kindle whole cultures and people to react in certain ways. It is important to examine what and why we are kindling something. Reasons can be self-serving or leading others to a different alternative. If we are going to kindle a spirit or movement, it must arouse people's feelings. Our words and actions must excite and work toward a positive project. Kindling something positive, which will better society, should always be the goals when we are leading in a new innovation or direction. Kindling emotions of love, kindness, joy and positive motivation should be the direction of our words and actions. There must be zero tolerance kindling negativity, anger, violence and hatred in the world. Throughout history, mankind has kindled many movements and worshiped negative ideologies because of words and actions stirring up emotions that were not based on kindness and God's word.

Kindling anything positive starts with words and actions based on God. Mentally, physically, emotionally and spiritually, we must follow this blueprint for kindling ourselves and others. Our salvation depends on it. God wiped out the whole civilizations who had lost their ways and not believing in him. Isaiah 27:11 says, "Its boughs shall be destroyed, its branches shall wither and be broken off, and women shall come to build a fire with them. This is not an understanding people; therefore, their maker shall not spare them, nor shall he who formed them have mercy on them." Kindling the wrong words and actions will have the ultimate price to pay. Every day, our words and actions kindle what direction our conversations, attitudes and reactions we have around others. If we notice we are not kindling good vibes or feel confrontational, it is time to change directions. Words and actions must invoke positive feelings.

Staying on point and kindling loving, helpful dialogue takes discipline and faith. Those days when we do not feel 100 percent, we must use our patience to kindle positive words and actions. Focus on God and ask for his help. Kindling love and kindness in these tough moments shows grace and maturity. Think about moments that could have gone terribly wrong had we kindled the wrong attitude or actions. We must be grateful to God for allowing us to have the right words and actions to handle the moment. Provocation should never be kindled in our words or deeds. It is easy to get caught in a wrong pattern, so don't. Start each day kindling words of joy saying thank you and showing gratitude for every little thing. It is the small habits that kindle the successes for larger moments. When we choose to kindle kind and positive words, the world becomes a much better place for everyone.

KEY

We all have keys that lead us toward success. Keys can be people, circumstances, behaviors, or knowledge. How we use these keys is important because it affects us mentally, physically, emotionally and spiritually. Managing keys takes practice with trials and errors. When we use our keys, they should be directed at positive outcomes, with great leadership. A decision to work for what we want is the key. Bring all our energy toward this decision and filter out any negative word or action, which will keep us from unlocking our door to success. When we discover a key, it is like a lightbulb illuminating. Once we discover the key, things will fall into place nicely. We may not know where the next key is coming, but when it does, we say thank you. Our keys should be for the good of humanity because what we do on earth is the scorecard we are handing in on Judgement Day.

Our keys can open the door for ourselves and others. Keys can give us explanations and clues we never would have fathomed. These keys so often are closer than we realize. Our words and actions are the keys to how life goes. Matthew 16:19–20 says, "I will give you the keys to the kingdom of heaven. Whatever you bind on earth shall be bound in heaven; and whatever you loose on earth shall be loosed in heaven. Then he strictly ordered his disciples to tell no one that he was the Messiah." Sometimes, we need to keep some of our keys to ourselves and let others learn by their words and actions. Life has to be lived in God's time. God will give us certain keys when he feels it is the right time. Everyone does not grasp the same keys in the exact moment.

Keys can be whatever works best for us. The same key may not work for everyone. Our words, actions, thoughts, maturity, and heart play a huge role in what type of key may work for us. One thing is for certain, the biggest and most important key is making God a part of our daily life and decision making. Sometimes, we are like a rowboat adrift, not knowing exactly what direction to go. God is the key as he knows before us which way to go and what the outcome will be. Listen for keys each day when we are praying. Look for small keys around us. Feel these keys opening our mouth, hands and heart to a positive, helpful and successful life. We never know when a key will be the opener to many locks that bind us. Keys can be big or small, and we must be grateful for them all.

KNEEL

How many times in our lives are we around people who speak, direct our actions, or hold titles worthy of kneeling? Growing up and playing sports, good coaches commanded attention with their inspiration and motivation. They gathered a team around them discussing strategy and showing good technique, and we knelt around them giving respect. Royalty in any movie or book when people visited a king or queen, their actions were to kneel in front of them. Kneeling shows absolute respect paying tribute to the person and position. The answer to the former question is we should be kneeling every day showing gratitude, love and respect. This is to Jesus as he gave up everything for us bestowing all our gifts. Kneeling to Jesus and using our words and actions in a positive light should be our daily goal above all else. When we kneel, we are telling him we are giving all to him in this moment and seeking mental, physical, emotional and spiritual guidance.

Kneeling cleanses us of our words and actions asking forgiveness. When we kneel in front of Jesus on our day of reckoning, we are being accountable of our earthly transgressions. Romans 14:10:12 says, "Why then do you judge your brother? Or you, why do you look down on your brother? For we shall all stand before the judgement seat of God, for it is written: "As I live, says the Lord, every knee shall bend before me, and every tongue shall give praise to God." So [then] each of us shall give an account of himself [to God]." Kneeling is healing, and when we speak and act with a servantlike attitude, we are living right. Kneeling gets rid of the "we are better than you" attitude. Kneeling shows mature actions that come from the heart.

Our biggest hurdle with kneeling is ourselves. We need to get out of our own way and live with humbleness and humility. The no one is going to tell us what to do and when do it line does not fit with kneeling. Kneeling brings peace, and with it, we surround ourselves with kind and loving people. When we kneel, our words and actions are no longer harsh. Kneeling is a choice we have to make each day for ourselves so the world feels right. When we kneel, we are taking control of our emotions and putting things in proper perspective. We are all on Jesus's team. Imagine, kneeling before him as he gives a preparatory speech leading us into action. Kneeling is contagious, and when we show others we are humble, they will want to kneel beside us. Kneeling gives us the feeling that in turn promotes the ceiling.

KISS

Kisses play important roles, tell incredible stories, and can have so many meanings. A kiss may be passionate, friendly, or derogative. Kisses are normally positive, and we think of them in a loving manner. Our words and actions can dictate whether we are getting a kiss or not. We all remember our first kiss with whom and where. We also remember a last kiss when a loved one is tragically killed. In many countries, kisses on both cheeks are a friendly greeting. When we are kissing, it should feel special. Kisses affect us mentally, physically, emotionally and spiritually. We know when we really kiss someone if it is something friendly or much deeper making our insides churn. Kisses can be a quick peck or long and passionate. Kisses usually bring about endearing words. Kisses can also symbolize how people feel toward one another when you tell someone where to kiss us. Kisses normally lead to happier words and times.

Kisses can open communications or say it all. Kisses are welcoming and personal. What one may feel about a kiss compared to another is open for interpretation. Kisses sometimes can be confusing when used as experimentation. Young couples begin to date and kiss. To one, it was an awesome experience; and to the other, it was average at best. Hard to know where we stood in that first moment. When we kiss with the right frame of mind, in a kind and loving manner, God knows our direction. Romans 16:16 says, "Greet one another with a holy kiss. All the churches of Christ greet you." Kisses should not just be routine but something special. When we kiss someone, it should come from our hearts and not just a haphazard, common occurrence. When we choose to kiss, we should be genuine in our words, thoughts and actions.

Some people are expressive and kiss everyone, and others are more reserved and only kiss in special moments. Knowing we are loved is sealed with a kiss. Kisses show support and say we care in trying times. Nowhere else is it more important than to show a loved one we care and let them know things are alright by a small kiss. Words and actions today are critical, and we have lost the art of the kiss. Kisses symbolize love, yet we see so much anger and uncaring actions in our world today. When was the last time a homeless person was kissed for kindness or the forgotten elderly person at a nursing home? A kiss shows gratitude and love from the heart. We do not have to kiss everyone we come across, but even blowing a kiss to someone will have a tremendous impact for their day. We never know when our kiss will turn someone's life around.

KINGDOM

Daniel 2:44 says, "In the lifetime of those kings the God of heaven will set up a kingdom that shall never be destroyed or delivered up to another people, rather it shall break in pieces all these kingdoms and put an end to them, and it shall stand forever." These powerful words sum up God's kingdom, and we need to show respect every moment. The word of God is absolute with rules to follow for running our kingdom. Our lives are filled with trials, people who have trouble following these rules, and emotions that carry us away from God's word. In our kingdom, we must establish control of ourselves building a stronghold mentally, physically, emotionally, and spiritually to honor him. It takes positive, loving and kind words practiced daily for our kingdom to flourish. Time each day should be spent giving ourselves to him by our words and actions, so we can run our kingdom by his rules.

In the earthly kingdom, what we do will affect how we are received in God's kingdom. The only perfect one is him, and we will make mistakes which he knows and understands. When making these decisions, are we purposefully disobeying the word, or are the mistakes honest ones done with a good intention? We must focus on gratitude for God's kingdom and all the gifts He has given us on earth. Our kingdom must run parallel to his kingdom, or conflicts will arise. How we deal with people, money, character flaws and other situations in the earthly kingdom is building our resume. We must distance ourselves from words and actions that are negative and go against God's kingdom. Tough choices must be made, and we must say to others we choose to live our life for God. When we succeed in wrestling with earthly choices, our path to the kingdom gets brighter.

The earthly kingdom is filled with tests about our character. We must surround ourselves with others who want to attain God's glory and help us from falling. When positive meets positive, great things are preserved and accomplished. Establishing a rich and glorious kingdom takes teamwork. We are only as strong as our weakest link in our kingdom. Set up a plan that makes us and our counterparts accountable to one another and God. Inside and out, we know when words and actions are causing us to move in the wrong direction. Protect the kingdom at all costs. If we do not have God's direction and support, we have nothing. Believe great things will be spoken and done even when times appear tough. When it is time to greet the Lord in his kingdom, we pray he will say to us, "Job well done."

KILTER

When our life is running in good working order, our words and actions seem to be in kilter. Our words flow effortlessly while talking or giving a speech. Our actions seem to be in perfect timing for what is needed in the moment. It takes only one unexpected turn to make things off kilter. People become off kilter, events go out of kilter, and emotions unkilter our language and deeds. Each day, we strive to remain in kilter. Our mental, physical, emotional, and spiritual health depend on kilter. Some things are out of our control like a rainy day ruining a picnic, causing the day to go off kilter. Others we are in control and with some kind, comforting, and well-thought-out words and actions, we can keep things in kilter. When we feel moments sliding out of kilter, we have the power and positive word of God to help us keep balance.

Good conditions most of the time work themselves out and keep things in kilter. It takes learned and experienced energy, belief, and words to change a negative circumstance into a positive one. There are those we know if something is off kilter, their whole day turns to chaos. Others can roll with the flow, and their calm and well-thought-out solutions put things back in kilter. The difference is our words and actions. If all we ever hear is pessimistic talk and watch negative behavior, that is what we will receive. Kilter needs positive words and actions so people can work out good solutions. Positive words and actions also keep our feelings in check so things do not get out of kilter. Staying in kilter also takes a grateful heart and a thankful attitude. Too many times, people get off kilter about a situation but forget to realize things could be much worse. Kilter means not taking things at the worst-case scenario.

We cannot control everything, but we can with our words and actions keep things in kilter. Mary Buchan in her book, *Over iT: How to Live Above Your Circumstances and Beyond Yourself,* says, "Those who are resilient can more quickly regain their equilibrium and spring back when they are thrown off kilter by the storms of their life." The key to kilter is flexibility in all circumstances because there are many right answers to different situations. Think and talk clearly not letting our emotions get the best of us. Kiltered people make good leaders who keep a level head so their words and actions do not cause additional strife. When daily living becomes unpredictable, turn to God's word for kilter. Talk and pray about whatever is concerning. Philippians 4:6 says, "Have no anxiety at all, but in everything, by prayer and petition, with thanksgiving, make your requests known to God." When we learn to keep kilter, it acts as our filter for peace.

KEEN

We all know those who are keen. We also know those who are anything but keen. As we live together in our great big world, middle ground has to exist. Growing mentally, physically, emotionally and spiritually, we need the keen and obtuse demonstrating life's lessons. The paradox of the cross and the law of attraction each show us the bottom line is faith and belief in the cause. 1 Corinthians 19–21 says, "For it is written: I will destroy the wisdom of the wise, and the learning of the learned I will set aside. Where is the wise one? Where is the scribe? Where is the debater of the age? Has not God made the wisdom of the world foolish? For since the wisdom of God the world did not come to know God through wisdom, it was the will of God through foolishness of the proclamation to save those who have faith." Keen knowledge is great, but a strong belief and faith whatever our endeavor is imperative. The naysayers who say this idea is not shrewd do not know how to believe and dream. Keen is what we allow it to be, and if we can put our body, mind and soul, behind something, it will turn into a positive and successful outcome.

Positive words and actions are what is keen. Developing outlets and surrounding ourselves with can-do people are how it is done. When book smart and common sense mesh with one another, this is keen interaction in a positive direction. We must be grateful for both because without one another, forward thinking and creativeness would not exist. It can be annoying in the company of someone who knows everything, just as it is being around someone who brings nothing to the plate. Thank God for both types because keen interaction would not take place. Keen needs to be for the goodness of all and not only for self-gratification.

Keen takes mental, physical, emotional and spiritual work. Working each and every day in a positive direction generating new and exciting ideas is keen. Keen work also leads to many failures, but the positive side is now we know what not to do. The smart thing to do is never give up. When our works begin to appear bland, keen answers come to the surface. We have to ask God each and every day for guidance no matter how trivial the situation seems. This is where keen and faith go hand in hand. Keen is only as penetrating as where we are in the moment. Stop and think before we do or say something. Our words and actions may not be keen. The power of persuasion and including all before making a decision is keen. There are times when a keen decision needs to be made when the life and safety of others hangs in the balance. In this instance, intelligent words and actions must take precedent. Keen and positive words and actions always make the grass green.

KNACK

We are all born with special knacks that we can use for positive uses. Some people have to work at a skill for years to become a professional while others just have the knack. Some painters, scientists, mathematicians, ball players, leaders, some just have the know-how. Amazingly, each one of us has a special knack. Using our special skill for the betterment of others hopefully is the direction. Mentally, physically, emotionally and spiritually, there are those who are gifted.

It is important to not be jealous for those who come by things naturally. It is frustrating to ask someone who has a knack, how do you do it? Usually they say, "I just know how." Wouldn't it be great if we knew how to untap these gifts? Our bodies tell us how we feel with our emotions, so we know ourselves best. That is how we know we have the knack for something. We can just feel it.

Developing knack takes hard work, patience and perseverance. Positive influences in the areas we want to succeed usually take a mentor to work alongside us step by step. Having that father who hits thousands of ground balls to us at third base, a grandfather who tutored us in the art of woodworking, or the study partner who sharpened our skills at math. Allow and thank all those people who were positive influences developing our knack. Building a knack takes thick skin because we need to accept constructive criticism as we go. If we do not know we are doing something wrong, coached correction brings perfection. C. E. Stowe, son of writer Harriet Beecher Stowe, said, "Common sense is the knack of seeing things as they are, and doing things as they ought to be done." Knack takes others, and we always have to be thankful for those who guided us.

Encourage and share our knack with others. Light someone else's torch to succeed as we give back by teaching them our knack. Our God-given talent he wants to see us do for others. Get the ball rolling by teaching our knack, coaching a skill, or projecting a positive influence. All knacks we can always look back and see a positive influence who helped us succeed. Network with others so we can develop areas of improvement. Those who have a special knack, people are somewhat reluctant to speak with because most times, they do not want to bother them or feel intimidated. Successful people want others to come to them to share a knack. Knacks build bridges and grows in family trees. This is why so many people in the same families seek the same professions. Law enforcement is one profession where we see generation after generation putting on the star. Sports stars share their knack from grandfather to father to grandson. When we develop our knack, we will never lack.

KIN

Our relations with our kin are supposed to last a lifetime. Sometimes, these make permanent marks. Kin should be happy, successful and supportive. Kin can also be a powder keg. The words and actions interacting with our kin make things positive or negative. Kin says blood is thicker than water. Sometimes, we overlook faults with our kin, when we shouldn't. If our kin are negative or doing destructive things for us mentally, physically, emotionally or spiritually, then it is time to cut the cord. Kin needs to be positive, happy, motivating and supportive. We expect more from our kin, and when it falls short, we feel disappointed because kin is supposed to be the closest unit. Kin should be trustworthy, standing by our side through thick and thin. When picking someone to join us as our kin, it is important to tell the whole story and not let half-truths stand in the way. Eventually, we learn everything about our kin.

Praying every day our kin relationships are successful is important. We must be thankful when our kin are supportive and stand by our side. When interacting with our kin, our words and actions should be positive and helpful. If we are struggling with kin, it is important to look to God for answers before we open our mouths. English lawyer and philosopher Francis Bacon Sr. said, "They that deny a God destroy man's nobility, for certainly man is of kin to the beasts by his body; and if he is not of kin to God by his spirit, he is a base and ignoble creature." We have to depend on God to help us with our own kin. With kin, we have to look at the best qualities and focus on the positive ones. There will always be a black sheep of the family.

For kin to get along sometimes, it takes an outside source to see through issues. When we are dealing one-on-one with kin, we sometimes stand too close to the fire. Kin are who we spend the majority of our time, share our deepest conversations, and depend on the most. If we do not have a kin member to share when times get tough, there is nothing wrong with seeking a counselor to act as an outside resource. Kin should be the easiest to communicate, but sometimes, it is the hardest because emotions can run high. Our kin should be supportive, fun to be around, and a true security blanket. If it does not feel this way, it is okay to reevaluate. Kin has to be positive for joy to exist and for those to coexist. Our words and actions play the biggest role with our kin. If we are not good to our kin, no one wins.

KICK

Kicking something requires steadfast determination. A will to get better, positive words for encouragement, and making our actions accountable are the beginning steps. People can kick all kinds of habits mentioned in the Ten Commandments to live a cleaner and more positive lifestyle. Mentally, physically, emotionally and spiritually, our life depends on kicking negative habits to the curb and enriching our life with positive, energizing and uplifting choices. It is not possible to kick negative out of our lives without a strong belief in God. Psalm 78:65–66 talks about how God had proven himself time and time again, and his people still did not follow his ways. "Then the Lord awoke as if from sleep, like a warrior from the effects of wine. He put his enemies to flight; everlasting shame he dealt them." When we do not kick continued negativity out of our life that angers God because he knows we can do better.

Visualization is important when kicking a habit. Not only do we have to imagine it, but we have to picture ourselves coming clean. Kicking something takes every ounce of determination, and we are using our strongest muscle in our body, the thigh. Focus on kicking negativity out of our life. When we do kick a negative habit out of our life, it is a cause for joy and celebration. Faith plays a tremendous role in kicking negativity. God will give us the strength when we choose belief. Kicks win games, kicks don't allow us to complain. When kicks are new, there will be few; but as we kick away the beasts, many more will come to the feast.

Kick away people, places and things that are not bringing positive to our life. This will take work, and persistence will pay off. Kicking away the past will uplift and renew us for future opportunities. Kick away the we can't do that attitude and replace it with we can! When we do this, we will kick life up a notch. Positive people and achievements will start coming our way. Kicking life's behind will give us confidence and a feeling of elation. Life will never kick us around again because God is on our side!

As we enjoy the fruits of our labor and successes from kicking the world's tail, we will have to learn how to kick back and relax. Some people have never been able to kick up their feet. Their personalities and willingness to keep kicking makes them tick. There needs to be a balance between work and play. When kicking back, learn what we like which brings us calm. Meditation and spending time with God will help us kick-start relaxation. When we find what brings us peace, kick out all other defeats.

KNOW

We know what we know because of all the things we have heard and seen. We have been told what to know, when to know it, and why we should know it. We have a choice to know what is true. We have a duty to know what is good and positive. Only we know what is best for us. Words and actions in our lives have always been dictated to us, and we are told why something should be as it is. As we grow mentally, physically, emotionally, and spiritually, we can sweep away the negative knows and replace it with positive. We learn to know we are not a sponge and have to soak up everything people throw at us. Knowing and sharing things that bring about the best in us and others is what should be our drive. Know when to listen, when to speak, and use the power of words to uplift the world.

When people ask us what do we know, are they genuinely asking us for a positive reason, or are they testing us for gossip to use in a negative fashion. Sometimes, it is tough to discern what we should tell people what we know. If what we know is harmful in our words or actions, then it would be better left unsaid or demonstrated. We all want to know the truth, and no one likes being lied to, but is it really important for us to be a know-it-all? We learn to know people's personalities are shaped by their emotions and upbringing. There are those who know if they are not the center of attention. There are also those if they know something, we have to pry it out of them. We all want to know the truth but at what cost?

John 8:32 says, "Then you will know the truth, and the truth will set you free." This is important when knowing about ourselves and being open and honest. We know we have sinned in our lifetime, and it is important to know the truth about ourselves. When we tell God about our failures, he already knew. God wants to know if we are willing to face our own truth. Knowing each mistake we make helps us grow as long as it is not intentional, repeated, or deliberately hurtful to others. Know our relationship with God and feel his presence each day. When we are confident in this area and have had successes, it is important to share what we know with others. Know positive, gratitude, joy, happiness, and success. Know how to share it with others so they can experience bliss. What we know can change someone's life with positive words and actions.

KNIGHT

Understanding a knight mentally, physically, emotionally, and spiritually requires depth. The words and actions of a knight represent chivalry and personal merit. The honor each of us needs to strive for with our words and actions should be knightly. Mean what we say and follow through as an upholder of a cause. Positive words and actions mixed with knightlike qualities is a win-win proposition. A knight trains for his adventures like we should with passion to succeed. The knight has symbolized battle and prestige for centuries. Knights get right to our emotions. In the book, *A Knight of Seven Kingdoms*, by George R. R. Martin, "A great battle is a terrible thing." The old knight said, "But in the midst of blood and carnage, there is sometimes also a beauty, beauty that could break your heart." We have to dedicate ourselves like a knight to conquer our language and behavior battles.

Knightly words and actions must be visualized for success and gratitude. Our words and actions when done with class will be like a knight saving the day. Listening to knights in battle as their armor clacks together with every blow, watching the chivalrous knight save the fair-haired maiden, and challenging others with their words and actions takes us to the edge of our seat: That's how a knight prepares. When we dedicate ourselves to live by a knightly code, we all can energize the world. A knight is a protector with his speech and actions. Like the Knights of the Templar or the Knights of the Round Table, we must live by a code to protect others from harm. Pray daily for knightly qualities in our personal lives and with our interactions with others. When we speak and act knightly, the world will bestow wonderful gifts upon us which are earned.

Knights accept accolade with humbleness and gratefulness. The sight of royalty knighting someone is truly exciting. Powerful personalities such as war heroes, inspiring thinkers winning a Nobel Peace Prize for humanity, and artists for their incredible creativity in their realm. The wow factor knights represent reaches toward the heavens. Having knightly qualities takes help from God to reach, maintain, and exceed expectations. Our words and actions can be just as powerful when we keep a positive focus and confer with him about everything, no matter how big or small. We are a knight in shining armor with words and actions to guide others positively in the right direction. We stand up for those who cannot stand alone. We speak words of wisdom in troubling times when others are mute. We open our strong arms with tender mercy for those who require comfort. We act as a knight for our family and the rest of the world.

KEMPT

Always make arrangements and try to plan a kempt lifestyle. Our words and actions also need to be kempt. While we cannot know everything that will happen in our daily lives, preparation for change keeps us kempt. Mentally, physically, emotionally, and spiritually, a kempt life provides balance. Checking our emotions and not letting others control our speech and actions is kempt. We all know people whose lives are a train wreck because they are unkempt in many areas. Avoid people and situations that make us feel unkempt. We have to believe in our own words and actions following through for kempt to work. We must project a positive attitude and have faith in God for kempt. Mark 4:38–39 says, "Teacher do you not care we are perishing? Then he arose and rebuked the wind and said to the sea, 'Peace be still!' And the wind ceased and there was a great calm."

We need to speak and act gratefully for kempt to multiply. Choose our battles because bickering unnecessarily causes an unkempt life. In my years of policing, the most ridiculous argument I ever had to arrest someone was for putting too much soy sauce on a hamburger! These people were unkempt in their speech, actions, attitudes and faith. No one person or family is perfect, but none knew the word kempt or how to apply it in their lives. Kempt takes positive mentoring and commitment. We all have work to do in our lives, but do we have a positive resource available to make kempt a reality? Unfortunately, many do not. Look ourselves in the mirror and choose to be kempt. Clear out bad words and actions that are not positive. Kempt people know how to restore order, organize a positive plan and build useful and meaningful life steps.

Choose a kempt mentor. When we follow others on a positive, kempt path, not only do we learn by example, but we are given the tools to enrich others. Decide our speech, actions, and attitudes, will no longer cause us to be unkempt. When we are searching for the right kempt word, thought or action, ask God for his direction. When we choose a life of kempt, we are no longer exempt. Accountability fuels our commitment to stay kempt. The work we do now will be rewarded when we stand before the Lord, our God. Get rid of all the unkempt clutter which degrades ourselves and others. Take the responsibility of the pillar which is strong and keep others kempt. Lead the way with our hands, feet and tongue to make others positive and kempt. Unless our intentions, words and actions are kempt, do not make the attempt.

KEEP

This word is one of the most important ones because it has so many meanings and directions to follow. Keep our words and actions positive and encouraging. Keep our nose to the grindstone. Keep focus on what we want out of life. Keep adhering to God's word and listen for his answers. When we keep going each day on a path that is positive, great things will happen to us which will help us grow mentally, physically, emotionally and spiritually. Keep speaking and acting grateful for all the good in our life. When we keep good company, we stay away from negative sights and sounds. Refrain from divulging secrets we were supposed to keep. Support people and causes that keep energizing and inspiring others. Pace ourselves comfortably instead of trying to keep up with the Joneses. Keep climbing the mountain toward success because if we think we can, we can.

Keeping our body, mind, and soul in top condition takes dedication and hard work. Staying on top of our game keeps us going each day. Finding what works for us giving the best results keeps us motivated. Ecclesiastes 10:18 says, "When hands are lazy, the rafters sag; when hands are slack, the house leaks." Keeping from getting lazy with our words and actions takes effort. When we hear others say negative or foul things, it would be easy keep up with them and participate. We need to keep away from this activity and have discipline. Our work is a reflection how we keep ourselves. Does our inner thought and direction we keep match the output? We must continually monitor ourselves so we do not keep a hypocritical image. Ask God to keep us on a righteous path to control our tongue. Ask him to keep us from overreacting in certain circumstances. Keep asking for guidance daily.

Keep updated on what is going on in the world so we can keep growing, but do not become inundated with everything going on because this can keep us negative. Know the difference to keep a healthy knowledge. We do not have to know everything, but it is good to keep up with what is positive and beneficial for the world. Keep doing good things for others and surround ourselves with those who want to do the same. Keep our promises to mentor, teach and act as a positive role model. Keep volunteering for great causes. Say and do things that keep us young at heart. Get to know others from different generations and keep contact. The knowledge we will keep from young and old will help us tenfold. We will never know when the friends we keep will help us act and speak.

KIT

Having a toolbox with all the necessary equipment to accomplish any job is the ultimate kit. Our life skills are the same. Speaking and doing things appropriately also requires a kit. Acquiring our life skills kit takes many years of experiences. How we earn or gain our kits comes differently for each of us. Hopefully, we were lucky enough to have good family, friends, mentors and experiences to positively develop our kit. How we mature mentally, physically, emotionally and spiritually depends on our kit. The important thing is knowing how to use our kit. Remember, even if everything seen and heard was not perfect, everyone has something they need to improve upon. We may not always have in our kit what it takes to complete the task. We must seek the proper tools from others to stock our kits. Most notably, we must look to God and learn from his word to improve our kits.

We must develop our kit bit by bit. Solutions to any circumstance can be found if we know where to look when rummaging through our kits. Think of things in our lives we need improvement. Focus on positive means to make our kits better. We have to channel and control our emotions to make our kits work properly. Knowledge and experience shape our kits for what we can do in the future. Preparation from yesterday, today, and for tomorrow must come from the tools in our box. Gratitude is one of the best tools we have. Gratitude demonstrates appreciation of others' words and actions. Thank-you is a tool that can be used in almost any situation. Please is a great tool in our kit seeking permission and acknowledging manners. Work ethic represents a huge tool in our kit because we are willing to make sacrifices for ourselves and others to achieve a great cause.

Our words and actions developed from our prosperous and grateful attitudes are the positive means for a healthy kit. Throw our heart over the bar in the area we want to achieve success. Remember, when we receive an accolade, the most important tool in our kit is giving God all the glory. 1 Corinthians 3:7 says, "Therefore, neither the one who plants, nor the one who waters is anything; but only God, who causes the growth." Our kit becomes full because of him and listening for him requires a loving heart. If we are filling our kit only for self-righteous endeavors, we are going about it the wrong way. Our kits are made full to help others, spread joy, and offer positive solutions for those in need. It is not about how many tools we have in our kit, but how we use what we have to make the world a better place. Make sure our kit has the tools for God's satisfaction.

KEN

People ken different words and actions which they are familiar. Their ken can be learned from many places. Family, friends or mentors shaped what words they heard and what actions they saw. Like the law of attraction, we only ken what our mind allows us. What we can envision we can do, so the sky is the limit. Our perception of words and how our reaction to them is our ken. Ken gives us insight mentally, physically, emotionally, and spiritually. How well we ken depends on the basics we have inherited. Our spectrum is what we believe in ourselves. Positive dialogue and how we regurgitate verbal knowledge reflects what we do physically. We have to experiment how we are going to react when new ken becomes available. Will we fix our ken or will we continue to go down the same path? If we have ken, we will feel empowered.

The greatest thinkers did not allow other's ken to manipulate or change their vision. Instead, they powered through with their newest ideas with the help of their ken. Ken allows us to dream, think and focus. Imagine knowing how to do something better verbally or mentally and not doing anything about it with our ken. Untapped skills lead to negativity and staleness. Do not let our ken go dim. Always seek those who brighten our day and push us to achieve better ken. Those who speak and act negatively only bring the same. Sharpen our ken with those who encourage, motivate and are positive. Ken takes time, patience and the help of God. He knows when our ken is able to handle experiences and grow. Mastering our own ken takes trial, error, and heart. Do not be afraid to test our ken. When we are confident with our ken, it is time to help others with their vision.

We always must keep developing our ken on words, actions, and topics. Positive words and actions propel our ken to greatness. If we know something important, do not feel like we need to keep this ken to ourselves. Ken leads to new development shaping the world. Proverbs 2:6–8 says, "For the Lord gives wisdom, from his mouth comes knowledge and understanding; he has counsel in store for the upright, he is the shield of those who walk honestly, guarding the paths of justice, protecting the way of his pious ones." When we do not know which ken to believe, turn to God and use it for good and positive things. Ken used with gratitude, mercy and helpfulness will always bring great reward. The greatest gift our ken can bring is when others are led to brighter paths with inspiration and hope. When we offer our best ken, we will always stay away from sin.

KINETIC

Our lives are put into motion every moment like kinetics. Our words and actions are the same way, but we must learn to control the kinetic activity so we don't say or act in an inappropriate manner. Kinetics are like the law of attraction; once the ball gets rolling, it goes fast. We have to be able to put on the brakes with our words and actions to control our emotions. Our kinetic lifestyles put us in places and positions we cannot always plan. Our language and actions must be positive. Living in a politically correct world with instant media outlets we must be careful of kinetics. Dynamic words and actions must be well-thought ahead of time and carefully selected. Kinetics transforms us, and we have to be grateful for its vigor. God still is in control of us, and kinetics are left in his hands.

Knowing God is in control of it all, how do we prepare ourselves for kinetics mentally, physically, emotionally and spiritually? We have to stay positive and intend to do our best with our words and actions. "Your life is a reflection of how effectively you balance potential and kinetic energy," states Steve Maraboli, *Unapologetically You: Reflections on Life and the Human Experience.* Sometimes, we cannot turn our mind off when we go to bed. Kinetic thinking signals we need to relax or change our words and actions. Physically, we are always in motion, and there are times we must slow down to give our bodies a rest. Emotionally, when things seem to be spinning out of control, we must slow our roll and evaluate our circumstance. Spiritually, when we are not connected with God in prayer, word, or action, we are living life too quickly. Continuing to stay kinetically going will burn us out in all areas of our lives. Slow down, God is in control!

Kinetics require ability that in turn needs balance. Our words and actions must be able to stand tall in all we encounter. When we use our kinetics, we are energetic. When our positive words and actions begin flowing, we become magnetic. When we get moving on that positive cause, our kinetics allow others to join and want to be a part of something great. Balance in our thoughts, words and actions is when we know our kinetics are working at full capacity. Kinetics allows us to find the right people at the right times for what is needed. Kinetics mixed with gratitude and prayer is a formula for success. If kinetics are not running smoothly, like a finely tuned engine, our lives will be chaotic and out of balance. Our positive words and actions start each and every kinetic reaction. Our will to do and say all that is good for the world is what kinetics should create.

YIELD

There are many times in our lives we wished we would have yielded prior to saying or doing something. We must learn from our mistakes with unyielding optimism. Positive words and actions in our lives generate a lifetime of yields. Our emotions play roles in knowing when to yield. Mentally, physically, emotionally and spiritually for growth, yielding is an important aspect. Judgement when to yield comes with experience and tutelage. A good parent, teacher, mentor, friend or liaison can teach us to yield in different circumstances. When things are not going our way and seem negative, we must yield to faith, gratitude and love. Take account of what we have, believe God gave us all which is good, and show loving direction. When we make this personal commitment every day, positive things will occur to stop and yield negative consequences. Yield to destructive words and actions letting them move out of our life.

Are our words and actions in line with how God would want us to speak and act toward others? Most of us would not be able to pass this test. Yielding destructive verbiage and behaviors is not easy. These learned behaviors have been a habit for a long time. Yielding to these temptations is taking the easy road. How many arguments could have been avoided if the parties involved had yielded their anger before speaking? When we yield, this is building a shield for our heart to grow stronger and more loving. Expect to be punished in some way when we choose not to yield. Numbers 12:11 says, "Ah, my Lord!" Aaron said to Moses, "Please do not charge us with the sin that we have foolishly committed!" Aaron did not want to pay the price after he did not yield to the Lord's word. Society has this same problem because people want to do and say what they want, but not yield to accountability.

People who yield from bad language and behavior are accountable to God, others and themselves. These are the positive life leaders we want in charge for decision making and planning. Think of examples in our life and the world who have yielded personal gain for the betterment of others: Parents saving for college instead of buying extravagant things, people giving their lives to the poor such as Mother Theresa, military personnel, police officers and firefighters who do not yield to unsafe conditions risking their lives daily for public safety. Having the capacity to know when to yield and when not to yield is a survival skill. Knowing there is more to do with a situation or there is nothing more we can do for a situation is imperative. Do not yield to negative things that the devil tries to snare us. Instead, promote a positive field that will develop a strong yield.

YEAR

Cultures and individuals embrace the word year as marking time and tradition. Comparisons are made about everything imaginable over this set time. Every mammal, animal and human have a birth date every year. Goals are made over a year establishing aggression or regression. Birth year, death year, leap year, good year and bad year. If we say a certain year, people remember historical feats, winning teams, songs, birthdays and anniversaries. Words and actions change throughout the years. In former years, the word bad meant bad. In recent years, bad can mean the complete opposite; good. Years are not what they appear. In our minds, we cannot accept and believe when thirty years have passed by time wise, but physically we feel it, not being able to do what we did in the past. Some years stick out more than others. In America, the years 1492, 1776, 1861–1865, 1929, 1941–1945, 1969, 2000 and 2001 have great significance and meaning, which are common knowledge.

Years decide what is acceptable, traditional, and unacceptable behavior for our words and actions. A generation ago, no swear words were allowed in the media. Now it is commonplace, and we hear abusive and obscene words and gestures every day. Genesis 1:14–15 says, "Then God said; Let there be lights in the dome of the sky, to separate day from night. Let them mark the fixed times, the days and the years, and serve as luminaries in the dome of the sky, to shed light upon the earth." Years mean something physically, mentally, emotionally and spiritually to everyone. We have 365 days and four seasons each year to reflect on our lives. Words about years strike conversations about the good old days or the year a loved one passed. There is so much meaning in the word year because it gets our motors running and our emotions churning.

Each of us is shaped by our words and actions based on our years on this earth. In our younger years, we may have said or acted immaturely. As the years pass, we probably have handled situations differently or chose to be silent. Years make us take accountability of our lives, pass along wise instructions because of our mistakes, and lead us to be better people. We need to embrace each year as if it is going to be our last. Truly loving someone for their character, flaws and all, takes years to appreciate. Years of friendship, fellowship and tradition is what makes us smile. Years of hardship, loneliness, and chaos makes us confused and sad. Living our years to the fullest and making each one a resolution to complete our goals brings joy and hope. Take each year and live our lives with no fear.

YOUTH

"Out of the mouths of babes." We have all heard this expression. Parenting is the most influential tool shaping youth. Positive words and actions should be the norm making youthful experiences shine brighter than the sun. Mentally, physically, emotionally and spiritually, we have a direct line what our children hear and see. When our youth are saying and doing things that are inappropriate, we can bet an adult had something to do with this behavior. Youth are inspired by what they see and hear, so that is our chance to do things correctly and get them on the right path. When it is time for youth to leave kid land and become an adult, hopefully, we have given them all the tools to say the right words and perform proper actions. The youth are our future leaders, workers and inventors, so we need to mentor them, so their lives are full of health and not filth.

When it is time for the youth to leave the nest, our words and actions should guide them to success. Timothy 2:22–25 says, "So turn from youthful desires and pursue righteousness, faith, love and peace, along with those who call on the Lord with purity of heart.

Avoid foolish and ignorant debates, for you know that they breed quarrels. A slave of the Lord should not quarrel, but should be gentle with everyone, able to teach, tolerant, correcting opponents with kindness. It may be that God will grant them repentance that leads to knowledge of the truth." We may do all we can for youth, but without daily prayer and reflection, they will not grow with confidence and make decisions with conviction. Positive words heard about themselves and others will keep them from feeling guilt stricken as adults. Previous generational issues should not be shouldered by the youth of the next era.

The fountain of youth, where lightheartedness leads to fresh ideas and kindness kills, represents all that is good. Words and actions should be valued by youth to express themselves positively and clearly. Youthful men and women will learn by their mistakes to live another day and fight another fight. Wishing we were young again to have another shot at redemption is wishful thinking. Youth have the opportunity to win the game of life when they have been taught correctly with positive words and actions. Listen to the youth speak and act today. Hear their excitement and feel their ideas. The world moves fast, and the youth of today have more ways with technology than ever to express themselves thoughtfully and intelligently. Enlighten youth with positive words and actions so we will see and hear their greatness come to fruition. Perhaps the youth can enlighten us with their intuition too.

YEARN

Yearning is a burning desire to do what we say and follow through with our actions. Our language turns exclusively to our focus as we yearn to get there. Our emotions churn as our awareness is heightened by our goal. Visually, we calculate each move we make and hear every word spoken as we yearn toward success. Positive reinforcement pushes us, teaches us, and shows us how much to yearn for something. Encouraging words pump us up, and our passion overflows like a love story. Songs of Solomon 5:4 says, "My beloved put his hand by the latch of the door, and my heart yearned for him." As we near our goal, we can feel every ounce of emotion as we yearn. Yearning involves mental, physical, emotional, and spiritual preparedness. Positive examples show us how to yearn, but make us aware we will not burn with the decisions we are about to make.

When we yearn, we also learn and grow. We have to have our mind and attitude right focusing on our goal. We must be thankful for our God-given abilities and make our concern what we yearn. Sometimes, we must realize what we yearn is not what God wants for us. It is important to slow down and listen to God's subtle hints. Yearning means our body, mind, and soul is churning, which can be chaotic and loud. This is when we need to adjourn and find a quiet place to prepare our words and actions together carefully. When all is well and our plans match God's plans, our yearning will spurn creativity. When we yearn for answers, think of this acronym to keep us on track. YOU ENVISION ALL REQUIRED NOW. Simplicity may be the key as we say and do only what we can handle in the moment. It is amazing when we take the extra time with our words and actions, how what we are yearning may flow more smoothly.

Learn by example when we yearn so we can pass it on to others when it is their turn. Our words and actions, when we yearned in the past, may not have been healthy. Whether we yearn about people, relationships, careers, or goals, make sure we control what comes out of our mouths. When we yearn, act as an intern soaking up all the positive ways to speak and act appropriately to achieve our goals. Mentor to others who are yearning, so they are not overwhelmed and heading down the wrong path. Pray and ask God if we are yearning for the right thing at the proper moment. How we handle what we yearn, when it does not go our way, is the true mark of mature words and actions. Through our hearts yearn for success. Speak and act with control over our emotions. In the end, what we yearn, we will earn.

YOKE

Our yoke is what binds us together making us who we are. We use words and create actions that come from our heart in our daily lives. Our yoke is our personal connection that others witness when they hear us speak and act. Positive words and actions should link our yoke for success. Everything in the world is interwoven by the law of attraction mentally, physically, emotionally and spiritually. How we say we are doing is how our day will go. Like cooking a sunny-side up egg yolk, we always want to keep it intact. Believe in such a strong yoke and implement it in everything we say and do. Talk to God throughout the day, so our words and actions represent a powerful and loyal yoke. Our solid yoke should remain untarnished. Make every effort to speak and act the way Jesus teaches to protect our yoke. Imagine our yoke as the spoke of a wheel holding it all together and moving forward.

Our yoke is blended together perfectly because he always knows before we do. Our yoke is delicately balanced. When negative words and actions make us feel stressed, use our mind positively quoting scriptures for a favorable outcome. Our yoke will always be protected when positive words and thought combined with proper actions take place. Yoke together all good thoughts and stop thinking about past failures or transgressions. Matthew 11:28–30 says, "Come to me, all you who labor and are heavy-laden and overburdened, and I will cause you to rest. Take my yoke upon you and learn of me, for I am gentle and humble in heart, and you will find rest for your souls for my yoke is wholesome and my burden is light." Speak and act gratefully about the yoke God has given us. Focus on our positive attributes until we know and believe our yoke is what makes us whole.

Everyone has a capacity to succeed, nourishing their yokes positively as a steward. Our yoke lives by what we love, understand and teach, so reach out to others. Our yoke grows even stronger as it is filled with joy and creativity. Positive words and actions from our yoke give others hope and a willingness to develop their yokes in faithful endeavors. Even if our yoke gets broke, it is the quality on the inside which matters. When we master our thinking, controlling our words and actions takes the heat from the yoke reducing stress. Treat our yoke better than a joke. Examine each word and action and how it affects our yoke. As we are cognizant about our words and actions, our feelings will tell us if we are protecting our yoke. A perfect yoke takes dedication and work.

YOU

You were born to speak positively, act righteously, mentor daily, and seek God with all our heart. You are the one, mentally, physically, emotionally, and spiritually, who has the choice to say and do great things. You can get the ball rolling surrounding yourself with successful people with positive influences who, through the law of attraction, keep doing good. You have hope and expectation as it says in Lamentations 3:22–24, "The favors of the Lord are not exhausted, his mercies are not spent; they are renewed each morning, so great is his faithfulness. My portion is the Lord, says my soul; therefore, will I hope in him." You have the ability to turn yourself around when speaking and acting negatively when you wait on God. You have to talk and act merciful and admit you make mistakes. You always have to say you can do this, so your motivation is done with passion.

You are the one who must control your emotions no matter the situation, so your words and actions encourage and do not discourage. Do not allow your emotions to cause you to speak and act in fear because God is in your corner. You need to pray for those who stir emotions, so they can find balance in their lives. You need your priority placed on God and not on earthly things to help keep your emotions in check. You must seek solitude daily and focus on what comes out of your mouth and what you do for emotional stability. You need to listen for God's voice in indecisive times to control your emotions for decision making. You will earn grace from God as you control your emotions and do not react to those who are troubled. You must remember everyone has turmoil, and you are the one who can be the peacemaker with your words and actions.

Your words mean commitment to others especially when you say you will be there. You have to follow through, raising your word to mountain-top status with your noble action. You create the most damage when you do not do what you say. If you lose your word and reputation in this world, you are finished. You should strive to make a difference every day with your words and actions. You need to work each day honoring God and his children, building a lasting legacy. Partnering this way, you will never be alone in the trenches. You need to be unique with your words and actions positively standing out, so others with troubles trust and follow you. You shall practice mentoring others with your words and experiences, lighting a path for success. You know the light of God surrounds you, the love of God enfolds you, the power of God protects you, and the presence of God watches over you, and wherever you are is God.

YAMMER

People all want to be heard. They yammer to us about what is going on in their lives. We yammer in times of positive events and calling for help. Yammering is what Chip Kidd says, "What people want, no matter who they are, is someone to listen to them. People have a lot on their minds, however trivial and if you're simply willing to sit there like a sack of dirt and let them yammer, they will tell it to you." We want our words to be uplifting, upbeat, and joyful. When yammering is not, we must be an active listener to recognize with God's help ways for positive mental, physical, emotional and spiritual changes. Others' yammering helps us learn patience and understanding because no one is alike, and it would be a boring world if we were. Yammering is a sign of wanting peace in every walk of our life.

Yammering can be complaining or telling others repeatedly about self. A gift of the mind and tongue to recognize our yammering is like a kill switch to say enough. We control our yammering when the mind tells the tongue okay, we have had our emotional say, and our tongue is going to get us in trouble. We all yammer at times with our spouse, friends, and family. When it turns negative, our spiritual warrior must save the day and say, "Convict us, Lord." Yammering teaches us to do better, dream bigger, and expect more from our words and actions. Yammering tells us we need more grace and a delicate touch because when we yammer, we push others away, instead of bringing them closer. Our conversations must be positive, and when we feel it going elsewhere, develop the ability to hear from God, stop and, if necessary, repent. If we are going to yammer, do it about God's word with gratitude and thanks.

Yammer to the east, west, north and south. No! Let's control what comes out of our mouth instead of yammering. Stand out as the one who uses correct grammar, not unrecognizable yammer! Everyone does not have the grace and mercy to deal with yammering. Act as the light to attract those who need their yammering to be heard. Offer positive solutions to negative utterances and combat yammering with God's word. Load our mind, body and soul with happy and grateful yammering, which is a refreshing path for others. Yammering can be good or bad, and we must know the difference and learn to turn the page. If we are yammering to tell tall tales, stirring up negative thoughts, or talking over others, quit! This idle chatter is demoralizing and reflects our spiritual immaturity. Yammer great things to others so they heal with zeal. Use God's words as ammunition so when we do yammer, it is to enamor.

YOGA

Yoga is a balance between our skills and actions. Mentally, physically, emotionally, and spiritually, we all can use yoga to cultivate our unspoken words into positive, life-altering dialogue. Yoga can also stretch our bodies to healthy ventures. Yoga, performed daily, can transform the body, mind, and soul, so a positive flow from the tongue, hands, and feet can create positive direction. Yoga can ease emotions, unclutter thought, and clear the path for us to hear God. Yoga builds flexibility in the body, which stimulates the brain. Flexibility and speaking positive, God managed, thoughts make yoga essential. Yoga helps us grow in like a butterfly coming out of its cocoon. Mistakes with our words and actions will happen, but when we use flexible, yogalike qualities, mixed with God's word, we will flourish and be forgiven.

Yoga is a confidence builder when we dive into it daily. Each day we stretch positively for growth, yoga can help us build our skills and balance our emotions. With yoga, we release any stressors for a healthier communication. Yoga can be summed up this way by B. K. S. Iyengar, "Yoga, an ancient but perfect science, deals with the evolution of humanity. The evolution includes all aspects of one's being, from bodily health to self-realization. Yoga means union—the union of the body with consciousness and consciousness with the soul. Yoga cultivates the ways of maintaining a balanced attitude in the day-to-day life and endows skills in the performance of one's actions." This balance allows for the positive law of attraction to kick in, and as our positive words and thoughts go, energy will flow. If we are well in the mind and body, our soul will advertise it to others with positive words and actions. Yoga helps us look inside and outside for happiness, love and joy to form.

We have to put our money where our mouth is, and yoga does this with breathing. Yoga teaches us to breathe rhythmically to slow down before we speak and act. Eloquence with well-thought dialogue will help through tough times and make the interaction better. Have gratitude for yoga and its balance it gives us. Our spoken words and actions will also become balanced. We all have God-given abilities, but do not bring them out ourselves. Yoga works on the conscious, so we can dig deeper within ourselves to bring out our talents. Yoga connects the mental, physical, emotional, and spiritual values at one level and pushes us to success. Yoga helps maintain peace in decision making whether to move forward, backward, or not move at all. Yoga keeps us centered and connects us with God. Yoga will unite all our positive words and actions, releasing emotions of love, joy, happiness and contentment, which will inspire others to victory.

YANG

Yang stands on its own. In the yang world, we have to realize not everyone has this ability. Words and actions must be examined historically, situationally, and with yanglike qualities to see if our masculine perspective is in tune with the world. Yang has always been associated with light, heaven and active principles. While this attitude of yang domination was good for our speech and actions, it may blind us to the perspectives of others. We must be positive and grateful. We must help those who cannot get to the yang and express themselves with well-thought, sensitive advice to uplift lives. A yang personality at times can be overzealous, talking and walking over others. A yang person must mentally, physically, emotionally and spiritually seek greatness, but at the same time recognize and acknowledge other people and ideas exist.

Yang personalities are aggressive in their words and actions. Most leaders come from the yang side and are not afraid to make important decisions affecting many. In doing so, yang must appropriately say positive words and create good environments. Yang personalities must remember balance is the key to capturing most hearts. *The Complete Works of Chuang Tzu* by Zhuangzi, it says, "So it is said, for him who understands heavenly joy, life is the working of heaven; death is the transformation of things. In stillness, he and the yin share a single virtue; in motion, he and the yang share a single flow." When yang attitudes mixed with negative words and actions take stage, yang drives a stake through the heart. This type of yang leads to isolation and ire. Yang can easily throw gasoline on a fire if they are not sensitive to others with their words and actions. Yang equals momentum, so we have to wait that split second to see if what is being said and done has integrity and loving intention. Yang must never be used for negative ventures or hurting others.

People should be the yang who inspires, motivates and teaches love, joy and happiness. Use our yang to have big shoulders to help others. Yang people mentor others and lead them to successes. A victorious life has much to do with the yang and positive reinforcement. Yang people do not worry about rolling up their sleeves and getting dirty. Yang people must see the big picture by saying and living better. Self-confidence and humility should be the way when yang personalities work with others. Yang personalities take care of their families, close acquaintances and themselves without looking to others for help. This attitude can get tricky when the yang may need help but can be unwilling to ask for it. Yangs usually say, "We can do it ourselves." It is important for yang personalities to be even keel and recognize when others want to help. Yang needs to slow down and listen to God for guidance.

YIN

Words and actions paint pictures, tell stories, start and end fights. Yin is feminine, mild, and even keel. Understanding your yin thoughts helps us say and act more grounded. On the other hand, yin attributes help us say and do things out of the box. When we yin, we win because we have to create our successes. Mentally, physically, emotionally, and spiritually, we have a choice as yin is pleasing. Choose to avoid negative words and actions which degrade, deflate, and defeat positive outcomes. Do not be the timid yin person who, when they walk into a room, others say, "There goes the wind." Yin people do not need to be so passive they let others walk on their speech and actions.

Yin people, do not be afraid to let others in. Think positively transposing dark into light and cold into warmth. Yin people look at things practically and can put on the brakes to keep things under control. Yin does not mean to take a back seat to anyone or anything. It is how we look at every decision and situation using yin experiences to measure what words and actions to take. Yin may not be a pie in the sky demeanor but sustains level-headed behavior. It is not a sin to question words and actions with our yin traits. The great thing is not everyone wants the same results or life. Yin fortifies our life and lets us know how and where we stand. Yin is mostly positive too, when it falls in line for effect on how we think, talk, and reason to make a good decision. Use our yin personality to teach others to reflect before they speak and act.

Thank God for our yin traits to show through. Gratitude how we see things and use our yin to teach and mentor others to win. Victory does not mean we are right, but we use our yin to come to a conclusion that comforts us all. Yin reinforces our experiences and teaches us to look into things before we stick our foot in our mouths. Philip Zimbardo from PictureQuotes.com says, "This world is, was, will always be filled with good and evil, because good and evil is the yin and yang of human condition." Knowing good and evil exist in the word, it is important to understand the yin inside of us. Opposing points of view does not mean our yin should be a different hue. Balance our yin to keep us at peace, but don't just make change to simply please.

YARE

Our mouths are yare each and every day to let us know what direction we are to go, what our day will be like, and if we honor others. Our speech and actions should emulate a cheetah, speedily racing with nimble movements through the air with agility so precise and flare. This picture in our mind represents yare. Our words and actions should be graceful, always encouraging and edifying all. Mentally, physically, emotionally, and spiritually, we break down our yare. Take our learned words and actions and with artful skill fit them into every situation using God's loving qualities. We are ready, set and talking faster than we can go. Yare as fast as a hare can be dangerous if we don't care. Speak and act aware so our yare does not wrinkle any feathers and get into others' hair. We may speak and act with yare, but are we doing it with God's prayer?

Yare is ready for action and eagerly prepared. Using God's word with yare will keep trouble from coming because our speech will be spiritually aware. Our speech and actions should be pleasing to God. Colossians 1:10 says, "That you may walk in a manner worthy of the Lord, fully pleasing to him in all things, bearing fruit in every good work and steadily growing and increasing in and by the knowledge of God with fuller, deeper, and clearer insight, acquaintance, and recognition." Our speech and actions seasoned with God's word will make our yare language beyond compare. A mind-set full of readiness and yare, what a pair! Surrounding ourselves with smart and spiritually yare-based language will endear others and will raise us to a level of leadership. Use our lively yare with confidence as we speak and act fair.

Maneuverability with our words and actions allows us to say the right things during situations, give us the reputation of having a charismatic yare. How awesome to be the person who everyone looks to having the yarelike flare. Stabilizing our emotions, nimbly asking God for speedy guidance and practicing gracious yarelike oration leaves positive impact. This unique quality is a gem to teach to others. Yarelike speech and actions take years of faith-based learning to master. When we can speak and act gratefully, positively, and eagerly, our yare blares like trumpets announcing an awe-inspired message. It would be a sin not to work with and pass yare qualities on to others who can help the world. Yaring is sharing our God-given abilities and teaching positive language for right actions. Reach out to those in need and intercede with our yare. Take the dare and use our yare to be the one who stands above the crowd, with speed, grace and agility.

YORE

Words we remember from yore. Famous speeches from historical figures, coaches and parents inspiring or chiding us to be more. Words from yore we want positive motivation that will allow us to soar. Yore words should never be used to keep score. Yesteryear becomes this year because we say and do what we recognize from yore. Yore is from the past, so we shall not dwell on words and actions that only take us back. God wants our yore inspired with positive words to open our body, mind and soul for our current chore. Mentally, physically, emotionally and spiritually, our yore shapes our core. Reflecting and learning from yore is important to know what to throw away and what to keep. Positive yore allows us to grow while negative yore puts us on the floor. Managing our yore is important, so we learn not to live long ago. Explore with our yore to open new doors.

We must talk and act grateful when teaching from our yore. Even if words and memories might not be positive from our yore, chalk it up to experience and turn it into something galore. When dealing with yore, look to Jesus and allow our true friend to help us mend. Yore should generate feelings of happiness, joy, and elation describing something that made us laugh so hard we cried. Alecia Elliott, on lyricist.com, describes yore this way in *Have Yourself a Merry Little Christmas.* "Here we are in olden days, happy golden days of yore, faithful friends who are dear to us gather near to us evermore." The memories of yore should bring words of lore. When teaching yore, God is our faithful friend who never leaves our side. Yore must be brought forward with integrity and passion positively linking old and new. Talk and teach positive yore with so much gusto people want an encore.

Yore words and actions are a proverbial storehouse for more. Mistakes are made, second chances are given, and we must remember our yore. Growing allows us to never forget our yore. Saluting those great people and their accomplishments, such as the veterans, from previous wars. Heartfelt words graciously thanking them for the price they paid is yore. Grateful words and actions are contagious when recognizing yore. There is no faster way to verbally and physically get people together to accomplish more, when recognizing the accomplishments of yore. The word of the Lord is a window from yore to show us what is in store. Yore shows us the past, lets us choose our words and actions for improvement, and kick-starts ambition to accomplish more from the lessons learned. Yore should never be this is how we have always done it; instead, yore should be a beacon pointing us evermore.

YES

Yes means joy, happiness, affirmation, with complete elation and outpouring of positive emotions—Yes! Yes has love flowing toward others engulfing them in kindness and surrounding them with peace and the Holy Spirit. We act and say yes with all our senses as we all can visualize to actualize the moment. Yes means we are faithful and thankful for our gifts God bestows. Five years ago, I owned five acres of land on a slope overlooking water. I had a dream of my perfect retirement home, having three levels of glass on the back facing the water, with the lower level as a workout area. The lot I sold out of necessity. Inching closer to retirement, I traveled to many states searching for lakefront property. After looking at thousands of homes on websites and in person, I could not believe my eyes! "Yes!" I screamed. "The house from my dream!" Three levels of glass on the back with the lower level as a workout area. (It was exact.) I now own that dream home. God has blessed me and not a day goes by where I don't have tears of joy. Yes! Thank you, God.

Another yes story which I dreamed came through God. My friend, Bill, passed away at age ninety-five. Bill was the grandfather I never had, the most well-rounded man I ever met, and my best friend. It was December, and I was terribly sick with the flu. I came home from work and slept seventeen straight hours. During this time, I dreamed of visiting Bill at his home. When the door opened, Bill was a little boy jumping up and down for joy along with his wife, Rachel, who also was a small child. The dream ended, and I awoke to check my phone because I had been asleep for so long. A voicemail from Bill's daughter told me, Rachel had passed away. The Holy Spirit interpreted my dream. Bill and Rachel were reunited in the kingdom of heaven as playful children. God gave me the biggest yes moment of my life. Thank you, Lord!

There are so many ways God tells us yes. Through dreams, people, words and situations. We need to be still, look and listen carefully for these moments. Some will answer questions and some will let us know we are on track. Galatians 5:22–23 says, "But the fruit of the Holy Spirit the work which his presence within accomplishes is love, joy, gladness, peace, patience, an even temper, forbearance, kindness, goodness, benevolence, faithfulness, gentleness, meekness, humility, self-control, self-restraint, continence. Against such things there is no law that can bring a charge." Yes encompasses all these positive traits when we focus our attention on God's word and deliver with our actions. Yes!

YEOMAN

When our words match our valiant actions, we build our reputation as a yeoman. We are not excused from yeoman service. A yeoman never gives up, and his words and actions encourage mentally, physically, emotionally, and spiritually. During life's challenges, our yeoman work brings God's favor. A yeoman never has a victim's mentality. As a yeoman, our self-image will be formed by how we speak and act. A yeoman brings trust, integrity, and something to believe in as he changes negative language into harmonious positive wisdom. A yeoman represents a conqueror who speaks and acts with confident boldness as he performs his job. A yeoman speaks and shows his craft like a priceless treasure. A yeoman is loyal like Daniel, who was cast to a den of lions because he stuck with his beliefs praying to the Lord. A yeoman truly must speak and act righteously, and if he does, he will be rewarded and left unharmed.

Yeoman must inspire others with their words and actions with a teaching, giving, and loving heart. Yeoman spend time with others and talk about how to become successful. A commitment to learning positive skills is a yeoman's focus on excellence. A yeoman brings stability to a rough storm, like Jesus calming the sea. Yeoman should follow a model of goodness and be the light for those who want more. We do not have to have riches to be considered a yeoman. Yeoman come from all walks of life uplifting with positive words and actions. Those who want to grow in the mind, overcome emotions, and develop a skill need to seek someone who speaks and acts godly and good. Who is the yeoman we can imitate? Jesus! Are we living the life with our words and actions so we can be a yeoman for others?

Solving these questions and turning our lives for the service of others is a yeoman.

An apprentice learns from the yeoman; as such, the yeoman was once the apprentice. Our words and actions are sometimes dull, uninformed and inaccurate because we have not found the yeoman to follow. III John 11 says, "Beloved, do not imitate evil but imitate good. Whoever does what is good is of God; whoever does what is evil has never seen God." Yeoman surround themselves with other yeoman for continued growth in their words and actions, giving instant credibility. Yeoman point us where to go so we grow. A yeoman has all the words, actions, traits, and integrity for us to follow and emulate. Find the burning desire to be the yeoman in our world. Yeoman must be the showman, introducing something new and amazing every day to make life bright and gay.

YARD

How someone keeps their yard tells a bigger story and usually is a reflection of their inner workings. A neat and orderly yard used for specific work and activities demonstrates a purpose mentally, physically, emotionally, and spiritually. A yard that looks like an episode of hoarders may want to put us on guard. This yard screams of dysfunction, negativity, sickness and a lack of motivation. Our yard signals words, actions and feelings whether positive or negative. We must create a yard that surrounds us with things which will make us feel good and successful. If our yard is cluttered with chaos, surrounding us our words and actions will show it. Our yard should describe ourselves with a signature, such as beautiful, orderly, clever or happy. One look at the yard and it says this person has it all together. Take ownership of our yard demonstrating how the 'sun shines on thee. Our yard should represent peace, love, hope and an incredible work ethic.

If we were born into or currently have a yard which is in chaos, the good news is it is only our current situation. Our yard will not define us forever. We can change and make improvements with positive words and innovative actions. God gives each one of us potential, but what we do with it and how we work at it will depend if we receive his gifts. Our yard is our life where we can implement positive steps to cleanse ourselves, bury the past, and seek a successful future. Never give up. Ross Perot said, "Most people give up just when they're about to achieve success. They quit at the one-yard line. They give up at the last minute of the game, one foot from a winning touchdown." Seek greatness inch by inch or three feet at a time. Do not compare our yard with others. Make sure our words and actions are positive, focused and on track so our yard is a storehouse which is serviceable.

When our yard is profitable with a life filled with stability, positive words, and calculating direction, share our experiences with others. Our yard should be where all come to gather for positive words, inspiration, and good times. We all remember as a child the yard we flocked to for fun, excitement and safety. Our inner and outer yards should match so we can provide motivational and positive guidance for others. As an example, we want our yard to be unsoiled, so people have the confidence in us to ask us how to fix theirs. Picture our desired yard and believe we can have it. When we put the work into action, our yard will flower beautifully. God views our yard as his sanctuary. Do not put anything in it we will later regret. We are special, so make our yard one to inspire and lead. Our yard, when we allow God to tend it, becomes a sanctuary.

OWNERSHIP

Words we speak and actions we take are our responsibility, and we must take complete ownership. Ownership does not assess blame or tell half-truths. Ownership handles things with accountability from self and God. 2 Corinthians 1:21–22 says, "But the one who gives us security with you in Christ and who anointed us in God; he has also put his seal upon us and given the Spirit in our hearts as a first installment." If our words and actions are through us and go into God's foundation, there is no reason not to take ownership. God knows what we are going to say or do before we do. Whether good or bad with our intentions, we must take ownership and tell the truth. Ownership is rough on our emotions because we have to be big enough to face the facts in front of others. Even if our words and actions are wrong, the truth sets us free when we take ownership.

Ownership requires a passion and a dream to fulfill greatness so joy, happiness, and elation can be shared with many. Ownership demands big shoulders to build on, rely on, and carry on. Words and actions do not always work out as planned, and in these cases, ownership shows courage and leadership. Ownership of our words and actions builds momentum, challenges our fortitude, highlights our aptitude, and fulfills our promises. The new ownership of the Chicago Cubs in 2012 took over a flailing organization. They told us what they were going to do one step at a time. Their words and actions were truthful and confident delivering their promise and taking ownership and the fans to a world championship in 2016. When a person or organization does not take ownership of their words and actions, it causes dissention and mistrust. Reputations become damaged which in turn brings negative emotions of anger, disloyalty and fear to raise their ugly heads.

Our words and actions must be faith based to bring out positive outcomes. Ownership means follow-through and commitment to benefit others mentally, physically, emotionally, and spiritually. Ownership demands for us to become a person of excellence. Talk and walk with integrity doing the right thing even when no one else is present. Let God be the boss, end of argument. Ownership recognizes this, so we must say and do things that pleases the Lord. There is no higher standard how ownership works with God. Say and do things for the right reasons, not because we want to, but because our ownership depends on it. Compromising ownership is a trip Satan wants us to take, tempting us with false securities that will only come back to haunt. Righteous ownership gives us favor and kinship with our Kingship. Always do what is right, and our ownership will take flight.

OATH

Taking an oath and saying the words commit us to those words truthfully and totally. Swearing an oath to God, country, organization and others is an assertive message indicating we will walk the walk and talk the talk. When we take the oath, we cannot do both. When we break the oath with our speech and actions, it has long standing ramifications for us and others. An oath means service, loyalty and integrity with our words and actions. Oaths are promises that put us in the middle of important situations affecting many lives. An oath says and implies we will take responsibility for our actions and others to keep the world free from evil. An oath is a way of shaping our speech, actions, and the way we live a life for ourselves and others. An oath means we will sacrifice our life for the good of humanity. Give thanks to those who take the oath with their words and actions because they will be the last ones to boast.

When we promise to live until death do us part, that is an oath, not idle words. We mentally, physically, emotionally and spiritually expect more from those who take an oath. Numbers 30:2 says, "If a man makes a vow to the Lord, or takes an oath to bind himself with a binding obligation, he shall not violate his word, he shall do according to all that proceeds out of his mouth." We must remember words, and actions still come out of the mouths of human beings, so no one is perfect. Those who take an oath speak and act similarly to accomplish a task. A command presence echoes and solidarity reigns when we take an oath. An oath says and represents not letting others down and working toward a positive cause. Never take an oath which we don't intend to honor and keep. An oath must be good for humanity.

Our life must move in the direction of our words and actions when we take an oath. Stop doing and saying negative things that defeats the oath we take in the presence of God. Our oath for ourselves and others needs to be positive, prophesizing victory, favor, and a faithful message. An oath must be a blessing and not a curse. Oaths should breathe life into our hearts. When we take an oath, it must have power for us to say and do the rest. Take an oath to never put ourselves or others down, always pointing to the Crown. When we say yes, we can, take others by the hand and lead them to follow. Make the oath we take a spiritual one, so our words and actions are positive and glorifying. Inspire others with our oaths, so we are known to keep our word truthful and good.

OPPORTUNITY

Opportunity knocks daily with our words and actions. What direction we take depends on the motivation we build and the opportunities we seek. A positive vocabulary combined with a can-do spirit opens opportunities mentally, physically, emotionally, and spiritually. Opportunities sometimes only come once in a lifetime, so it is our choice and free will to be ready and grab it. Ephesians 5:15–17 says, "Look carefully then how you walk! Live purposely and worthily and accurately, not as the unwise and witless, but as wise (sensible, intelligent people). Making the very most of the time [buying up each opportunity], because the days are evil. Therefore do not be vague and thoughtless and foolish, but understanding and firmly grasping what the will of the Lord is." We need to speak and act with purpose and spend our time wisely so opportunities do not pass. Each time we open our mouth could be the moment!

Opportunity has little to do with being rich or poor, strong or weak, or smart or obtuse. Granted, we cannot change our lineage or background. Once our cards are dealt, let us choose to make the most for ourselves and run to opportunities with determination. Abolish negative words, thoughts, people, and seek only positive opportunities. The law of attraction talks about how our current situation is only that, current. Opportunity come get us! Choose to work harder than others, take advantage of every conversation and understand where it can lead. How we respond will determine what opportunities are made. Muster every ounce of energy in our body and positively take the attitude we are unstoppable. When we believe, others will too, and the land of opportunity will open its doors to us. Refuse to accept anything other than the chosen person God has made us and help others make their mark.

When we use our potential and seek all positive opportunities, we carry the torch to light the way for a better world. Whether our gift is time, money, verbal or physical talents, mentor others with these special opportunities. Share and learn with others gratitude we obtained from not resting on our laurels. Each day create opportunities for ourselves and others living on purpose and not taking no for an answer. People who use their time wisely and on purpose do not say they are "busy" as an excuse. Instead, they say they are seeking their opportunities and priorities. Teach others to avoid unopportunistic activities that are not productive. Opportunity is not all work and no play because balance is a necessity. Let God direct us in the right direction to keep opportunity seeking on track. Opportunity will motivate and stoke our fire.

OFFERING

Our offerings must be sincere and come from the heart. Verbally committing to some charity and actively following through completes the offering. When making an offering, do not procrastinate. Life seems like we are nickeled and dimed constantly from people and organizations wanting an offering. Mentally, physically, emotionally and spiritually, offerings deplete our time and pocketbook. Offerings can become draining if we do not treat them as a blessing and a positive experience. Our words and actions concerning offerings tell us who we are in Christ. Are we making offerings which make us look good or doing it to glorify God? Malachi 3:8–9 talks about tithing and offerings this way. "Dare a man rob God? Yet you are robbing me!" And you say, "How do we rob you? In tithes and offerings! You are indeed accursed, for you the whole nation, rob me." Do not make an offering unless it is given joyfully.

Offering freely brings us joy, love, hope and fulfillment. We shall give to those in need so we can plant a seed in them to succeed. Offerings say we have an attitude of gratitude for all God has given us. When we give an offering, it is a choice. Our words, actions and feelings must be positive toward the offering; otherwise, we undo the great atmosphere we created. Each time we make an offering begins a fulfilling project. Offerings can be a one-time deal or a philanthropy for a lifetime. The truest offering we can consistently make is tithing for the Lord. The Bible says if we offer 10 percent of our assets for Christ, we will benefit many times. Offerings can be contagious in a public setting, but that is not when giving is paramount. Our offerings are most relevant when they are silently given.

The anonymous donor, the unknown trust and gold coins which magically appear during the holiday season; these are exciting and add wonderment to offerings. Offerings may be big or small, but the best part is it brings people together for a worthy cause. Good feelings ensue, and generosity pours for those in need of offerings. Offerings give new direction and faith to those who have lost hope. Offerings give an individual a second chance, a community new safety apparatus and technology means to cure life-threatening diseases. Offerings have a global impact and purpose, which feeds, clothes, and educates those who otherwise would have nothing. Our words and actions make the difference and help the cause thrive. Challenge ourselves and others to always give generous contributions because we never know when we may be on the other end. Always say yes to legitimate offerings because God knows if we gave our all.

OBEY

Obey is a word that starts debates about gender, social, religious, legal, marital and worldly issues. Obeying means following the rules or laws that govern the common good and safety of humanity. Mentally, physically, emotionally, and spiritually, obeying gets us in touch with our feelings of certain topics that gives us perspectives. Our speech and actions are affected by obeying because either we agree or not. Obeying and disobeying allows us to get our juices flowing verbally and nonverbally. Obeying deals with our God-given rights, Bill of Rights, free will and living with a purpose. Whether we obey or not shows what side of the fence we want to live, speak and act. Obeying recognizes authority, conformity and adhering to values. Joshua 5:6 says, "Now the Israelites had wandered forty years in the desert, until all the warriors among the people that came forth from Egypt died off because they had not obeyed the command of the Lord."

Our speech is instrumental in solidifying our personality and whether we will use it to obey or disobey norms. Obeying usually goes along with a positive, productive citizen. Obeying focuses on order, recognizing authority and our words and actions fall into step. Disobeying usually oppositely brings negativity, confrontation, and vile language. Obeying the First Amendment for free speech and assembly is great because we can use the laws we were given to verbally protest in a positive, peaceful and lawful manner. When disobedience to the First Amendment process occurs and disrespect reigns, chaos ensues. Obeying is a way of conveying positive and intelligent speech and actions. Those who obey have paid the price and understand their words and actions have consequences. Obeying gives legitimacy to causes using constructive words and actions to make a point. Using obeying words and actions builds a platform where commonality increases relationships.

Obeying words and actions get more understanding than negative rhetoric. Obeying verbal and nonverbal procedures starts and keeps dialogue going even if parties do not agree. We all recognize times in our lives when our words and actions did not obey, and oh, did we pay! We must be grateful the majority of people go with the program and obey. A general standard is set on a level playing field when people obey. This gives each side an equal chance of succeeding when obedience is used. Positive words and actions encourage and support obeying societal norms and laws. We need to use our words and actions fruitfully to teach each generation positive skills and show the value in obeying. Obey today and teach the world what to say.

OPTIMISTIC

The bright side of life begins with always believing, speaking, and doing things optimistically. Making the decision each day to do our best and find the good in every situation is acting optimistically. We should surround ourselves with people who talk and act with enthusiasm. Mentally, physically, emotionally, and spiritually, it can be easy to fall into a rut attracting negative people and situations who drain our optimism. Choose optimism or be prepared for a life of darkness. Genesis 1:3–4 says, "And God said, let there be light, and there was light. And God saw the light was good and he approved it; and God separated the light from the darkness." An optimistic person lifts us up, encourages us to thrive, and always delivers us with the help of God. Optimistic people attract with positive energy and send it out with a frequency others see, hear and feel when they walk into a room.

Our words and demeanors say it all, and immediately, people sense our mood. Leaders, no matter how many setbacks, always prevail because of their eternal optimism. Positive people who live, lead, and speak with optimism are favored. This kindled spirit can motivate a cause, carry a team, and push us to our optimum capacities. Optimistic people say we can, which flips the switch causing others to want a piece of the pie. We must look for the good in every situation no matter how bleak and seek optimism. When the odds say no, we must say yes. Optimism changes lives and removes people from their current situations. Decide to change our words and mind-set only to optimistic. Having faith and gratitude allows us to conquer the world. Optimism will lead to internal and external happiness, so keep achieving, believing and receiving.

Keep optimism burning by staying focused with our words and pursuits. Look in the mirror and tell ourselves we are good, and we are loved every day. Then use our positive words, actions, and attitudes to complement others, giving them an optimistic outlook. Optimism provides momentum and where there is enough becomes a train streaking down the tracks of life. Remember this acronym: Only People That Initiate Momentum Inherit Something Monumental. There is no better reward or feeling than watching someone's life brighten with optimism as they change their perspective and overcome their challenges. Optimism changes and saves lives. Optimism unveils the light of God surrounding us, the love of God enfolding us, the power of God protecting us, and the presence of God watching over us; wherever we are, God is. When we talk and walk in God's footsteps, we cannot go wrong. Optimism gets the job done with each setting sun.

OBJECTIVE

The eyes are always on the prize, so if our words and actions are uncertain, our objective will be lost. Focus on what we want, visualize having it now, and project positive thoughts completing our objective. Repeat positive phrases that keep us motivated toward the objective. Life has objectives for us to achieve mentally, physically, emotionally, and spiritually. Honoring God with our words and actions should be our top objective. Do not let our words and actions deceive us because Satan always lurks to jerk us off course. The active involvement with God in our objectives means we are never going for it alone. Do not let any emotions blur our objective, but use them as positive reinforcement to complete our task. Our words and actions should inspire encouragement, incite movement, and tell the story with objective in hand. Create our objective, which comes from the heart, with love and positivity.

Proverbs 4:23–27 declares, "With closest custody, guard your heart, for in it are the sources of life. Put away from you dishonest talk, deceitful speech put far from you. Let your eyes look straight ahead and your glance be directly forward. Survey the path for your feet, and let all your ways be sure. Turn neither to right nor to left, keep your feet far from evil." Decide, deviation from our objective is not a choice or opportunity to quit. Pay the price with all our blood, sweat, and tears to conquer our objective. In our lifetime, we will have a handful of true friends who encourage our objectives. People with drive will build the opportunities for their objectives. Do not be the one with all the potential who does not fulfill their life's objective. Stand up and stand out as the one who has exhausted all efforts, sought every avenue, and finished objectives no one believed we could achieve. How bad do we want our objective?

Mentors who have completed their objectives paved the way for us to find ours. Positive people with a never-say-die attitude are ones to emulate as our momentum pushes us toward our objective. There are many different words and actions that will lead us toward our objective. Keep an open mind to different skill sets as we reach for our objective. When one way does not lead us closer, then try something else. Ask questions and remember sometimes, the most unlikely place we look will be the answer to our objective. Stop and act grateful during the process because the smallest part may be the key for conquering our objective. Life is a lonely path when we seek positive objectives because we need to clear out all the naysayers, logical reasons why we can't, then live like no one else now for our reward.

ORGANIZED

Organized words and plans say a lot about a person. Organization means taking our time to think rationally and intelligently through a situation. Organized people live for today, tomorrow, and the future. Positive skill sets surround organized people like time management, job knowledge, and leadership. They have all their tools organized in place and immediately go there. Organized people measure twice and cut once. The organized ask questions, work deliberately, and describe in detail. Mentally, physically, emotionally, and spiritually, it is important to say and act organized. Organized always used to be a prideful norm, but today, too many people are averagely living in a chaotic state. Now, living, talking and acting disorganized has taken over in the world and is an acceptable norm. God does not want us to be disorganized. Colossians 2:5 says, "For even if I am absent in the flesh, yet I am with you in spirit, rejoicing as I observe your good order and the firmness of your faith in Christ."

Organization is an important skill we can learn as a child or even as an adult. We can organize time, money, space, words and actions. Rid ourselves of clutter because it stirs up negative emotions and feelings. Organization says we are productive people living with purpose. Even if we were born into a household of dysfunction and disorganization, use it as an example of how not to live. Organization makes us feel better about ourselves because the perpetual mess is gone. Organization makes our body, mind and soul clear and calm. When we watch someone complete a task in an organized manner versus a disorganized one, we see a huge difference. In the end, if disorganization costs us time or money, we will be unhappy. Think of the brick layer leveling, tucking, and measuring making the wall straight. Our words and actions must be organized the same way keeping our lives in perfect balance.

Giving directions takes verbal and articulate organization. Without exact understanding, someone may lose their way, misinterpret an important order, or become completely disorganized. We must feel grateful when someone has their act together and their organizational skills leading a clear way. Organization is like a puzzle; if we can match the pieces, we have a clear picture. On days when our life feels jumbled, ask God for help. His grace and mercy toward us will bring peace to slow us down and make organization possible. Do not confuse organization with quickly completing something so we can check it off a list. Organizing takes quality time, has a core like a heart, and serves a greater purpose for others. A well-run life is organized, and if our words are confident, competent, and calm, we believe in the system. When we are organized, it demonstrates we know how to prioritize, most importantly, keeping God first.

OPPONENT

A worthy opponent deserves respect with our words and actions. We play the game to win, with the hope the costs are minimum for us and them. An opponent for the ages initiates a great game, and when it comes to an end, is a shame. A formidable opponent brings our character to the limelight. Will our opponent remember us having dignity and class or speaking and acting with sass? Our emotions during competition can bring out the worst of us or leave our opponent with peace and grace, knowing we did not cause disgrace. How we react to success and failure lets our opponent know how the game will go, blow for blow. Rivalries need to be bittersweet, so our opponents, after the fact, will sit down with us and pat us on the back. Opponents can be strong, weak, mild or meek. Our words can be the same and come with a streak. Respect our opponents, and they will honor us back.

Words are strong indicators when they come from the heart, and our opponents bring them to the surface. As our opponents grow to rivals, the words and actions build contention, do not let it pull our thoughts and tongues afoul. Competition is healthy, but when opponents become the focus of evil words and hatred, it is time to hold our tongues. When so much effort is cast toward negativity with our words and actions, it is a waste of time. The truth of the matter, our opponents, or ones who have done us wrong, do not care how it makes us feel. Change our ways and sow good seeds, and this will bring us victory against our opponent. God warns us not to have useless disputes with our opponents in 2 Timothy 2:15, "Be eager to present yourself as acceptable to God, a workman who causes no disgrace, imparting the word of truth without deviation."

It is easy to twist our words and actions against our opponent. Our demeanor must not get caught up in negative language and actions. Resist the momentum in a group setting to defile our opponent. Speak and act positively representing good sportsmanship and class whether we win or lose. Having an opponent in life makes us want more, achieve greatness, and live with a chip, not allowing us to settle for less. Whether our opponent is a person, obstacle, health issue, money situation, or us as our own worst enemy, have an attitude of gratitude and say, "Thy will be done." We can beat any opponent if our words and actions are positive and God filled. Our opponents help us build a resume of life that reflects our works toward humanity. Our words and actions shall bring out the best in us, so there are no opponents which can defeat us with God on our side in the great game of life.

OPINION

Everyone uses their words and actions delivering opinions about every topic. Our opinions must be presented in a positive, godly way, or it is nothing but ridicule and self-righteousness rearing its ugly head. Opinions are how we think about things, and it is a choice. The golden rule concerning opinions is only give one when asked and make it glorifying to God. Mentally, physically, emotionally, and spiritually, our opinions are important to us because they reflect our words and actions coming from our heart. Opinions can help or hurt. When asked, make our opinion count as enriching, teaching, and caring. If we offer an opinion which is critical, do it in a way that builds up instead of tears down. No one wants to earn the reputation of being opinionated, constantly sticking their nose where it does not belong.

Positive words, righteous actions, and a dutiful heart are the ways to go if someone asks our opinion. Ask God for guidance before giving our opinions. 2 Peter 1:20–21 states, "Know this first of all, that there is no prophecy of scripture that is a matter of personal interpretation, for no prophecy ever comes through human will; but rather human beings moved by the Holy Spirit spoke under the influence of God." So if our opinions are seasoned with a strong dose of God's loving word, then and only then should it be said. Opinions do count when our words are fruitful and not rotten. Opinions must be backed up with real experience and knowledge. Too many times, opinions are given loudly and with no background in the specific area. Opinions with no merit often come from those who are hurting or unsure of themselves. They want others to think they are knowledgeable and deflect attention away from their own turmoil.

Work, study, and think with mercy and gratitude on life's situations regarding opinions. Carefully and with love in our hearts form opinions which we are qualified. There is nothing wrong if someone asks us our opinion and we reply, "I do not know." This is better than giving someone wrong or opinionated advice. Trust and respect is earned, which others see us quietly going about our business, but routinely assisting others flourish with insightful opinions. Hopefully, our words and actions will build a pedigree; and when we speak and act, the whole room will go quiet with anticipation. We all are children of God who need guidance with others' opinions from time to time. In these moments, become still, stop, look, and listen as life will unfold giving us the answer we need. Opinions may be free, but there is nothing written in stone we cannot get a second one. Opinion does not give us dominion.

OVERBEARING

The incessant talker jumping from one topic to another without taking a breath. The drill sergeant screaming in our face for us to shape up or die trying. The nosy neighbor we cannot separate ourselves from as they follow us from our mailbox to our door telling us everyone's business. These are examples of overbearing people with their words and actions. We all know our own overbearing characters, and we learn to not be like them. Proverbs 25:7 says, "Let your foot be seldom in your neighbor's house, lest he have more than enough of you, and hate you." Words and behaviors shape us from our youth, and we remember overbearing language and incidents that sparked negative emotions. A swearing, intoxicated family member demonstrating overbearing, damaging behaviors causing anxiety and fear.

Overbearing demeanors and negativity rob us of light and life. Stop the cycle and switch to encouraging language with a positive, over-bearing love of God and the world.

We must be grateful overbearing people, language, and actions exist to recognize how not to live. Disturbing words and actions freeze us in our tracks registering on the overbearing scale. A picture is worth a thousand words, and it may take audio or video of some-one and their raucous displays to make a difference with the over-bearing. These extreme behaviors channeled properly can turn into positive energy bringing victory to the overbearing. Their actions and words may be saying they are starved for attention. Overbearing can change to sharing, caring, and loving words and actions with only time invested and a good ear. Everyone is not created equally, and they handle their battles excessively. Overbearing language and displays usually get the same results back like the law of attraction. Overbearing reaps what overbearing sows. Overbearing people lack grace, peace, and calm in their daily lives. Help the overbearing calm their storms, so their rants do not become the norm.

Overbearing proclaims we want to be heard, seen, and under-stood for what we say and do because we are important too. Speak confidently, slowly and with God's objectives around the overbear-ing, so they can recognize a calmer and quieter path. Nurture the overbearing to soften their words and actions teaching them stability instead of chaos. Patience is an important virtue when listening and observing overbearing dialogue and drama. Take the stage away and remove the overbearing from their comfort zones. As a law enforce-ment officer, when an overbearing individual was removed from their safe and comfortable environment, accountability and unknown caused them to speak and act differently. The bottom line, we must take control of the overbearing with our conversation and actions to change the outcome. Overbearing must learn to speak and act differ-ently, or they will be left alone. Pray for the overbearing, so they can find tranquility in their body, mind, and souls.

OBSTACLE

Mentally, physically, emotionally, and spiritually, obstacles may be placed in our paths to keep us from where we need to go and grow. An obstacle of a car wreck with life-threatening injuries and the long recovery process. The obstacle of having a stroke and losing our speech and ability to communicate. Conquering the obstacle of fear from going out in the public and interacting with others. Overcoming obstacles of our past transgressions and sins helps lead a fruitful life filled with grace. These are obstacles that have been witnessed by us, and these people did not quit. Instead, they had faith, believed the obstacles were only temporary, and picked up the pieces. Give thanks to God with our words and actions and amazing works will occur. Matthew 17:20 says, "Because of your little faith, amen, I say to you, if you have faith the size of a mustard seed, you will say to the mountain, 'mine from here to there,' and it will move. Nothing will be impossible for you."

When we decide to live with a positive mind-set, speak and act with gratitude, and ask God for help, there is no obstacle we cannot move. Obstacles may be large or small, but our attitude is we will win them all. Obstacles do not have to be tackled alone. When we join others in a cause, a focused attraction can bring the obstacle down. Humans together have moved literal mountains as their obstacle, building the Transcontinental Railroad across the United States. The massive Great Wall of China was built over twenty centuries on obstacle-filled terrain. Space was explored, and a moonwalk occurred defeating many obstacles along the way. Obstacles make us think outside of the box, join unlikely company, and inspire us to new and exciting adventures. The challenges obstacles give us, tap all our emotions, mobilize our work ethic, and bring solidarity to our words and actions.

Obstacles can be mountains made out of molehills because our words and actions blow things out of proportion. Is the weather "rainy today," or "oh my goodness, the sky is falling!" People who fear everything are like Chicken Little and create more obstacles. These obstacles can be passed on generationally if not nipped in the bud.

We must have the ability to get out of our own way first, cleaning up our words and actions, so we can bravely and positively face our obstacles. When we rid ourselves of the victim mentality, we can survive, thrive, and help others with their obstacles. As our words and actions resonate with positive confidence and godlike assurance, move out of the way obstacles for all we are is a nuisance. Pray, think and laugh at any obstacle in our path.

OUTLOOK

Everyone has lived through a past and is experiencing their now moments with words and actions to determine what outlook they have for the future. Hopefully, a positive outlook is the forecast with their words and actions flowing like milk and honey. Each of us has a story shaping our outlook from the words and actions chiseling our demeanor. Fast forward to adulthood and have the eyes we looked through as a child still hold the same outlook today? We should guess life happened, and our outlooks changed quite a bit. A child's outlook is uninhibited, fresh, and whimsical. Our attitude of the sky's the limit, dreams are only a reach away, and our outlook is to infinity and beyond. Outlooks like these have exciting adjectives describing magical experiences. The action verbs take us from an adventure land to outer space leaving an outlook with zero boundaries. These incredible and fun outlooks may be some of our best memories.

Our outlook demands positive and forward results. To really achieve something monumental, outlooks cannot be average or good enough. If idle words and actions flow from our bodies, it is time to light a fire under our behind and start moving. Outlooks must have purpose for us to live fruitfully and for the good of others. In Brainy Quotes, Steve Jobs said, "Everyone here has the sense that right now is one of those moments when we are influencing the future." There is no better time than now to talk and produce positive results for a bright outlook. Changing our views mentally, physically, emotionally, and spiritually is a choice we have to make to improve our outlook. Outlooks can change from different angles, degrees, and heights. Walking in a large city we see tall buildings. On the ground, we feel dwarfed by these metal and glass monsters. Our outlook changes drastically from the 103rd floor looking over the city. Our outlook is now one of feeling on top of the world.

Outlooks are a view from the outside in when viewing ourselves. We see little results produced, so it is time to fix our plan. Speak and act gratefully because we have God helping us develop our standard operating procedures. God sees and hears us talk about our plans; he intercedes when we are drifting off course and checks our plan to see if it lines up with his outlook. Talking and working with God daily on our outlook is the perfect check and balance system. As we mature with our relationship with God, our outlooks will change and happen in his time. When our outlooks do not seem bright, take a breath and a step back. Joyfully smile and declare God is on our side, and we are in control to make our outlook better. Inside and out make our words, actions, outlook and ourselves positive beyond the shadow of a doubt.

OUTREACH

Words and actions should communicate to others we are approachable, helpful and have an outreach for anyone less fortunate. When we outreach, we need to show compassion, humility, and a willingness to guide others to prosperity. There are outreach services throughout most communities and assisting these agencies is doing God's work. Those who are blessed by the Lord need to recognize all who are needy and outreach to them mentally, physically, emotionally, and spiritually. Joel 2:18–19 says, "Then the Lord was stirred to concern for his land and took pity on his people. Then the Lord answered and said to his people: see, I will send you grain, and wine, and oil; and you shall be filled with them; no more will I make you a reproach among the nations." Rely on our words and actions to outreach and monitor our senses to recognize what important service someone is drastically needing.

Outreach is not only about standing tall when others are in need, but learning lessons for life. Each one of us will have ups and downs in life's journey, and we never know when we need others to outreach to us. Never be ashamed to admit when we need an outreach intervention. Speak and act gratefully to those from the outreach who serve the Lord and us. Their loving kindness and willingness to step in for and with us, grant us mercy. Our words and actions set in motion the law of attraction for an outreach. Positive words and kind actions along with a pleasant disposition will allow the struggling to know to outreach to us. An ally, friend, counselor, teacher or listener is what we can find during an outreach. An outreach is successful when the person helped becomes the one who wants to mentor to others.

Jesus' whole life was dedicated to outreach as he performed miracles, healed the sick, and provided teachings for us to live our lives. These lessons teach us how to use our words and actions to give back each day. Outreach is important because our life on earth is short, and we are living for eternity. Outreach magnifies our words, actions, and shows what is inside of our heart. Outreach is a blueprint for successfully helping those who cannot help themselves. When we outreach, just because, we will be blessed tenfold down the road. Outreach spreads joy, love, happiness, confidence, and an unbeatable spirit. Think of all the wonderful things people have outreached to us. Say thank you from the bottom our heart and begin an outreach to others in need. Whatever our talent may be, put ourselves to work and spread our teaching, so we will be outreaching.

OCEAN

The massive power of the oceans are metaphors for the significance of our lives through our words and actions. So much of each are significant how we live on earth. The depth of the oceans reminds us how our words and actions play key roles affecting others. Words and actions have boundaries like the ocean. Psalm 104:5–9 says, "You fixed the earth on its foundation, never to be moved. The ocean covered it like a garment; above the mountains stood the waters. At your roar, they took flight; at the sound of your thunder, they fled. They rushed up the mountains, down the valleys to the place you had fixed for them. You set a limit they cannot pass; never again will they cover the earth." The waves and calm represent ups and downs in life and how our words and actions correspond. The ebbs and flows of the ocean can play games with our balanced emotions.

Words and actions have so many life-sustaining values as the oceans supports species of fish, crustacean, and mixes with the air in the atmosphere. When people disagree with each other, they say they are oceans apart. Our words and actions generate motion, and we cannot let our emotions bounce and separate like waves in the ocean. The steady and positive use of our words and actions can create a soothing mood as the ocean waves slide upon the shore. Misuse or deliberate use of our words and actions can unleash a tsunami destroying everything in its path. Our speech needs to be clear and inviting like the ocean overlooking the horizon. Navigating our words and actions to stay on top of the waves is the key to living our lives and surviving the ocean. Our speech and action needs to be inviting and rhythmic like listening to the soft, melodic cadence inside a seashell.

Learning to usefully use our words and actions in a positive manner compares to a captain navigating the ocean finding buried treasures. Oceans have brilliant colors, magical sounds and an artistic karma that captures the imagination from young to old. Our words and actions are built the same way over time, conquering our trials and softening the blows with eloquence and soul. We want to conquer the oceans for our own and never leave an opportunity alone. Whenever we mentor with our words and actions make the effort so life is not blown. In 1492, Columbus sailed the ocean blue discovering new lands and stepping on native sands. We need to continually explore our words and actions to find new ways to communicate and demonstrate to others all the invigorating things in the world. Be grateful for the ocean with all its character and hues, so our words and actions can describe all of life's panoramic views.

OCCUPATION

The occupation we choose reveals a lot about ourselves. Our occupation can serve humankind positively like our words and actions. Words and actions teach, preach, and reach out to others making a difference; and it bestows honor on our occupation. Choosing our occupation gives us a purpose, and our words and actions can improve our legacy or hurt it tremendously. Mentally, physically, emotionally and spiritually, we must delve into our occupation and create the best scenarios with our speech and deeds. Too many times, occupations become targets because of one ill-advised word or egregious incident. Do not let one bad apple ruin what so many honorable men and women have done to make an occupation cherished. Remember, the majority of people say and do what is right when working in their occupation. If someone is saying or doing wrong things to defile an occupation, those ignorant ones must be dealt with swiftly and harshly to maintain integrity. Make our occupation a proclamation of quality and class, instilling holiness that lasts.

People should actively participate in their chosen occupations to willingly change behaviors, honor family traditions, and serve the good of mankind. As we choose our noble occupations, the pride, honor and joy we feel doing the job needs to exude enthusiasm with our words and actions. Get excited about teaching, coaching and mentoring others to generate a special feeling toward our occupation. Whatever occupation we choose, hold it close to our heart and speak and act grateful for the opportunity. Leviticus 21:8 explains, "Honor him as sacred who offers up the food of your God; treat him as sacred, because I, the Lord, who have consecrated him, am sacred." Always look at the bright side of everything we do concerning our occupations. Anything that needs fixing is up to us to edify with our words and actions. Make our occupation with our words and actions one where everyone wants admission.

Our occupation should yield preparation, motivation, and adulation with our words and actions molding a joyous career. Occupational paths come from unique experiences which blend positive language and a yearning for success. We remember who helped us achieve more and who picked us up off the floor with their magical and motivational lessons for overcoming. Whether it was a laborer or a cop, the victory they spoke came from their occupational leadership putting us on top. Occupations quickly teach us what will be our priorities and the type of preparation we will have to endure. Every occupation has teachable life skills and directional values. Have faith and ask God for guidance when deciding on our occupation. The feeling will be right, and the confidence will flow when an occupation stimulates us to grow. Cherish the words and actions that encourage our journey and give us elation as we choose our occupation.

OVATION

Accolades come fast and furious today marking each landmark, goal, event and celebration with people using their words and actions as ovations. Standing ovations for individuals, teams, or an accomplishment usually leads to speaking words of thanks and praise. Ovations are outpourings of emotions symbolizing joy, happiness, pride and exhilaration for a job well done. When it is our turn to say a few words and project the right attitude after an ovation, we need to do it with humility and dignity. Always recognize those who helped us achieve and give all the glory to God who made us believe. As we anticipate the ovation, controlling our jubilation and holding back tears of joy may be difficult. The ovation tells us great work, keep it up, and we are with you without saying a word. Speaking after a heartfelt ovation gives us a chance to tell our story with inspirational words, positive steps and God-given wisdom he has instilled in our lives.

Ovations can be for a friend or foe. It is easy to celebrate with the one we know and love giving them ovations, but it is equally important to recognize those we do not know. Give ovations to players on opposing teams for outstanding efforts and especially when they incur any injury to say we are with you in your healing. God gives us our speech and actions to use for praise or persecution. Make our ovations ones earning grace. 1 Corinthians 7–9 says, "Therefore, neither the one who plants, nor the one who waters is anything, but only God, who causes the growth. The one who plants and the one who waters is equal, and each will receive wages in proportion to his labor. For we are God's coworkers; you are God's field, God's building." It is important our ovations minister to others creating a foundation on how and when to appropriately praise good works.

Paying homage and welcoming with an ovation generates good feelings and brings comfort. Accepting an ovation touches all our sensations. Ovations are mind numbing, knee knocking, gut wrenching, and thoroughly humbling. We hope when we speak, God will keep us from sounding meek. Pray the words roll off our tongues from the heart as we start to quiet the ovation saying thank you. Our ovation is a creation we will never forget. Many of the professional organizations are paying tributes with ovations to military families at their home games. They invite the families to the games talking to their loved ones on the jumbotrons, then the ovation roars as the soldier comes out of the crowd reuniting the family. These special ovations send thousands into tears of joy. Whether we simply say yay or yell until we are hoarse, ovations ignite the light and inspire us to keep up the good fight.

OBLIGATION

Mentally, physically, emotionally, and spiritually, we are born and raised with certain obligations, and our words and actions should follow suit. We have an obligation to daily see God in life, seek his presence and live by the commandments he has made. Family is an obligation we must continually work on to keep blood ties intact, teach our children right from wrong, and share life's lessons together. We have an obligation to reap our awards in life, maintain financial good standing and put in an honest day's work. We have an obligation to speak and act with positivity, integrity, sincerity, and wisdom. An obligation to worldly laws whether in our opinion is agreeable need to be followed for peaceful daily initiation. When these obligations are challenged, the safety and welfare of others are put in danger. An obligation of compliance is necessary to keep our lives running smoothly.

Obligations with our words and actions is important for recognizing and honoring where we are on the totem pole of life. We have an obligation to act and speak respectfully and professionally to our elders, bosses and dignitaries. Whether we like, respect, or agree with them, it is our place to act as a servant like the Lord. Psalms 116:12–16 explains, "How can I repay the Lord for all the good done to me? I will raise the cup of salvation and call on the name of the Lord. I will pay my vows to the Lord in the presence of all the people. Too costly in the eyes of the Lord is the death of his faithful. Lord, I am your servant, your servant, the child of your maid servant; you have loosed my bonds." Obligations come with a price, and when we dutifully carry them out, we are rewarded graciously.

We attract our obligations with our choices like the law of attraction. Choosing a career, spouse, or any other word or action obligates us to speak and act appropriately for the situation. When our words and actions do not coincide with our obligation, trouble is coming our way. Violation of obligations with our words and actions destroys character, brakes up relationships and questions our integrity. Once our obligations are breached, trying to restore others' faith in us is difficult at best. The only one who truly forgives us is God if we ask for his forgiveness for not carrying out our obligations. Obligations when completed gives us favor, leads to positive fellowship, and opens new doors for advancement. Finishing obligations that are ethically or morally challenging brands us as a person of merit who speaks and acts righteously when tough times arise. Our obligations, when followed with proper communications, equals a lifetime of edification.

OBSCENITY

Our language and how we use it is a building block for our heart and soul, and when obscenity is included, we only add poison. Obscenity used as a noun, verb, adjective or adverb smears vocabulary and makes us sound uneducated. When our emotions steam over and obscenity spews from our tongue, we have lost our good and calm demeanor. When we cannot articulate a sentence and add obscene words, it makes us seem rough around the edges. Obscenity pollutes the air and dilutes our good intentions. When our obscene words and actions are attached with God, it makes our Lord and Savior sad we are using his name in vain. Think through what we are going to say before we say it and slow our emotions, so obscenity does not become the norm. When we speak and act obscene mentally, physically, emotionally, and spiritually, we only sound nasty and do nothing but demean.

There is no place, time or event for our words and actions to leak obscenities. Even when we are angry and emotionally charged, there are clean words that can be used to get our points driven home. Ephesians 4:29 says, "No foul language should come out of your mouths, but only such as is good for needed edification, that it may impact grace to those who hear." If our words are clean, pure and obscenity free, our character and reputation will remain polished and respected. As a supervisor many years in law enforcement, tough times stressed our bodies, minds, and souls. We remembered those who kept their cool, where obscenities did not fly at the drop of a hat. Those were the ones we could count on to communicate professionally. Those who speak polished, act calmly with confidence, and avoid using obscenities are prized in the eyes of the Lord.

Consistently reading, writing, and studying books like the Bible, dictionary or thesaurus helps mold our words and actions in place of obscenities. Our word choices shall be positive, vivacious and accurately describing what we are saying or doing instead of obscenities used for slang. Speak and act with gratitude and clarity so all ears may partake. Obscenities open our body, mind and soul up to sin with our words and actions. Make a name for ourselves by eliminating obscenities from our life and lead a life of love, walking with God. Great orators are sought after to develop youth, spread positive and inspirational messages, and mentor society away from obscenity. Insightful thought, eloquent words and righteous actions make a transition possible getting away from obscenity. Preparatory work and self-control helping change obscene language and behaviors are a cognizant choice. Start each day as if it were our last, to speak and act like Jesus.

OMNIPOTENCE

The power of the Almighty God has no one to compare, and his omnipotence reigns over the heavens and earth. God knows us before we are born, knows what we are going to say and do before we do, and decides the outcome with his omnipotence. God lives in all of us, so we must take advantage of the best teammate possible and speak and act to honor our omnipotent friend. Our words and actions are a choice to get our minds right. Our omnipotent God inherited our sins from us, so we shall owe him our lives to surround him with love, kindness and a loyal heart. Omnipotence resolves every situation, and our words and actions must align with our big God. God gives us grace but still allows us to make choices. Making choices which do not honor the Omnipotent One teaches us to speak and act considerately by our mistakes. Omnipotence still allows for repentance when our tongues and bodies of work do not measure up to him.

We must live with a thankful attitude mentally, physically, emotionally, and spiritually that our Omnipotent One loves us and wants us to succeed. Whenever we struggle with life, remember to look to our omnipotent God. Matthew 19:26 says, "Jesus looked at them and said, 'For human beings this is impossible, but for God all things are possible.'" Stay positive and never give up on our dreams. Say we can, we will, and we are going to succeed through our omnipotent Father. Jesus walked this earth living in the flesh, taking away all our sins, performing miracles and getting resurrected to heaven to demonstrate his omnipotence. This power and awe of his omnipotence should bring us to our knees and filter our words and actions edifying him. No one is perfect, but we must strive to live perfectly in his omnipotent word. Body, mind, heart and soul make the choice to fall in love with our omnipotent God.

Spread the good news of our omnipotent Lord. Help others speak and act with respect toward God and all his works. Open the box to teach the knowledge of omnipotence. God's omnipotence and how he covers all our days' work, words and emotions let us know everything will be okay. Believe in God, achieve ourselves, and receive the omnipotence so we can do anything. We are a gift from our omnipotent Creator, and we must speak and act with specialness about ourselves. Positive words and believing in ourselves helps us to do the same to and for others. Glorify our words and actions recognizing all the good we can do for the world understanding omnipotence. The strength of omnipotence and applying it to worldly issues when we get people together can conquer anything. Omnipotence gives us clarity, and knowing this is in our corner, we can solve any equation.

OMEN

Words and actions play a vital role shaping our past, working through the present and developing our future omens. Think of the things we have said and done, which later came to fruition, and we say that was an omen. Dreaming too involves interpretation of words and actions which when we learn the results has many omens. There are positive and negative omens that come from our words and actions. We must stop the negative talk and work toward good results because like the law of attraction, we reap the omen we sow. The Bible teaches us to have simple faith in Jesus, act like servants and fishers of men. When we speak and act positively with grace, our omen will be good. If we stay holy with our words and actions and follow his commandments, our omens will be prosperous. History gives evidence with all the omens promised how groups still exist.

Omens are good and evil. Our words and actions set our beliefs. When we choose to live in the flesh and not by God's plan, we are playing cards with Satan who would love to create a negative omen. Acts 20–28:30 says, "Keep watch over yourselves and over the whole flock or when the holy spirit has appointed you overseers, in which you tend the church of God that he acquired with his own blood. I know that after my departure savage wolves will come among you, and they will not spare the flock, and from your own group, men will come forward perverting the truth to draw the disciples away from them." Omens can be warnings for us to speak and act better. Build a loving heart, so our words and actions resemble a true and thankful life. Omens can teach us to stay on the path of righteousness. Biblically, a tremendous amount of omens have come true.

Omens teach us to monitor our words and actions, and if we live with the fear of God, we will say and do the right things. Speak great, act better and create positive omens. When omens do come to fruition, do not be surprised by them because we have the ability to control them with our works. Simply put, omens are a good versus evil proposition. Our past experiences taught us what was right and wrong. Our emotions tell us with feelings whether we are creating light or dark omens. Omens are a dangerous game when our words and actions are not following a godly direction. Choose to build a legacy for ourselves, others and the world with positive words and actions that will make only good omens. When omens enter our conscience, speak and act grateful for their existence. Omens can help us correct our wrongs and also tell us when we are on the sunny side of life.

OPPRESSION

Oppression by negative words and actions affects people mentally, physically, emotionally, and spiritually. Take charge and turn negativity into positive influences that will take the oppression off our shoulders. Complement others at all times lifting up the oppressed. Smile with confidence letting all know oppression is not part of our world. Oppression is a form of bullying by verbal, physical or psychological tactics. These small people have their own negative features, and they hide them by pouring oppression on others. Speak and act courageously sticking up for ourselves and others who are not strong enough saying we will not be oppressed anymore. Make it an obsession to rid the world of oppression. When we say or do any expression, make it one of love, kindness, joy and happiness. Live each day and find the good points of view instead of dishing out oppression stew. Learn to smile and laugh avoiding the oppressive path.

Oppressors are those who only want to add stressors to our lives. Verbally, they want everyone to follow their orders causing dismay. Oppressors want us to do the work as they sit on their hands and smirk. Matthew 23:2–4 says, "The scribes and Pharisees have taken their seat on the chair of Moses. Therefore, do and observe all things whatsoever they tell you, but do not follow their example. For they preach but they do not practice. They tie up heavy burdens [hard to carry] and lay them on people's shoulders, but they will not lift a finger to move them." What's right is right and what's wrong is wrong. Oppressors need to learn a lesson about their negative words and aggressions. When someone has a grip on us and all they want to do is oppress our life, it is time to tell them enough is enough. Make it our mission and alleviate oppression.

One kind word will brighten someone's day where oppression will make it gray. Create a positive space where everyone may come and learn to stifle the oppressive crowd. When we are on the brink of uttering an oppressive word, imagine if Jesus heard. Our words and actions must capture grace instead of being oppressive and falling on our face. Say positive things loudly and proudly and dismiss oppressive ones profoundly. Our words and actions tell everyone who we are, so it is up to us to live above par. Speak and act possessively of our good name and never let an oppressor put it to shame. Positive finds glory and negative creates soot. We have a choice to fight oppression and give it the boot. Stop the cycle of oppressive words and actions because eventually, it will point back to our own dissatisfaction. Positive words and actions beat oppression any day and makes everyone say hurray!

ORIGINAL

An independent action, thought or word for the first time created would be an original. When Eve ate the apple from the Tree of Knowledge, this represented original sin. Originality is a fresh approach to how things have always been accomplished. A new song, invention, discovery, all are original, and our words and actions should represent us like no other. We are an original created by God, and no one has the same fingerprint or DNA. We must be grateful for our originality, so we have the opportunity to stand out in a crowd. Everyone has their own original mental, physical, emotional and spiritual capacities. We are derived with original God-given talents. Each original blessing by word or action may touch multitudes for generations. Hebrews 3:3–4 states, "But he is worthy of more 'glory' than Moses, as the founder of a house has more 'honor' than the house itself. Every house is founded by someone, but the founder of all is God."

Originals may be blessings given because God wanted us to say or do his wish, or come from extensive thought and work. If we are lucky enough to have an original gift that no one else has, use it for the greater good. Einstein, Edison, and Franklin were given brilliant minds which created original ideas. Use our original talent to entertain. When a pitcher has been touched with the original gift of a lightning bolt for an arm it brings the crowd to their feet. Original means unique, special and the only one. Our words and actions must carry our original personality without a doubt. We should be remembered by our original speech and actions how they glorified others positively. Tell the ones we love in an original way every day. Inspire with an original message that will be repeated for a lifetime. Originals only come by once in a blue moon, so speak and act with a new tune.

Originality has its price because everyone wants and wishes for those rights. When we are original, people want to duplicate our style, steal our thought and guile. It's tough being number one, second to none, with everything we say and do on pay for view. As an original, we must have thick skin for those who want to question our origin. When our original words and actions are used in a humanitarian way, very few will be dismayed. Made original is a thrill completed by sheer will and dynamic skill. Original touches emotions and opens the world to bigger oceans. Original words and actions motivate people for a cause, which produces thunderous applause. When our words and actions are original and come from a righteous heart, people recognize our work of art. Original speech and works neither plagiarized nor usurped, when presented with good taste will be remembered as chaste.

OVERCONFIDENCE

Our words and actions show others our confidence or overconfident levels dealing with every topic opponent or pressure. Emotions can make us calm, cool, and collected or take us to uptight, hot and bothered. We never can underestimate life's everyday obstacles. Overconfidence stems from success with our past speech and actions. What or whoever our opponent may be, we have to always give maximum effort. Eventually, overconfident words and behavior get us beat in sports, finances, relationships and the commandments. We need to speak and act with humbleness and humility because it is not our job to even out the inequities of life acting overconfidently. Never act overconfidently toward God's word. Deuteronomy 1:41 talks about soldiers not taking the Lord seriously. "In reply you said to me, 'we have sinned against the Lord. We will go up ourselves and fight, just as the Lord, our God, commands.' And each of you girded on his weapons, making light of going up into the hill country."

Overconfidence is a sign of immaturity mentally, physically, emotionally and spiritually. Do we believe we are smarter, stronger, and near the same level as God? If our words and actions reflect this attitude, it is time for a big setback. When we are overconfident, we say and do things that are irrational trying to win the battle of life. Overconfidence comes from everyday desires and goals. There is a fine line between using our words and actions in confidence aligned with God's intuition and overconfidence trying to handle everything ourselves. Overconfidence dulls our senses as our hearing others stops, seeing right from wrong ceases, our taste becomes bad, our touch is like a hammer, and our smell becomes rancid to others. These are metaphors, of course, but overconfidence breeds bad speech and behavior. When we speak and act overconfidently, we become detached from God's way.

Prayer through our words, actions, and always keeping a kind heart guards us from overconfidence. Success multiplies overconfidence unless we remember our humble beginnings in everything we say and do. We were not always the big fish in the pond, and it was God's grace which has given us our glory. People who are grateful and acknowledge God first stay even keel and avoid overconfidence. When we prayerize, picturize, and actualize with our words and actions, life is a humble confidence. As God commanded all the Pharisees, kings, tribes, and disciples to obey him, their overconfidence and fears caused them to worship idols and magic. Doing wrong overconfidently landed severe punishments. Stay focused on the Father, Son, and Holy Spirit with our words and actions. Overconfidence is treatable as we help others achieve their ambitions, are honest how we made mistakes with our words and actions, and thank God for all our gifts.

ORNERY

People have good and trying days; and sometimes their words and actions become ornery. We all want to feel composed and empowered before we speak and act, but orneriness sometimes breaks the ice in serious situations. Orneriness with our words, actions and a sense of humor is good as long as it is used appropriately. Ornery dialogue and behavior is usually associated with stubbornness, surliness, grumpiness cantankerousness, and bad-tempered people. Dealing with these types of individuals many times requires us to speak and act ornery back. American Christian Author Philip Yancey says, "The more we love, and the more unlikely people we love, the more we resemble God who, after all, loves ornery creatures like us." Our ornery words need not be cussed, but they need to make a point.

Using the Law of Attraction words and actions laced with orneriness may only be understood by ill-tempered ones. This conversation or demonstration when realized by the ornery one makes them understand how ridiculous they look and sound.

When conversation and events are flowing positively with progress, that is not the time to introduce orneriness. We must know when to speak and act with orneriness because the timing must be perfect to steal the show, but not kill the flow. In serious circumstances involving life and death, at no time should anyone choose to speak and act ornery. Our pedigree should stand for kind, happy, and pleasant words and actions. When we deal with ornery people, hopefully, we can sway them our way. Some people are naturally ornery and dyspeptic with their personalities. Learn why they are ornery, and if it is because of outside influences, try to get them the help they need to live a happier, balanced life. When ornery words and actions are not healthy leading to a positive lifestyle, it is time to make a choice and change.

Each person's perception of ornery words and actions changes with the times. Orneriness used to be reserved for vaudevillians, comedians, and comics. Now orneriness is run of the mill with our words and actions for shock value. Movies and television programs with their ornery words and actions have created new stars. There has to be a limit to ornery words and actions when they become distasteful, disrespectful, hurtful or adding no positive value. Even God became ornery when he knocked the money changers tables over, but it was to restore order, change behaviors, and obey his commands. The gratitude we should share is knowing when ornery words and actions cross the line. We all have been shaped by words and actions since our youth, and when orneriness appears, we know it. Do not let our hearts be taken over by orneriness. We live in ornery times, but it is up to us to create our words and actions using them for a positive, uplifting, and God-given purpose.

UNITY

Words and actions need to unite us with people and circumstances. Our unification must be inside and out, mentally, physically, emotionally, and spiritually. We cannot unify others unless our own shop is in order. Focusing on positive words and actions and following through with the body, mind and soul leads to unification. We have a choice to unify or nullify. Unity takes ridding ourselves of self-serving attitudes and living with generosity, humility and spiritual endurance. When we speak and act, unity must flow naturally like a waterfall. Unity is having a grateful attitude and a pure heart helping us think before carrying out our words and actions. Bringing people together through our words and actions is a unification process which, when done with love and compassion, sprouts us unlimited successes. When unification of our words and actions hits barriers, ill will arises, and coexistence is difficult. Unity breaks down all walls to help the common cause with positive words and actions.

Leaders use their words and actions in the body like in Ephesians 4:2–6, which says, "With all humility and gentleness, with patience, bearing with one another through love, striving to preserve the unity of the spirit through the bond of peace: one body and one Spirit, as you were also called to the one hope of your call; one Lord, one faith, one baptism; one God and Father of all, who is over all and through all and in all." Unification with our words and actions comes as we rely on God's word and believe even when we cannot see. There are so many stories in the Bible where unification of the body, mind, soul and people occurred with faith. Unity in words and actions accomplishes tasks and gels people together with energetic teamwork. In the most trying times and desperate situations, unification is imperative to win battles and eradicate evil brewing.

Use unity to create the best for the world. Unify and challenge ourselves to find a cure for diseases killing humanity. Unite to find answers to political, social and economic gaps. Unity does not always lead to the perfect environment, but when positive words and actions are infused, there is a chance the stars will align. When we unite, we take flight, and put on an amazing fight. It should not take tragic events shaking a nation to its boots for unification to occur. Let's not wait to speak and act with unity during a tragedy, but instead, unite proactively instead of reactively. Unifications stand alone with a strong signal when we are ready to go onto a playing field and are aggressively seeking the moment. Positive words and actions along with unity causes our opponent to flinch knowing what is coming.

UBIQUITY

Ubiquity with our words and actions is here and now. It is important to live for today, open-minded, and with positive words and actions that create a ubiquitous foundation. We are favored and blessed with grace to live ubiquitous lives where we can go anywhere or complete anything. Life is a fun choice, so it is up to us how much ubiquity we relish. The more positively we speak and act, the doors of antiquity close and ubiquity opens. The universe is plentiful, so we must mentally, physically, emotionally, and spiritually stay in tune with God's word and listen for ubiquitous opportunities. Choosing free will to accomplish anything we imagine, dream, or design when mixed with gratitude is an ubiquitous combination for success. There are no boundaries, no limits, or negativities from the past constructing our words and actions. Only positive, prevalent chances will fulfill our ubiquitous destination.

We must continually remind ourselves to live for today in this ubiquitous world. No one knows what tomorrow might bring. Ecclesiastes 9:7 says, "Go, eat your bread with joy and drink your wine with a merry heart, because it is now that God favors your works." When we have ubiquity, never waste this precious time with inactivity. The time is now to speak and act with positivity and passion because ubiquity may go out of style, like fashion. Do not procrastinate, do what we say we are going to do, and speak all things which are true. Ubiquity is here and now, but when we speak and act, never run afoul. Make it a vow for love, kindness and peace, so the rug does not get pulled from under our feet. There is no time like the present to speak and act with good works. Remember, ubiquity is balanced because God makes the timing perfect.

Ubiquity is the place to be laughing, loving, and living with glee. Moments like these develop the family memories. Ubiquity means we were placed in the right place and time. We cannot explain with our words and actions how we avoided getting hurt, what made us help someone, or avoiding strife. Ubiquity is the unforeseen guardian angel who lives close by, who we cannot ask why. Speak and act gratefully as ubiquity leads the way and saves our day. As sure as the sun rises and sets, ubiquity is quite the asset. Ubiquity allows us to share and care adding a special flare for each visit with a loved one beyond compare. Ubiquity is the last word spoken, the final kiss, living and working with bliss. Speak and act with energy, love and style, because ubiquity means here today and gone tomorrow. As ubiquity unfolds, we may have only one attempt to break the mold.

ULTIMATE

Ultimate is climbing to the top of the world, achieving the most, speaking with grace and wisdom, and doing great things for others. In wanting these ultimate accomplishments, there was a path we took or will take in the future with our words and actions we must examine. Mentally, physically, emotionally, and spiritually, we shall pay the ultimate sacrifices if our words and actions do not edify others or glorify God. There is nothing wrong with lofty goals of wanting more, reaching the maximum or working toward promotion. The important thing is enjoying the ultimate ride and learning contentment in the moment. We were created in the ultimate and perfect image of Christ. Moving to our ultimate destination has hills and valleys that test our words and actions. Ultimately, we must be thankful for obstacles because they help us mature and grow.

Our words and actions explain and demonstrate where we are in our search for the ultimate. Are our ultimate avenues paved with our say or God's way? Psalms 86:11–12 proclaims, "Teach me, Lord, your way that I may walk in your truth, single-hearted and revering your name. I will praise you with all my heart, glorify your name forever, Lord my God." Ultimate success in anything is a positive and motivated attitude and heart. This recipe toward our final point is great, but without godly patience and contentment, we may not reach our ultimate goals. Stop, look, and listen to ourselves along each step of the ultimate journey. Say and do positive things complementing along the way. Our ultimate attitude should be one of gratitude, making lemonade from lemons each day. Our ultimate goal should be to leave something positive everywhere we have stepped or with anyone we have shared our passion.

Ultimate means the best with our words and actions. The integrity, credibility, personality and humility will ultimately make us unlike the status quo. Choose the right words and actions every time by engaging our brains with ultimate and constant training. Recognizing others' emotions, and listening intently ultimately will help us find the right words and actions for every circumstance. We must add positivity to lives helping others reach their ultimate dreams too. When traversing our path to the ultimate end, when the roads get rough, reach into our travel bag and pull out words and actions that glorify God and others. This will not only pull us through the mire, but take our minds off of our ultimate ego, ourselves. Earthly goals and achieving successes are tremendous, but our ultimate desire must be pleasing the Lord. Reflect on our words and actions each day to check if they are up to God's ultimate standard.

USEFUL

Our words and actions must be useful, filled with love and kindness. When our words and actions are not useful for someone, a circumstance, or creation, they are better off unsaid or undone. It is useful to say the appropriate word at the correct time and do the right thing always to empower. The importance of usefulness means no one has to carry our baggage or worry about us uttering inappropriate words. Our useful words should help others through the difficult times. Our useful actions must display giving to those in need.

We never know when our useful language and positive work ethic will be received with mercy. Hebrews 13:1–2 reads, "Let mutual love continue. Do not neglect hospitality, for through it some have unknowingly entertained angels." Our useful words and actions may endure forever in someone's heart. When we give the time and make the effort with a thankful attitude, usefulness grows and positivity flows.

Everyone and everything has a use and a purpose. We must believe in our words and actions; otherwise, we are not useful ourselves. Useful people do not want to sound average, look mediocre, or take a free ride. Their mind-set portrays usefulness, a positive mental attitude and a choice to do good for others. Useful people do not wait for someone else to inspire them. Useful people are the first ones rising, raring to go and the last ones to rest when the job is done. Useful words and actions direct and correct with compassion and wisdom. When we speak and act with God's favor, there are no limits to our world. Useful people encourage, develop and conquer inspirational feats, which others say cannot be done. As useful people achieve the best, they pull others along who want to emulate success. When we choose to speak and act usefully, it will keep our body, mind and souls youthful.

Useful is what useful does. Our words and actions build a resume, and our results are determined by God, if our usefulness was good enough. The most derogative put down in the world is to be called or thought of as useless. Do not ever let this slip off our tongues about anyone or anything. Useful means positive, encouraging, happy and hardworking. If someone is struggling, speak and act usefully picking them up and helping them bud. When we have useful verbal and physical skills, it is a sin if we do not help others fulfill. Our lives depend on useful because if no one says the right thing or does the work, everyone would become a jerk. Usefulness moves us forward through life. The biggest complement anyone can give us is to tell us we are useful. When all is said and done, let our tombstone read, "Here lies a useful person, who gave their all, for all."

UNDERSTAND

Understanding with words and actions takes on many dimensions. Mentally, our understanding how to do something could be life or death. Physically, we must understand any limitations to stay healthy. Emotionally, we must understand what changes our moods and causes us to experience joy or what takes us to the breaking point. Spiritually, we must understand God's word and follow it infinitely with our hearts. We must understand good versus evil and follow righteous words and actions as our guidance. Understanding ourselves and learning what we need to improve is being open, honest and a priority. God gives favor to those who admit their mistakes and truly understand the need for change. Daniel 12:10 says, "Many shall be refined, purified, and tested, but the wicked shall prove wicked; none of them shall have understanding, but the wise shall have it." When we understand the only perfect person was Jesus, it gives us all room for improvement.

Leaders understand what it takes to make life full of enthusiasm and stoke the fire keeping our dreams aglow. Choose positive thinking no matter what the incident, outcome, or where we are in life. Understand our dreams, wishes, and needs will rise to the top when God says it is time and our words and actions match his will. Stay focused and understand the answer we want most may not be ready for us yet. Our positive words and actions used energetically and repeatedly are building the bridge of understanding and maturing. Understanding the peaks and valleys when trying to obtain a goal are tests to see if we are ready to receive it. When we understand the power of joy, happiness, giving and team building, our toolbox to live overflows. Each one of us is uniquely gifted by God, and we must understand this principle. There are people we meet every day who are strategically placed in our lives for us to tap their greatness to achieve success.

Learning and understanding positive experiences outside our comfort zones are vines of growth to help us and others. Everyone uses words and actions uniquely, and by witnessing these magical exchanges, we understand how God uses everyone differently for his service. No matter how we use our positive words and actions, we must understand God has a purpose for us. God does not cherish whiners and complainers with their negative thoughts, words, and deeds. Remember, there were only two original descendants who made it to the Promised Land. They understood faith, believed without seeing, and were positive with their words and actions. As followers of Jesus, we must honor him with positive words and actions. We must understand, others who are not followers are watching us to see how we react to successes and adversities. Understand, when we speak and act with positivity, we are leading as role models for others to follow.

URGENT

It is urgent to get to our destination. It is urgent to say the right thing to everyone, everywhere, and all the time. Urgency has become the new norm on how we speak and act without grace and distinction. Here is an urgent message; it is time to get back to basics where God, family, and work are our priorities. When we are talking and doing things in urgency, we are missing out on perfect peace. God has a plan for us mentally, physically, emotionally, and spiritually; and more times than not, urgency is not in the equation. Our urgent words and actions are caused by anxiety, manufactured stress and going too fast. Trying to say and do things urgently causes mistakes with our mouths and bodies. Slow down and think before we speak because we are not breaking an urgent news story every minute of the day.

Urgency has its space when an emergency is taking place. Then it is time to speak and act urgently with command when we need to give a helping hand. When our words and actions need to be urgent, it will help stop the turbulence. Urgency is anything but complacency. Urgency is living on purpose and not letting the grass grow under our feet. Urgency is taking charge to save us from defeat. Sometimes when we are urgent, we miss the boat or don't hear the beautiful note. When we speak and act urgently too often, we must remember to stop and keep in touch. Our urgent words and actions may cause us to be rude, when in fact we need to change our attitude. Colossians 4:5–6 says, "Conduct yourselves wisely toward outsiders, making the most of the opportunity. Let your speech always be gracious, seasoned with salt, so that you know how you should respond to each one."

Urgency teaches us what needs to be done and what can wait, like planting our garden filled with faith. We must urgently seek the Lord with charm and grace so our words and actions do not forsake. Urgency is transparency because when we are acting and speaking fast, we may not always remember what we said or did last. Speak and act on purpose sending our message across so our urgent mouth and body does not get us lost. Speak and act thankfully, our God is not an urgent God, as he always warned us about breaking the laws which he made. When it is time to punish us for our sins, it is because of poor choices we made. The only urgent things we should speak and do is love the Lord and our neighbor through and through. When it is time to pick and choose, did we speak and act too urgently, or did we spread good news?

UNCOUTH

When things do not go as planned, our words and actions must not reach an uncouth level of negativity. Uncouth language and works is no better than misguided youth. Ephesians 4:29 says, "No foul language should come out of your mouths, but only such as is good for needed edification, that it may impart grace to those who hear." It is up to us to change our uncouth words and actions and use humility and humbleness. Rid ourselves of uncouthness by acting as a fire starter using God's word to fight back. Train the body, mind, and soul eliminating uncouthness by buttoning up the lip. We must be in touch with the Holy Spirit as we speak and act so uncouth does not become the truth. Create new life and passion for others using inspirational words and actions. Ask God each day to leave uncouth out of our vocabulary and demeanor.

Thankfully, uncouth words and actions can always be defeated by God's word. Discover the unlimited power as it changes our hearts as we learn God's word and uncouthness fails to cross our path. A positive attitude and making it our job to speak with God daily will eliminate us from uncouthness. Fill a box with our words and actions before we speak, so there are walls holding uncouth back. When our emotions are raging and we are saying, "We will get you back!" Our pride was hurt, so our words became uncouth. Take a deep breath, close our eyes, go for a walk, or any other pressure-relieving mechanism we need to kick uncouth down the road. When we speak and act with uncouthness, it is keeping us from going to the place God intended for us. Speak and act gratefully in every circumstance so our grace and favor never waiver. Make it a daily plan with prayer to eliminate uncouth from our roots.

Think how wonderful it would be if all our words and actions were uplifting instead of uncouth. Parents either spread good news or plan on uncouth being used by our youth. Uncouth hurts like a bad tooth, and unless we fix it, the damage gets worse. Honor God with our words and actions. Do not pollute the air with uncouth words. Mentally, physically, emotionally and spiritually, we must realize we do not need others to lift us up or pull us along. Only uncouth people refuse to discipline themselves enough. When we speak and act uncouthly, that shows how uncaring, immature and self-centered we are. Grateful people do not want to act uncouthly because it really only calls attention to all our insecurities. Uncouth is ugly sounding, terrible looking and is like putting lipstick on an alligator. Overcoming our uncouthness will be rewarded in heaven.

USURP

Our words and actions occasionally result in causes and effects in our lives. If the words we have spoken and the actions we created usurped us from results or changed a decision to be now unfavorable for us, how do we react? Life is not always fair, but we mature and grow when usurpations exist and are able to go with the flow, not letting our emotions override our mouths. Speaking and acting out about usurpations only burns bridges which we may need to cross another time. Speaking outwardly how we were usurped creates negativity because anger, bitterness, and resentment prevail. If we are usurped about anything, we must give it to God and say he has other plans for us. We may feel wronged, but only God has the ultimate authority to usurp things for us. Usurpation is sometimes a blessing in disguise because had we been given what we wanted, it may have led to our demise.

How do we handle usurpation with dignity, class, humility and acceptance? Mentally, physically, emotionally and spiritually, we see ourselves one way and are usurped taking us in a new direction. Getting let go at a promising job only to acquire a better one. Speaking out when no one else will and someone says at least he did the right thing. Taking a risk that goes against the norm. These are usurpations that people recognize our character and hard work. When we are usurping someone or something, do it with tact, love and class. How we do it and say it will be remembered for years. Usurpation is sometimes our ticket to a new life filled with gifts bestowed by God. Complaining when we are usurped only brings more agony. A positive attitude and controlled speech make usurpation a small feat. When we are usurped, hold our heads up high with grace and proudly walk out of that place.

When we are usurped, do not pout, the Lord will provide security with clout. 1 Kings 2:15–17 says, "Adonijah, son of Haggith, went to Bathsheba, Mother of Solomon. 'Do you come as a friend?' she asked. 'Yes,' he answered, and added, 'I have something to say to you.' She replied, 'Say it.' So he said, 'You know that the kingdom was mine, and all Israel expected me to be king. But the kingdom escaped me and became my brothers, for the Lord gave it to him.'" Handling ourselves with God's words and actions when we are usurped is more favorable than a nag who continues to complain. God always has bigger and better plans for us when we are usurped. Usurpation teaches us how to speak and react getting that monkey off our back. When we see others who have been usurped too, have gratitude and show them the muse. This inspiration and understanding usurpation will allow others salvation. Dealing with usurpation in a godly way will always help others find a new way. When we are usurped, believe in God because he has a funny way of evening out the odds.

UNSHAKABLE

Life happens quickly from every direction, and we need to fortify ourselves mentally, physically, emotionally and spiritually for an unshakable foundation. When we are unshakable, our words and actions are a reflection how much work we have accomplished, and we react in a godly manner. Fear may rear its head in any situation, but through training, our words and actions positively with God's word, we will never be shaken. When we believe everything will be alright, unshakable is gratitude with fight. When we see someone who is unshakable, it is unmistakable the charisma and strength they project. Acts of courage, voices of calm, unshakable messages leave us in awe. Unshakable, like Rome, was not built in a day. Unshakable takes a positive focus with ice water running through our veins. Unshakable means fighting life's battles through the pain and glory. When we build our cathedral, our words and actions become unshakable grace.

Knowing we have to face difficult dilemmas, make tough decisions, and do it anyway is what makes us unshakable. In these troubling times, Psalms 16:8 says, "I keep the Lord always before me; with the Lord at my right, I shall never be shaken." Remove ourselves from the flesh which is shakable and into the Spirit which is unshakable. There is nothing we cannot say or do when we believe the Lord walks besides us, two by two. When our tongue is out of alignment or we trip and fall, there is no worry as God makes us an unshakable wall. We only allow shakable things to penetrate our wall if we choose weak-mindedness or physical surrender. Unshakable men and women choose life and not death. Positive words with loving and joyous actions equals unshakable which is unbreakable. Speak and act gratefully finding the good in everyone and everything, and we will be an unshakable being.

What have we done with unshakable faith each day to show the Lord we have earned our way? Jesus takes away all our sins to give us unshakable favor. He did this, so we build an unshakable support system for others using positive words and actions. Pick up the shaken and all who are tired and aching. There is no rest for the weary when life comes with a flurry. Gratitude and thinking positively makes the invisible, visible, the impossible, possible, and the shaken, unshaken. Positive words and actions with an unshakable faith fill our hearts with glory, mercy and grace. "What can we do for you?" This is the servantlike and unshakable attitude we should choose. Unshakable people laugh at fear and put it to rest. When our hearts are filled with joy, our unshakable words and actions follow suit. Unshakable people who are the best, give the boot to negativity and inspire the rest.

UNANIMOUS

Unanimous words and actions are positive because agreement occurs, and progress comes to fruition. Our words and deeds must unanimously edify people and make the world a joyous place. Unanimity is not always the result as words, actions, and opinions differ when attempting to come to a decision. When a unanimous decision is not made, our words and actions need to be respectful. Today, there are two instances where unanimous is the only answer: loving the Lord and following all his commandments and a jury convicting someone of a crime. In all other instances, our words and actions deal with majority rule or minority pools who are not unanimously heard. Unanimous language and acts are usually confident because the message is bold, confident, and courageous with the destiny approved. The great things about the unanimous word of God is it cannot be approved by any other authority, it cannot change, and there is no better way to live our lives.

Act 4:32–33 states, "The community of believers was of one heart and mind, and no one claimed that any of his possessions was his own, but they had everything in common. With great power, the apostles bore witness to the resurrection of the Lord Jesus, and great favor was accorded them all." In a positive and loving community, the integrity and trust with our words and actions give us blessings and favor. When we speak and act unanimously, it says committedly a project or cause moves forward. Unanimous means without a doubt. Unanimous clears the deck from underhandedness and equals the responsibility. Unanimity says and does with tranquility and calmness. Unanimity takes faith and belief in one another, so the outlook is extremely bright. God's love is unanimous and enriches us daily for growing and tithing. Unanimous is a model for our words and actions coming together building community and continuity. When we accept others and they tolerate us, it is a unanimous relationship.

Using words and actions for a unanimous outcome takes patience, perseverance, and kindheartedness. We all can agree to disagree about lots of things, but when we are unanimous, energy flows and positivity grows. It is easy to go with the tide to keep peace, but unanimity takes dedication to a cause and many times done without applause. Unanimous means we have been through the bends and brakes, and our plan will go through with no mistakes. Unanimity takes commitment and a special way of life. We are special people who came to the forefront to unite. When unanimity with our words and actions drive the race, there is no such thing as second place. Unanimous is glorious, the top of the heap. Unanimous words and actions better follow through because if we don't, people may say we just went along too. When our thoughts, words, and heart are unanimously filled with God, he will always help us.

UNCONDITIONAL

We were unconditionally created for a purpose by God, and through our words and deeds sometimes we make mistakes. Thankfully, our God forgives us when our words and actions are not up to reproach. Mentally, physically, emotionally and spiritually, positive words and actions should empower others, enlighten a moment, and build unimpeachable character. Our words and actions should unconditionally uplift others in their situations guiding them to their best. We need to speak and act grateful unconditionally for all we have no matter if it is big or small. Knowing God will provide for us unconditionally, and we are never alone should send chills up our spines. Unconditional love, devotion and understanding by our friend Jesus is all we need. Our unconditional God is one prayer away, and the results will come in his time. We need to learn to speak with God about all our issues. He knows anyway, so there is no topic which is unconditionally off the chart. Our words to him should be bold, valuable, and absolute, so he knows we are unconditionally repairing our souls. God knows if we are using our words whole-heartedly or haphazardly.

Ephesians 1:3–6 says, "Blessed be the God and Father of our Lord Jesus Christ, who has blessed in Christ with every spiritual blessing in the heavens, as he chose us in him, before the foundation of the world, to be holy and without blemish before him. In love he destined us for adoption to himself through Jesus Christ in accord with the favor of his will, for the praise of the glory of his grace that he granted us in the beloved."

The transition of unconditional love toward everyone is a tough hurdle to leap when others have hurt our feelings or caused anger. Unconditional forgiveness is something we all have to work at every day because if we do not let go of these negative emotions, it will not let us have a clear frequency to God's blessings. Our prayer channels will clog, and our spiritual focus will evade us. A clear conscience and unconditional, positive focus will give us discernment as we listen for God's message. Tell God unconditionally we give ourselves to him and acknowledge to do what he wants with us. When we choose this unconditional stance, positive energy will flow, and our senses will be more receptive. Let our words and actions flow unconditionally with grace as we forgive everyone face to face. Speak and act like St. Michael rebuking wickedness with the glorious and unconditional word of the Lord. Open our mouths with joyous words, create a positive atmosphere doing for others, and make our hearts bleed unconditionally for God. When our body, mind, and soul are unconditional, our life becomes bountiful.

UPWARD

Motivation, inspiration, perspiration, sacrifice, creativity and gratitude are ways we impact others with their upward journey using our words and actions. We face many challenges each day, and the words we hear and the deeds we see mentor others upward for a better life. Upward is a reflection of positivity, compassion, transition and explosive energy. Thinking of upward, we immediately visualize Jesus and living with him in heaven. Upward means advance or promotion to a greater place. Our words and actions need to praise which will raise those upward from their current conditions. Mentally, physically, emotionally and spiritually, we fight everyday issues that try to pull us downward. Our words and actions seasoned with God's wisdom are our first line of defense against negativity. This alliance keeps an upward demeanor from spiraling out of control. When we keep our focus upward with positive words and actions, there is no better way to help us win the race.

Accept upward as the only direction to go when we fall and stub our toe. We cannot do anything for him except speak and act courageously. Talk is cheap, and deeds are weak unless our motives are pure and moving upward toward the peak. Powerful words and actions transcend us with spiritual faith, so we can see what we believe. Acts 1:8–9 says, "But you will receive power when the Holy Spirit comes upon you, and you will be my witnesses in Jerusalem, throughout Judea and Samaria and to the ends of the earth. When he said this, as they were looking on, he was lifted up, and a cloud took him from their sight." Dedicate and generate positive words and actions for upward movement to glorify him and others. We never know when an upward glance, a positive stance, or an unbelievable chance will be seen and heard by the man above, so he can fulfill our walk of love.

Everyone wishes, dreams and prays of an upward life, and no one wants to cause unforgettable strife. Respecting others' feelings, opinions and ways of life takes patience, practice and an upward vice. Upward should not seem awkward, it must be awesome. Deliver the upward word everyone wants to hear. Victory in any situation takes courage to move upward even when we are scared. We must give it all to God and stop self-serving ways if we want our lives to move upward and out of the haze. In our upward journey, look and see how we got to this wonderful place and never forget those who encouraged us with their inspiring grace. Say thank you to mentors who sacrificed for us and baked us into this delightful, upward crust.

UNLEASH

Unleash every ounce of our loving kindness to others with our positive words, actions and energy touching their hearts. There are not enough grateful words and deeds to honor God for giving us his Son and unleashing all our sins. He is aware of all we say and do before we unleash it to many or few. Unleashing all our burdens on him allows us to mature and grow, so we do not keep making the same mistakes. Jesus unleashed words to us, so we live and treat others with love and respect. Language and deeds unleashed by us occasionally are caused by our emotions getting in a rush. Think before we speak and act because the ignorance we unleash may leave us flat on our backs. Controlling our thoughts and words takes years to master, but when we do unleash, it brings worlds of peace. Unleash it all to God.

Smiles, laughs, stories of encouragement, and tears of joy flow when we unleash words that make others grow whole. Unleash God's words and deeds letting everyone know how much he loves them. 1 Colossians 1:13–14 says, "He delivered us from the power of darkness and transformed us to the kingdom of his beloved son, in whom we have redemption, the forgiveness of sins." No matter what goal or dream we want to accomplish, it is always attainable when we unleash positive methods for success. Push ourselves to the limit, and when we think we cannot go any further, endorphins are unleashed and teaches us better. Energy unleashed all at once could be dangerous for our words and actions and can lead to poor health. Stress needs to be measured a little at a time to keep us mentally, physically, emotionally and spiritually calm. This way, the monster inside does not become unleashed. Knowing how, when and where to unleash our words and actions will lead to satisfaction.

Let go, unleash all negativity in our body, mind and soul. Describe ourselves with every positive word and unleash actions that show we are whole. Believe and have faith in us and unleash all the demons that destroy much. God knows we all were made for success, so unleash all the creativity so we can do our best. Surround ourselves with those who unleash encouraging samples and use their positive experiences as prime examples. We never know when a positive person is an angel in disguise, so stop doubting ourselves and start unleashing productive lives. No one is perfect, and sometimes, we have unleashed our own wrath, but do not worry my son, God has forgiven our past. We are good, and we are great, and this is the attitude we must take. Unleash ourselves with positivity, humility and class building our confidence to last. Unleash courage about who we are because we are God's star.

UPHOLD

People have good intentions to uphold what they say and do, and it is immeasurable when they follow through. We need accountability with our words and actions because when we uphold these promises, we make others believe. The same is true when we uphold the word of God and reap our blessings too. We must decide if we are upholding ourselves full time with our speech and deeds or are we part timers sowing little seed. Attaining quality life values depends on our words and actions, so we can mentally, physically, emotionally, and spiritually grow. Uphold what we think, believe and say or do because there is only one chance at being true. When we uphold laws, customs, beliefs, words and actions, we grip naysayers and tell them we get no satisfaction. Upholding positive speech and deeds takes work, as anyone can criticize using jealousy as an evil vice. Even if we are the only one to uphold our ground, our destiny is sealed safe and sound.

The ratio 70:12:3:1 is critically important how we understand and uphold our positive way, earning trust each day. In biblical times, Jesus traveled with seventy people gathering information ahead of him. Only twelve were chosen as disciples to uphold his words and actions. A mere three were trusted enough to uphold the vision of God. Finally, Jesus, the only son of God died for all our sins, upholding all of us in his father's name. Imagine the power we have in us upholding our abilities and staying the course. Psalms 14:4–5 says, "Will these evildoers never learn? They devour our people as they devour bread; they do not call upon the Lord. They have good reason, then, to fear; God is with the company of the just." When we uphold God's word and are tested, we receive favor, blessing and grace, so we can feel his presence.

Upholding takes courage and a survivor mentality with our words and actions. Some are born with an upholding demeanor, and we must be grateful for these warriors in the world. David defeated Goliath upholding his words and actions saying, "I come against you in the name of the Lord." When we uphold with our language and deeds, this honor gives us all our needs. Uphold love, kindness, and happiness spreading it wherever we go. Uphold all that is good and positive in the world teaching the misunderstood. Speak and act with humbleness and humility demonstrating servantlike qualities upholding dignity and class. When we uphold what is right, the Holy Spirit gives us incredible insight. Choose our words and actions wisely, keeping our enemies closer than our friends. When we uphold all these positive values, they will lead us to God, our true friend. Speak and act bold because upholding cannot be bought or sold.

UPLIFT

Vocabulary and deeds generate energy, and we must decide to use them in an uplifting manner. A shift in our mind must take place as we choose to use positive ways to speak and interact with others. Mentally, physically, emotionally, and spiritually, surround ourselves with others who uplift instead of deflate the room. When we encounter those who are not glorifying others or dragging themselves through the mud of life, it is our responsibility as a human being to uplift them turning negative into positive. If our counseling and mentoring does not uplift them, then it is best to separate ourselves from those adverse situations. Positive words and actions do not magically occur. Uplifting takes practice by monitoring our own language and pursuits to put on the brakes when negative starts to flow. Environment is key, and everyone has different experiences making them either positive and uplifting or negative and rotting.

When we are not saying or doing things in an uplifting manner, sometimes we may get called out by others. Historically, when ancient civilizations strayed from the path of righteousness and God's words and commands, the wrath came down in demonstrations of plagues and natural disasters. God himself will intervene. 2 Samuel 22:10–14 says, "He inclined the heavens and came down, with dark clouds under his feet, he mounted a cherub and flew borne on the wings of the wind. He made darkness the shelter about him, with spattering rain and thickening clouds. From the brightness of his presence coals were kindled to flame. The Lord thundered from heaven, the Most High gave forth his voice." Today, positive speech and pedigrees that are uplifting are being replaced with acceptance of everyone who is different for shock value. Values, goodness and wholesome personality are no longer the mark, and muttering has replaced uplifting.

It is time to take back the word and action arena, and if it is not uplifting, do not say it, do it, or follow it. Let grace, gratitude, and integrity act as our uplifting leaders and demand excellence. Uplift until our dialogue and works create original masterpieces to inspire others. Average is the easy way out, and when we only strive to fit in, our uplifting abilities start hanging out with sin. Find a positive group or start one of our own that uplifts and only talks about ideas from God's throne. Powerful thoughts, words, and deeds is all the uplifting anyone should need. Uplift in every way we know because we need to battle Satan's shadow blow for blow. Uplifting is gifting from above with our speech and actions turning into happiness, joy and love. Thank you, Lord, for creating us to speak and act with purity and to be uplifting to others.

UNCANNY

Opportunity is truly amazing when we believe and set our focus on something. It is uncanny how magically what we want appears to come true. Our words and actions must energize our frequency to say and do the uncanny when others do not have faith. Matthew 8:25–27 says, "They came and woke him, saying, 'Lord, save us! We are perishing!' He said to them, 'Why are you terrified, O you of little faith?' Then he got up, rebuked the winds and the sea, and there was great calm. The men were amazed and said, 'What sort of man is this, whom even the winds and the sea obey.'" The correct words and deeds coming together at the right moment causes awe, an instant uncanny credibility. Our speech and ways need to incite excitement and uncanny wonderment. The more perceptive we are about people, places and events, our uncanny language and skills can invigorate the world.

Uncanny is a keen knack that allows us to find our way back. Gratitude has purpose, and the way we say it or do it is an uncanny jewel. Uncanny is a tool on the same plane of above, and when we use it properly, glides as peaceful as a dove. Knowing what to say and do in certain circumstances with uncanny rhetoric and wit allows us to control the venue. Building our legacy with uncanny verbal and positive skills with no doubt will pay our bills. God uses each of us in many uncertain and uncanny ways to help pick up the pieces for those who stray. Thank you, Lord, for uncanniness that will be used to rid the world of loneliness and invent creativeness. As our positive language and means develops our engine, uncanny will be reserved for plenty.

Where will we be when we unleash our uncanniness? Is it a moment of candor when uncanny needs to be tender? Will it be a time of laughter when uncanny will be remembered ever after? Uncanniness makes us wanted for our speech and labels our actions as unique. God's words and actions are all uncanny because there are so many deep parables and teachings showing us the way. When something cannot be explained and we do not know where to go, uncanny unlocks doors for wisdom to flow. Uncanniness takes faith in many ways, so we will always know just what to say. Uncanniness develops character and grace, so we can go, do or speak any place. Uncanniness is developed through the Father, Son, and Holy Spirit; and through our life, we can tell it and live it. As our years pass and wisdom grows, uncanniness is a trait undeniable through faith.

UTILITY

Words and actions must energize like a utility outlet generating power, which serves a positive function or purpose. A utility must be useful, and if our speech and deeds are not constructive in content and form, they are not worth uttering or doing. What may sound and feel like a motivational utility for one does not work the same way for all. The utility that fills all our needs verbally and actually is God. Romans 5:6–8 says, "For Christ, while we were still helpless, yet died at the appointed time for the ungodly. Indeed, only the difficulty does one die for a just person, through perhaps for a good person one might even find courage to die. But God proves his love for us in that while we were still sinners Christ died for us." When we seek and rely on this utility with all our hearts, great creativity grows and charismatic verbalization flows.

We must positively bestow a grateful attitude toward utilities we use each day. Mentally, physically, emotionally, and spiritually, all utilities have a purpose, which are connected somewhere to someone. Utilities must be used for the common good and not for evil purposes. Utilities, such as water, in its purest form serves billions to drink and generate energy allowing us to survive and run the world daily. Another utility is electricity, which although unclear how it is made, serves everything we do or will be doing in the future. Without these incredible and God-given utilities, life would exist at a snail's pace. Positive words and deeds are in the creative process each and every day, so more utilities are available, which make our lives more efficient and easy. Trial and error and innovative speech and works tied with faith makes new utilities possible. Utility comes from the mouth and hands out of necessity.

Why can't the world function collectively with its speech, actions, beliefs, and intentions for utilitarian purposes? Greed and self-centeredness come from the flesh making utility the mark of identity. Our words and actions concerning utility must be clear, concise and positively delivered, so there are not any selfish motives. Utility should be useful to all, provide an uplifting experience and be done with God's approval. We must be vigilant with decision makers to see if their words and actions are reasonable for future utility to move forward. True utility should cause trust, leadership, creativity and cohesiveness to reign. A good utility will verbally and monumentally stimulate pride, gratitude, elation and a positive atmosphere. When we need a new utility, pray to God it will be created for the good of humanity by men and women who say and do the right things and are willing to take responsibility.

UNABASHED

Our vocabulary and works take a lifetime of living, learning, and earning our stripes developing into an unabashed specimen. Seeing and hearing people react to every emotion created by God challenges us to speak and act unabashed. Circumstances moving from childhood to adulthood are different for everyone, so perception and perspective may not be always unabashed. The unabashed person takes good things from successes and mistakes, and from their experiences creates a gift with wisdom. Proverbs 1:24 states, "That men may appreciate wisdom and discipline, may understand words of intelligence; may receive training in wise conduct, in what is right, just, and honest; that resourcefulness may be imparted to the simple, to the young man knowledge and discretion." Decisions of how, when, where and why we communicate and demonstrate with unabashed skills goes hand in hand with God's word. It is an inner feeling of peace that tells us the time for unabashed to be released.

Confidence with word selection and delivering useful presentations is an unabashed skill set. We are a work in progress accumulating mercy and grace from God because we are willing to study His unabashed word and laws for living. Our strength, character, and work ethic shape us mentally, physically, emotionally, and spiritually into an unabashed person. Knowing the difference and practicing unabashed oration and discipleship is a positive choice followed up with a can-do spirit. We know when our effort and others is not at an unabashed level. Energy feeds off God's grace delivering hope, love and happiness with our unabashed talk and pursuits. Keeping ourselves continually motivated takes consistent, burning desire and attracting like people who share the unabashed light. The gift of gab and sewing the abashed seed must come from the heart. If our heart is not committed to a cause, God knows it, and unabashed rhetoric and principles are out of balance. Unabashed means we are built to last.

Living a positive life filled with poise, charisma, and charm are unabashed principles that only an attitude of gratitude can command. Our attitude is fed by what we observe and hear, and keeping an unabashed, thankful stance is much more soothing than troubled rants. Keeping an unabashed attitude may take selecting different friends or choosing a new location of residence. We know what we need, and if garbage is coming in, unabashed goodness is not coming out with our words and actions. Tough choices made by us today save our attitude and keep unabashed from getting trashed. Positivity and thanks fill us up full to the brim because we are emulating him in an unabashed way to brighten everyone's day. Our attitude of a servant giving verbal help and advice is just as important as unabashed pursuits opening other's eyes. Pray with vigor and zeal because God gives us his love unabashedly.

UNAPPRECIATIVE

Climbing the ladder to success many times takes years of influential words and meaningful traits learned from others, and we should never be unappreciative to them for their insight. Thank you and please opens many doors with our expressions and performances because if we are unappreciative, others will be unwilling to get involved with us. Recognition with positive phrases and works kindles joy, happiness and good thoughts toward us so they know we are not unappreciative. Always be intentional with positive compliments or pursuits. Occasionally, we may be forgetful, but not unappreciative, yet to someone, it may still sting. Ecclesiastes 9:14–15 reads, "Against a small city with few men in it advanced a mighty king, who surrounded it and threw up great siege works about it. But in the city lived a man who, though poor, was wise, and he delivered it through his wisdom. Yet no one remembered the poor man."

Throughout history, civilizations do well for a while but then become unappreciative toward God's word. The unappreciation comes from the flesh and believing in something else or trying to do things on our own. God warned disciples, kings, Pharisees, tax collectors, and citizens about the obedience of his laws, but we say immoral terminology and perform unappreciative acts constantly. Deviating from faith and belief destroys us mentally, physically, emotionally, and spiritually; and the more unappreciative we are, increased wrath will be unleashed upon his people. Do not speak or act unappreciatively toward God and his works for any reason because this only reflects immaturely with self-centeredness. God promises an abundant life filled with positive works when we tap into the potential he gave us. Our taproot dies and so do we, when we are unappreciative toward God and his works. Unappreciation should never come from our lips or leave our fingertips.

Living each day with excitement and a positive outlook is a choice and means to not let unappreciativeness creep into our lives. No matter what our mental state, physical condition, emotional roller coaster or spiritual connection, stop for a second and take inventory. Unappreciation go away. We are not going to feel sorry for ourselves today. Examine what we do have which is probably more than most and give the glory to God our host. Unappreciative words and actions occur when we stop counting our blessings and drop our responsibilities. We need to be positive and responsible to God, our family and ourselves to knock an unappreciative attitude off the shelf. Learn to stir up passion with our terms and mechanisms showing positive and possible as the options and solutions. When unappreciative moves out from our lives, thankful, grateful, and appreciative come back and live in our heart making a house a home.

UNSTOPPABLE

We are an unstoppable machine when positive energy flows. We can do anything! There will be no negativity with our words and actions, only unstoppable prosperity leading to victory. Pay attention to what we say and do only focusing on the unstoppable view. Say thank you to the Lord with his powerful words motivating us for our unstoppable surge. Practice makes perfect talking and mentoring in positive ways because unstoppable should be the only game played. Motivational speaker, Les Brown, says, "Life takes on meaning when you become motivated, set goals and charge after them in an unstoppable manner." Each day declare with unstoppable zeal, "I am a winner!" and expect only the best. Our future is unstoppable when we believe because our faith takes over allowing us to achieve. When we envision success, we see an increase in our mind-set motivating us to unstoppable feats. Awake each day and take charge of our tongue, so we will act like the unstoppable one.

There are no excuses allowed with our words and actions if we want to be considered unstoppable. We must sacrifice and work hard to be unstoppable saying and doing the right things. Unstoppable takes a positive mental attitude and encouragement with our speech and demeanor. We must exude unstoppable passion as we talk and work toward the prize. We need to catapult ourselves over any obstacle in our path showing unstoppable spirit. Unstoppable is a promise never to quit and always say what is legit. Mentally, physically, emotionally, and spiritually, we are unstoppable when our foundation is solid because of positive mentoring and coaching, developing our words and actions. We remember those who pushed us to our unstoppable levels. The inspiration we gained from their words and deeds filled the unstoppable gauge to pass on to others in need. Make our speech and demeanor an unstoppable example of positive creativity.

God is our unstoppable pillar of faith. His words and examples lift us to unstoppable heights, touching the stars he made one night. Our God is not mediocre, average, or plain, but an unstoppable leader giving us wisdom, love and belief in his name. There is nothing to compare of God's unstoppable words and deeds when faith supports our cause and fills our needs. Our words and ways when parallel with his give us unstoppable favor. Have his words etched in our brains for an unstoppable combination to get us through all pleasures and pains. When God's words and actions touch our hearts, we become unstoppable, off the chart. The only things keeping us from an unstoppable will and place are words and means that degrade and disgrace. Speak and act gratefully because unstoppable desire and God's power will take us higher. We are the unstoppable example for generations to come.

UNDERESTIMATE

1 Corinthians 6:18–20 says, "Avoid immorality. Every other sin a person commits is outside the body, but the immoral person sins against his own body. Do you not know that your body is a temple of the Holy Spirit within you, whom you have from God, and that you are not your own? For you have been purchased at a price. Therefore, glorify God in your body." We must not underestimate God, our opponents or our remarks and conduct. What we say and do has a bearing mentally, physically, emotionally, and spiritually on others and ourselves. Speaking and acting positively all the time is a challenge, but keeps us on a good course and makes us not underestimate anything. We do not want to deeply offend the Lord or any other

person by underestimating our words and actions. When we underestimate, we do not show respect, obedience, love or awe of feelings.

Comments and activities need to be edifying, not underestimating others value. Underestimation may be purposeful or unintentional. Our utterances and movements should be pleasing and uplifting. It is a much more comfortable atmosphere being surrounded by positive people talking greatness and working together for better and empowerment, instead of underestimating. Our words and actions are sacred to God because he redeemed all our sins, so we never want to underestimate them. When we speak and act, the words and deeds that follow should give others a feeling of awe and excitement, not underestimating their abilities and status. When we do not underestimate, it gives others a feeling of belonging and importance. Underestimating people, speech, or mannerisms can get us hurt. As a law enforcement officer underestimating leads to complacency and that is when mistakes are made. Never underestimate others' language or conduct because if they are direct and negative toward us, then they are conspiring against us.

It is a sacred gift not underestimating life. Speak and act gratefully giving credit where it is due, so we do not underestimate a situation causing a feud. Never underestimate the words from God as that is where we will be judged. When we underestimate, it bites us in the end because we did not think clearly and plan for the consequences much to our chagrin. Discovering our maturity occasionally results from underestimating the world we know when our verbal skills and comments fall far below. Thankfully, we grew, putting the past behind us, and learned underestimating is bad news. We now are a bright ray of light never underestimating anything in or out of sight. God's rhetoric and his positive insight now cohabitate within us, making us a dream team never underestimating a thing. Underestimating speech and activities is a habit of the past, we are now loving, focused, and built to last.

ULTERIOR

The words which come from our mouths and the works we do, are they pure for the cause or are ulterior motives driving us? Straight shooting with our words and actions is what we would all like to face daily, but unfortunately, others conceal their ulterior plan. Ulterior speech and deeds are inferior because they do not take courage to be untruthful. Mentally, physically, emotionally, and spiritually, we are out of balance when ulterior ways enter our language and pursuits. Ulterior is a disguise selling something that really does not live up to expectations. Rhetoric and acts that are ulterior have no positivity except for self-centeredness because usually, we are deliberately taking advantage of someone or something. Our words and actions define us, and when others see we are ulterior in nature, our relationships and reputation suffers. Choose to speak and lead with superior grace and rid ourselves of ulterior ways.

There are causes and effects that are consequences when we use ulterior words and actions in our daily transactions with others. It feels like a punch in the stomach when people use ulterior methods to deprive us financially, relationally, or exponentially. When it comes to God's word and studying it, are we lovingly developing it to know him or are we ulterior to be seen and heard? We cannot have an ulterior heart in anything we say and do because God knows the truth. Matthew 24:4–5 says, "Jesus said, to them in reply, 'See that no one deceives you, for many will come in my name, saying, 'I am the Messiah', and they will deceive many.'" When it all gets said and done and people are deceitful, their ulterior ways are exposed. Pray when we have negative intentions to say or do ulterior things and hope to meet a guardian angel with wings.

Speak and act gratefully each day so we stay on the path of righteousness and escape ulterior melee. We surround ourselves, like the law of attraction, with those who speak, act and think the way we do. Give positive reinforcement with true words and deeds and eliminate ulterior factions. It is refreshing when we are around others who positively impact people with their language and means, and not ulterior methods. Do not be afraid to use our positive words and actions to call out ulterior forces. God gives us the strength to conquer all which is ulterior. It is up to us to not be passive with ulterior people. If we are proactive, we use God's word, sword and shield to defeat ulterior yields. The cure for ulterior is using our speech and deeds for nothing other than positive feeds. Let us chip away at ulterior so the surface is smooth, so we all improve.

UNIVERSAL

Universal language and behaviors do not fit all situations. Using universal words and actions maybe common and acceptable for some purposes in generic instances, but separation of worldly and eternal means are two different realms. Compromising our words and actions for sinful tirades and deeds does not equip us for salvation. Our emotions at times become overloaded, and we may want to say or do something in an angry spiteful response, but that is not universal restraint as a Christian. Do not damage our spirit by going along with others sinfully as a universal spirit. 1 Peter 4: 4–6 states, "They are surprised that you do not plunge into the same jump of profligacy, and they will vilify you; but they will give an account to him who stands ready to judge the living and the dead. For this is why the gospel was preached even to the dead that though condemned in the flesh in human estimation, they might live in the spirit in the estimation of God."

When we use our words universally not separating flesh from spirit, judgement from Christ will come. Those unwilling to discipline themselves and to learn to universally suffer as Christ did will always ask why me? Our words and actions plant seeds, and we have to allow them to universally come to fruition in God's time. Nothing we can do or say will occur until he is ready. Frustration may take place as we wait, but this is how we are universally tested to see how we will use our words and means. Stop focusing universally on the flesh. We are only here for a short time. Universal prepares ourselves for the life in heaven we will share with God. When we focus universally on God first, mentally, physically, emotionally, and spiritually, our words and actions will turn into grace.

A positive attitude of gratitude and a thankful heart is where our words and ways must flow universally each moment of every day. It does take work to stay on track, but when we turn the corner and make the universal change with our speech and deeds, we are like a generator supplying power to all in need. Our powerful and grateful words and actions lead us to the path of universal righteousness. God forgives us of our sins, allows us to repent, and changes our language and behaviors to lend a universal helping hand. Our priority on earth is to spread joy, love, kindness, and happiness universally so others want to emulate us, and be like God. We are all his disciples. We must choose to lead by example with our positive words and deeds for solving earthly situations with universal and spiritual means. Committed and universal to Christ means there is no reversal.

UTMOST

No matter who is the person, what is the topic, or how we feel, when we talk and engage, we need to have the utmost respect. Utmost is how we should boast as our words and actions shape the direction the situation will go. When our language and deeds are not first-rate people, see through this and hesitate. We never want anyone to question if we are giving the utmost effort because we will then be second guessed. Speak properly and boldly with the utmost attention to detail. Act graciously in every venue with utmost care because we will never know when others will compare. The greatest compliment anyone can give us is when what we say and do, is done with utmost gratitude. Utmost comes from the heart and lives inside us with faith. God, our Father, shines down upon us each day, and he is the utmost, no comparisons can be made.

Colossians 1:15–20 states, "He is the image of the invisible God, the firstborn of all creation. For in him were created all things in heaven and on earth, the visible and the invisible, whether thrones, or dominions or principalities of powers; all things were created through him and for him. He is before all things, and in him all things hold together. He is the head of the body, the church. He is the beginning, the firstborn from the dead, that in all things he himself might be preeminent. For in him all the fullness was pleased to dwell, and through him to reconcile all things for him, making peace by the blood of his cross [through him], whether those on earth or those in heaven." When we act as a servant, ask for his mercy for our mistakes, and believe his words, we will receive the utmost grace.

Utmost is first place because if we are anywhere else, we are only running the race. Our words and actions should always typify the cream of the crop because it would be epic failure if our utmost was a complete flop. Pray each day so we are energized as our speech and deeds plants the utmost seeds. Are we going to be remembered as the person with potential, who turned into a ghost, or the one whose effort was the utmost? It is up to us to decide how we speak and act mentally, physically, emotionally and spiritually for our life's journey. Disregard all negativity, speaking assuredly because utmost is our place. We were made for success, and our language and pursuits are the utmost roots. Give the world our utmost each and every day with everything we say and do because we are always on display.

UNIQUE

People have qualities which fit their personalities, and their words and actions are unique. The unique language and deeds hopefully are used for good seeds. Our speech and behaviors form the core, like oblique muscles, and this strength is unique because everything starts from here. Unique rhetoric and pursuits are incomparable, which makes them so sharable. A unique verbal or active skill causes others to stop in their tracks and sit back and chill. Immediately, dialects tell everyone where we are from when the unique accent flows from the mouth it says, east, west, north or south. We then laugh at these unique verbal and character differences and say it is their mystique. What we see and hear is always different wherever we go, but when unique stands out, it peaks our memories and causes them to flow.

Mentally, physically, emotionally, and spiritually, we were all created to be the perfect unique. God gives us so many ways to share our unique verbal and nonverbal cues. Mentor our unique experiences, sing a song, or do whatever helps us communicate a positive message all day long. Life is too short to allow our unique traits to go to waste. Unique is good and unique is great because it gets us going with faith. Use our unique building blocks and positive self-esteem forging a thankful attitude for all to see. Unique can stand on its own, so our speech and deeds sew incredible seeds. Only God knows the greatest plan he puts inside, it is up to us to pull unique to the outside. When unique becomes comfortable for us and we can stake our claim, our words and actions will help others win life's games. When unique is everything we say and do; that is Almighty God, kindly blessing you.

Unique does not mean a selfish vocabulary or demeanor should exist, the opposite is true. Give all we have with our wisdom and grace and show off unique as a solitary place. Do as God did in his unique way, as John 3:16 says, "For God so loved the world that he gave his only Son, so that everyone who believes in Him might not perish, but might have eternal life." The unique decision gave the world eternal salvation. When unique advice better others' lives, there are no sweeter words or complementary works. Kindness, compassion, love and gratitude should be our unique attitudes. Make our uniqueness distinctive and matchless as we build our fortress. Quality is the key for what we say, and we provide a unique perspective, innovative in every way. Sharpen our words and actions every day, so our unique lessons never get stale and leads us in a passionate way.

EPILOGUE

Thank you! *T.H.A.N.K. Y.O.U.!* Readers, thank you for sticking with me. Mentors, family, friends, coworkers, teammates, thank you for inspiring and encouraging me. It is my hope that you feel uplifted and more grateful from reading *T.H.A.N.K. Y.O.U.* I also hope you feel better off and more thankful than when you began this gratitude journey. Remember, each person is a gift from God and instilling positive words and actions in every circumstance will make the difference in the world.

BIBLIOGRAPHY

Books:

Brown, H. Jackson. *A Book of Love for My Son.* Nashville, TN: Rutledge Hill Press, 2001, p. 190.

Byrne, Rhonda. *The Secret.* Oregon: Beyond Words Publishing, 2006, p. 169.

Curtis, Bryan. *A Call for Courage: Words of Inspiration from America's Presidents.* Tennessee: Rutledge Hill Press, 2002, pp. 28, 35, 97, 99, 107, 110, 112, 120.

Greene, Robert. *The 48 Laws of Power.* New York: Penguin Books, 2000, pp. 104 and 176.

Holtz, Lou. *Winning Every Day the Game Plan for Success.* New York: Harper Perennial, 1999, pp. XIV and 52.

Lounsbrough, Craig. *An Intimate Collision: Encounters with Life and Jesus.* Greenville, SC: Emerald House Group, Incorporated, 2013.

Maraboli, Steve. *Unapologetically You: Reflections on Life and the Human Experience.* New York: Better Today, A, 2013.

Martin, George, R. R. *A Knight of the Seven Kingdoms.* New York: Bantam Books, 2015.

Paone, Anthony, J. S.J. *My Daily Bread.* USA: Confraternity of the Precious Blood, 1954.

Peale, Norman Vincent. *The Power of Positive Thinking.* New York: Prentice-Hall Inc, 1953, pp. 24 and 70.

The Board of Trustees of the Confraternity of Christian Doctrine. *Saint Joseph Edition of the New American Bible.* New York: Catholic Publishing Co., 1992. All biblical quotes.

Zhou, Zhuang. *The Complete Works of Chuang Tzu*. USA: Penguin Classics, 1994.

Movies:

Patton. DVD Directed by Franklin J. Shaffner. United States: 20th Century Fox, 1970.

Websites:

Sir Francis Bacon. Google. Accessed June 7, 2017. https://todayinsci.com/B/Bacon_Francis/BaconFrancis-Quotations.htm.

Les Brown Quotes. Accessed June 8, 2017. https://www.brainyquote.com/quotes/authors/l/les_brown.html.

Mary Buchan. Good Reads, Xplore Inc., 2017. https://www.goodreads.com/author/quotes/4836845.Mary_Buchan.

Edmund Burke. Brainy Quote.com. Xplore Inc., accessed June 6, 2017. https://www.brainyquote.com/quotes/quotes/e/edmundburke119389.html.

Alecia Elliott. Lyricist quotes.com. Accessed June 8, 2017.

Horace. Brainy Quote.com. Xplore Inc. Accessed June 9, 2017. https://ww.brainyquote.com/quotes/quotes/h/horace152505.html.

Steve Jobs. Brainy Quote.com. Xplore Inc, 2017. Accessed June 8, 2017. https://www.brainyquote.com/quotes/quotes/s/steve-jobs416894.html.

www.azquotes.com/author/7989-Chip_Kidd 2014.

C. S. Lewis. Brainy Quote.com, Xplore Inc. Accessed June 6, 2017. https://www.brainyquote.com/quotes/quotes/c/cslewis151465.html.

B. K. S. Iyengar. AZ Quotes.com, Wind and Fly LTD. Accessed June 8, 2017. http://www.azquotes.com/quote/532619.

Ross Perot. Brainy Quote.com. Xplore Inc. Accessed June 8, 2017. https://www.brainyquote.com/quotes/quotes/r/ross perot101658.html.

Adlai E. Stevenson. Brainy Quote.com, Xplore Inc. Accessed June 7, 2017. https://www.brainyquote.com/quotes/quotes/a/adlai-este391610.html.

C. E. Stowe. Google. Accessed June 7, 2017. thinkexist.com/quotation/common_sense_is_the_knack_of_seeing.../145812html.

Harriet Beecher Stowe. Brainy Quote, Xplore Inc. Accessed June 7, 2017. https://www.brainyquote.com/quotes/quotes/h/harriet-bee155742.html.

Philip Yancey. Accessed June 8, 2017. https://www.goodreads.com/book/show/21816684Vanishing graces.

Philip Zimbardo. Accessed June 8, 2017. Picture Quote.com.

NOTES

NOTES

About the Author

Growing up in the competitive environment of Northwest Indiana and succeeding in sports and life granted Tom Mavity avenues for personal development. God, family members, friends, coaches, teachers, co-workers, and other mentors shared their words and actions leading Tom's growth mentally, physically, emotionally, and spiritually. Playing sports and graduating from Wabash College generated work ethic, integrity, sacrifice, team work, and valuable life skills on and off the field. Working over two and a half decades in law enforcement and witnessing all types of behaviors demonstrated positive and negative ways of living. Always striving for excellence, a dream came leading him to share this extremely strong message. Using positive words and actions instilled with gratitude will lead people to success. Live each day with an attitude of gratitude and say thank you!